DICK GENTRY

AT THE FOOT OF THE SOUTHERN CROSS

*An American Editor Offshore
in The Cayman Islands*

woodlord

First published in digital eBook formats in
Great Britain in 2009 by EBOOKS-UK

www.ebooks-uk.com
www.ebooks-america.com

eBooks-UK, P.O. Box 36, Chesterfield S40 3YY, UK.

This revised edition published by Woodlord in 2010

Copyright © Dick Gentry 2010

The right of Dick Gentry
to be identified as the author of this work has been asserted under the
Copyright, Designs and Patents Act 1988.

A CIP catalogue record for this book
is available from the British Library

Designed and typeset by Keith Mason for Woodlord Publishing
Chesterfield, Derbyshire, U.K.

Cover design Copyright © Keith Mason 2010
This edition in paperback format
copyright © Woodlord 2010

WOODLORD

P.O. Box 36, Chesterfield S40 3YY, Derbyshire, UK
An imprint of eBooks-UK
a division of eSites-UK Ltd.

ISBN-978-1-906602-08-6

Frontispiece

"Now I saw in my dream, that the big highway up which Christian was to go was fenced on either side with a wall, and that wall was called Salvation. Isaiah 26:1.

Up this way, therefore, did burdened Christian run, but not without great difficulty, because of the load on his back.

"He ran thus till he came at a place somewhat ascending; and upon that place stood a cross, and a little below, in the bottom, a sepulcher. So I saw in my dream, that just as Christian came up with the cross, his burden loosed from off his shoulders, and fell from off his back, and began to tumble, and so continued to do till it came to the mouth of the sepulcher, where it fell in, and I saw it no more."

-The Pilgrim's Progress

ACKNOWLEDGEMENTS

Joe Crocker, and later Ringo Starr, put into music how I feel about this book. They "had a little help from their friends." So it was with my manuscript. I had help from many friends all along the way. Most have to go unnamed because their names are lost to memory even though I recall their kindnesses. I gave my real, first-ever friend's name to the Cayman Police Commissioner. I gave a few pseudonyms to other real characters in this book.

Roy, Fred and Buddy were childhood friends, and I cherish my fellow Marines, especially those who have said goodbye—GySgt Jim Breslin, former Georgia Sheriff Slick Jones and high-school friend Sgt. Jack Bowles.

Professionally, there's Bill Southard, my first editor, now gone; my first editor/mentor, Joann Byrd, who's now so recognized as a journalism professional she has her own web site, and the journalism professors at Ole Miss and Eastern Washington University who kept the fire going when I almost blew it out.

Mechanically, Joann, my wife Martha, my daughter Alison and her friend, Judy, read the manuscript and told me what they thought. Ursula Gill, former editor of The Caymanian Compass, was of immense help and I had editorial and typing help from Carol Henderson.

Keith and Jane Mason, who salvaged, edited and published my book are now my favorite Limeys. And speaking of the English, today I try to remember our colonies were founded by the English and except for a few bumps in the road, America and England are pretty much facing the rest of the world shoulder to shoulder...

It has taken me more than 15 years to complete this. I meant it to be comical, because I am a humorous person. When I first read it cover to cover, there was little laughter and a tear or two.

However, I enjoyed every minute remembering, and writing...

DEDICATION

To Martha

I hope you enjoyed the dance.

ABOUT THE AUTHOR

Dick Gentry is a former seagoing Marine and an award-winning writer who has worked in newspapers and magazines across America and one foreign country. His career in journalism spans more than 40 years.

Gentry and his wife Martha, a registered nurse, live in the Georgia mountains north of Atlanta.

Born in Tupelo, Mississippi, he began his professional career in 1962 as sports editor of the *Artesia Daily Press* in New Mexico. This was right after the University of Mississippi barred the enrollment of controversial civil rights champion James Meredith. The riot there has been called the first American insurrection since the Civil War. Gentry served as editor of the school's daily newspaper in the summer of 1962 just before the battle began. He was a first-hand witness to the rebellion.

He was executive editor of *The Birmingham Business Journal* in the mid-1990s. In between, he has been city editor of the *Ocala Star-Banner* in Florida, a staff writer for the *Spokane Daily Chronicle* in Washington State, executive editor of *Hawaii Business Magazine*, and editor of the *Atlanta Business Chronicle* and the *San Diego Business Journal*. He graduated from Eastern Washington University in 1980.

During recovery from a stress-related illness in Texas while working for the *Beaumont Journal* in the early 1970s, he penned an impulsive letter to the managing director of the only newspaper in a tiny, Caribbean nation. To his surprise, he received a reply. Thus began the adventure of a lifetime in The Cayman Islands, recorded in this manuscript, *At the Foot of the Southern Cross*.

CONTENTS

7

9

PROLOGUE

On March 29, 2006, a Subcommittee on Oversight in the U.S. House conducted a hearing on Offshore Banking, Corruption, and the War on Terrorism. One of those who testified was the respected Robb Evans, CEO of Robb Evans & Associates, California attorneys who specialize in recovering fraudulent offshore funds, who told the assembled congressmen:

" I am a retired banker, and what I have been doing for most of the last 10 years is getting the money back, the money that has been stolen, the money that has been laundered, and trying to get it back to its rightful owners. First of all, I think when you are talking about terrorists' money and the other kinds of money laundering, you have to remember very clearly that the terrorist financing is small dollars. It is clean money going bad in small amounts as opposed to what you are talking about in sanctions, which is very large dollars. They are very different problems, and they are critical.

"I would just like to point out that there is an island that does more money laundering than any other, and that is Manhattan. The island that does most of the money laundering in the world is Manhattan, but I would like to talk about a couple of other (places).

"What we do in my organization is we trace money, and we try and recover it for the victims of fraud, and we do it mostly on behalf of the United States Government. I want to share with you very briefly, just to try to straighten out maybe a little bit of reputational risk here, one batch of money that went to two different islands (one of which was The Cayman Islands.)

"This is money that was stolen in California, and it was routed to The Cayman Islands. We traced the money to The Cayman Islands, and we did a good deal of work in terms of doing the forensic investigation work, and we went down to The Cayman Islands to try and recover the money, and we shared the information with the government there.

"Here is what the government did. As soon as we showed up and shared the evidence, the first thing they did is they started their own investigation of the bank in question, which was an active bank in The Cayman Islands. They confirmed our findings, and they ordered the bank closed and liquidated. After getting

proper authority from their courts, they provided us with all of the bank documentation so that we could go onward tracing the money elsewhere around the world. They arrested and prosecuted the bank officers and the local launderers. We had a prosecution going in California. They sent two witnesses from the Cayman Government to help us in our case, and they gave us the money back for distribution to the victims.

"Now, as part of our tracing of that money, we followed a large bloc to yet another island, and this island nation is about to get a major handout of United States aid. We tracked $8 million to Vanuatu. We went down to Vanuatu, just as we did in The Cayman Islands, to share the information we had, to show them the documentation. We went with a written introduction from the staff of the Board of Governors of the Federal Reserve.

"The Vanuatu authorities refused to meet with us. They tried to confiscate the money, which was clearly documented as money stolen from consumers that needed to go back to consumers. They tried to confiscate the money for their national treasury. In spite of repeated requests to discuss and try and resolve the matter in some fashion, in some kind of asset-sharing program or anything else, they have completely refused to for years now.

"The bank in question where the money went to in Vanuatu continues to operate. Its largest single deposit is this stolen money, at least as nearly as we can tell. The same bank is under indictment in the United States for States for money laundering, and its executives are fugitives.

"...What I would suggest to this Subcommittee is that the fight against international money laundering goes on on many levels. There are little leaks, and there are big leaks. Please do not forget the little leaks. These are critically important, and in your position, you can do a good deal to stop it. By putting the pressure on these small jurisdictions to shape up and try and do the right thing rather than try and profit from it, you can turn that around.

"Now, in The Cayman Islands, I know the Caymans have been lambasted pretty thoroughly here today, and my job is not to defend them at all, but they got the message years ago. They have been extremely cooperative in our recovery efforts, as have a number of the other former British colonies. Not true every place else."

IN 2004, Natasha Lance Rogoff, a field producer for "Tax Me If You Can" for the public television show FRONTLINE, included the following during a rare broadcast on tax havens:

11

"For the U.S. Treasury, offshore jurisdictions like The Cayman Islands pose a double problem: (1) they can offer American corporations and individuals attractive financial deals and access to capital markets at a much lower cost than U.S. banks in America, and (2) they can guarantee virtually complete secrecy about financial deals and assets held by Americans, in accordance with Cayman confidentiality laws (except in the case of criminal activity)...

"Over the years, the Cayman authorities have moved several times to tighten regulation and oversight of their financial centers - particularly to stop criminal money laundering and financial deals by drug traffickers. Starting with the Mutual Legal Assistance treaty with the U.S. in 1990, Cayman authorities have set up measures to facilitate the exchange of information between the U.S. and Cayman. In July of 2000, Cayman authorities required local banks, law firms and financial institutions to exercise greater due diligence to identify suspicious clients and required that they report all suspicious transactions to the government's Financial Reporting Unit (FRU). And in November 2001, The Cayman Islands concluded a tax information exchange agreement (TIEA) with the U.S. that provides for exchange of information relating to U.S. federal income tax...

"However, the tightened Cayman regime did not specifically target tax evasion by foreign citizens. Moreover, Cayman's privacy laws make it extremely difficult for industrialized countries to follow the trail of money as it passes from reputable U.S. and European financial, accounting and law firms to The Cayman Islands, making it difficult to investigate tax abuses...

"While the tax agreements somewhat bolster the U.S. government's ability to prosecute corporations and individuals engaging in tax evasion, the agreements are limited, and in most cases do not allow the IRS to investigate suspected corporations or individuals unless there is a court order or strong evidence of criminal activity. As one Cayman official stated, "Despite excellent fishing in the Cayman waters, no fishing expeditions are allowed..."

"If the IRS wants to investigate potential wrongdoing by a U.S. corporation or individual, it must request information from Cayman's chief justice on a case-by-case basis. Unfortunately, this painstaking process is inadequate to deal with the numerous cases of tax fraud perpetrated by U.S. citizens and corporations. Furthermore, the IRS does not have sufficient resources to pursue investigations of wrongdoing on a case-by-case basis..."

THIS ALL MEANS that if the U.S. Government thinks you are a shark who has violated U.S. laws with your secret account in The Cayman Islands, it has the means—though difficult to navigate—to cook you. If you are only scampi, you're probably safe from the pot.

The very latest ingredients stirred into the brew came at the G20 Summit in London in Spring 2009 when there was general agreement among the participating nations that tax havens in general were bad for the taxing authorities of those participating nations, particularly England, France, Germany and the U. S. British Prime Minister Gordon Brown is possibly Public Enemy No. 1 of tax havens and said at the recent Summit that England has for 20 years tried to force tax havens to share their deposits information with taxing authorities and he promised "there will be an agreement at this summit." There was some movement toward a resolution.

During his campaign, President Barack Obama said there was "a building (in George Town, Grand Cayman) that houses 12,000 corporations... That's either the biggest building in the world or the biggest tax scam in the world." It is neither. U.S. Senate Finance Committee member Chuck Grassley claimed the building—The Ugland House—has been the source of "much debate" in the Senate floor. "It's time the Finance Committee found out what's really going on there."

The Ugland House was not present when I lived in George Town, but today it is a short trip down the sidewalk from my old office. And, I could see the former office of Maples and Calder from my window. Now, it's the largest law firm in the country, and may have helped the wealthy Norwegian shipping magnates build The Ugland House. And, it was the old Maples and Calder who sent me a letter during my last days in Cayman. I was excited. I thought it was probably an invitation to a grand cocktail party. Unfortunately, it was a letter evicting me from my house.

I'm guessing Maples and Calder today conducts a lot of legal work from The Ugland House and perhaps owns part of it. The principals of Maples and Calder that I knew in the 1970s claim no association with the firm today. Mr. Maples is a British Member of Parliament and I was told Mr. Calder has a smaller law firm in Cayman. I remember both men fondly.

As for what is "really going on" at The Ugland House, Senator Grassley, I'll tell you myself: Owners and/or managers of capital around the world who wish to protect certain legally-gained

13

assets from prying-eyed tax-collectors have formed legal offshore companies to protect those assets. *In its simplest form, a tax haven is a country with very low or nonexistent taxes which welcomes offshore depositors and does not report information about these depositors to anyone. Obviously, that is annoying to many home nations of these unknown depositors.*

Here's a recent press release relating to fallout from the G20 from Maples and Calder reacting to a tax information exchange agreement (TIEA) signed by The Cayman Islands and New Zealand: "This is the 12th such agreement (with another country) signed, and the Caymans have been 'promoted' by the Organization for Economic Cooperation and Development (OECD) from a so-called 'gray-list' to the 'white-list.' The OECD praised the Caymans for "setting a good example" for tax havens.

Although the issue has not been fully settled as of the time of this writing, The Cayman Islands have agreed to provide certain information to requesting nations, including the U.S. As noted earlier, the Cayman government is already providing requested information upon legitimate requests for those accounts suspected of criminal activity. What the future holds for tax havens in general and The Cayman Islands in particular is beyond my ability to predict.

UNTIL VERY recently, The Cayman Islands were virtually unknown to Americans. For myself, I had no idea what I was getting into when I accepted a job working for a small newspaper there almost four decades ago. One of the reasons few knew of the Caymans was because it was off the track to tourism until after W. W. II. There was no air service, no air conditioning, and mosquitoes drove everyone crazy. It was grim.

As the 1950s unfolded, a trickle of tourists, drawn by rumors of the most beautiful beach in the Caribbean, began to explore. In the late 1960s, offshore banking enterprises discovered the tax-free Caymans. There was regular air service and the mosquito was defeated. Growth was inevitable.

I arrived just as the offshore banking boom began in earnest. Most Americans have no idea what an offshore bank is. At the time, I didn't either. I quickly found that I would be working for the only news outlet in the country. There was nothing else, although you could get some news and sports on shortwave from Armed Forces Radio. I learned I was in complete charge of the newspaper and its accompanying printing company.

In spite of the fact that the author is a simple Mississippian with soft feet from walking on pine needles most of his early life, this is not a religious book as the title might imply. The only religious acknowledgement I make here is: I thank God for allowing me a beginning, middle and finale in life. So many friends missed that great opportunity.

This is not about a reporter who rose to great professional heights. I never made it to the really big show. I have written more obits than feature stories. This is a small story I wrote for myself because I wanted to remember it. When someone asked me what it was like down there, I told them to read Don't Stop the Carnival by Herman Wouk. That was fiction; my story is true.

From Tupelo to Texas, from Hog Sty Bay to Batabano, we're off.

1

THE LAND OF THE CROCK

Looking down from my window, I saw an enormous, elongated pancake poured on a gigantic blue griddle. My first surprise was its dimensions. I could see from one end to the other as we approached. It was absolutely flat with very few landmarks inland, and surrounded by the vast, consuming Caribbean Sea. There were no high buildings, trees or hills to be seen and the other two portions of this three-island nation were nowhere on the horizon. No wonder it took so long for somebody to discover this forlorn-looking pebble.

The Costa Rican jetliner braked to a stop a dozen or so yards from an open, tin-roofed building that might have been a tobacco barn except for the concrete floor and long tables visible inside. For a moment I thought we were lost and had somehow blundered into backwater Mexico. But there was no mistaking the faded sign over the entrance to the big rustic structure: "Cayman International Airport."

The weather was a shocker after the late-winter chill of south Texas. When the hatch door opened, the smell drifted in with the heat. It wasn't unpleasant, just different. In fact, given a choice between the sickish sweet aroma of the greasy, belching refineries around Port Arthur and the inexplicable scents in Cayman, I wasn't complaining.

There was this oddball hint of decaying vegetation chopped up with exotic spices. I didn't know it then, but Cayman had no sewer system, or fresh-water wells. Hundreds of septic tanks around the capital, George Town, were adding their obnoxious aroma and there was the hint of rotten eggs that I would learn was dissolved minerals from the minuscule aquifer beneath the limestone.

I wondered what Dr. Roy would look like? I only knew he was ancient and had been one of the first dentists in the country. I wasn't positive who was going to meet me. Perhaps no one? That idea was unnerving.

16

Looking at the congenial faces watching us as they waited outside in the hot sun, I saw a peculiar bunch. The faces reflected a light to dark-brown hue and most looked through yellowish-brown eyes, or pale-blue ones diluted occasionally with gray. As they anxiously peered at us, I thought the eyes sparkled and blinked and bedazzled or faded with the accidental brightness, or dullness, one sees looking up at the heavens at night. The faces radiated more pleasantness than handsomeness. I recognized the composite of skin and eyes among many of them as a familiar mixed-race mulatto concoction I had seen growing up in the segregated and recently violent Deep South. And since I had never known a person of color very far beyond skin tint— even after my exposure in the Marines—I was abruptly anxious about that, too.

I would soon learn these colorful faces reflected a multi-generational, genealogical soup—the flotsam and jetsam amalgamate of black, white, Latino, pirate, scalawag and other assorted misfits and adventurers interrupted unfortunately, in more recent decades, by the arrival of bankers, lawyers and other more sophisticated thieves. I hardly knew where I was, much less what it was. Like all of the arrivals before me, stretching back almost to the day Columbus's son spotted and recorded these tiny islands on the Great Mariner's fourth and final voyage, the Caribbean was a legacy to plunder and despoil. If there is such a thing as genetic memory, many of these people seeing me step off of the jet probably wondered: "What's this new white boy after?"

Other faces were disappointingly normal; almost identical to those who watched us leave from Miami International Airport. These misplaced gawkers were probably tourists waiting to return to Miami or expatriate Brits waiting to welcome more skilled employees from England. I thought of myself as a tourist, not a potential employee. I had already made up my mind this trip was a mistake. We retrieved our bags from the unattended pile on the tarmac and hauled them inside to place on wooden tables and wait for the unhurried customs inspection.

When it was my turn, the inspector looked at me through bottle-lensed glasses and smiled. He poked through my overnight bag and asked where I would be staying? The way he said it wasn't menacing. He had an accent. It was certainly English, but with an unusual singsong lilt.

"I don't know," I said, "I'm just here for an overnight trip."

"But you have to know where you're goin' to stay tonight or you can't come here," he sang in the quaint little idiom. He looked directly at me and said, a tad sternly: "We don't let you sleep on the beach. You've got to be somewhere. It's the law, you know!"

17

I wasn't sure where I would go if he bounced me off of the island, since the jet was already rolling down the tarmac. I thought it left rather abruptly for its final destination, San Juan. The thought crossed my mind I should have stayed aboard.

"What are you doin' here?" he asked, and I became a bit edgy. He was a middle-aged Caymanian, quite tall with gray hair visible beneath the official Cayman Islands Customs Department cap.

"I'm here to talk to some gentlemen about a job at the newspaper," I stammered. He looked at me with renewed interest. "You mean *The Caymanian Weekly?*" He pronounced it, "Cay-MON-yon."

"Yes sir," I said. "I'm here for an interview." He stood up and looked at me steadily.

"Dr. Roy, he's here to get you!" he said, quickly closing my overnight case. He put a sticker on it signifying approval by customs (a small, colorful, cartoon drawing of a turtle in a pirate's hat), snapped it shut, picked it up and motioned for me to follow him.

That was my astonishing introduction to the clout of the individual who was waiting for me outside in the sun. I was impressed as I followed the customs-inspector-turned-porter toward the doorway.

At another counter a line was forming. This was the second checkpoint where a uniformed immigration officer waited to stamp your passport with the visa giving permission to visit—if you had a place to stay.

My escort took me to the front of the line and handed my passport to the official. "He's here to see Dr. Roy," he told the second man, who immediately stamped my passport and ushered us outside.

Once in the bright sunshine again my "porter" handed me my suitcase and pointed in the general direction of a small band of people. There, standing in the middle of the group, holding court, was Dr. Roy. There was no mistaking him.

Dr. Roy was a very tall, slim, graying, slightly bent Caucasian with a hawk-like nose, narrow-set, bluish-gray eyes and the severe countenance of a man clearly blessed with an air of natural command. He wore prescription glasses without shades and his hair was closely trimmed along the sideburns and neatly combed. He wore a starched white shirt and tie, which made him stand out even more from the crowd around him. The hard-edged harshness in his face was accentuated by huge bushy, gray and black eyebrows. He spotted me as I approached and broke away from the group to walk toward me. He was almost as tall as I. Perhaps 30 years ago, he would have matched me evenly. As I was to learn, he could be a fierce adversary—treacherous, even dangerous—when crossed, or slighted.

"Mr. Gentry?" he said gruffly, holding out his hand, "I'm Roy McTaggart." He smiled and welcomed me to Cayman. It was one of

18

those smiles that might have been genuine, but it radiated little natural warmth.

We walked the short distance to his car, a dusty, green, 1969 Dodge, and we exchanged a few pleasantries about my flight down. He spoke with the same curious dialect the customs inspector had used.

Riding the two miles along Shedden Road from the airport to the town, I began forming an uneasy opinion about my host and potential employer. At age 82, he was still a robust and imposing figure. I could imagine him even more intimidating in his younger years. He appeared to be struggling to be open and friendly, and I wanted to appear at ease with him. In reality, it was rather tense and I found myself beginning to seriously wonder, "What in God's name am I doing here?"

"We are going directly to a meeting of the board of directors at the Cay-mon-yon," he said. "Everyone will be there, except Billy, so you don't have to worry about him."

I had no idea who Billy was, so I wasn't worried and I didn't probe further. I knew absolutely nothing about the newspaper or the staff. I had no idea there was a board of directors. I thought Dr. Roy owned everything outright. He owned just about everything else.

"I own that building," he said, pointing to the four-story Barclays Bank building on Cardinall Avenue, "and that," pointing to a grocery store. "And that's mine too," he said about another large building on Cardinall Avenue as we drove past. A sign over its porch read, "McTaggart Tobacco Company." He had once received a royalty on every ounce of tobacco that came into the country. If you smoked a cigarette, you made Dr. Roy a bit richer with every puff.

By the time we pulled up in front of *The Caymanian Weekly*, I was fidgeting and wanted to hurry the process. I wanted to get through the bullshit and get the hell out of this strange flat, foreign little three-part country with its sing-songy people and anomalous smells and return to the familiar stench and slow, steady drawls of Port Arthur, Texas and environs.

2

A GOOD SMELL MAKES A DIFFERENCE

The offices of *The Caymanian Weekly* were in the central part of the dusty, main square of George Town. There was only one block that could be considered "downtown" in Grand Cayman. Church Street, which ran all the way along the western side of the island of Grand Cayman, composed the western boundary of the town. Fort Street and Cardinall Avenue were the north and south arteries of downtown proper, and Edward Street was the eastern boundary. The offices of *The Caymanian Weekly* were on Edward Street, in a white, one-story, concrete block building facing west. It was a five-minute walk west to George Town harbor.

Concrete block was the favorite construction material in the country. The Caymanians thought they had an endless supply of sand from the beaches and with no lumber available except for what was imported; building blocks were an easy, profitable solution for the construction industry's biggest supply problem.

There were two large rooms of equal size in *The Caymanian Weekly* building. High on the front wall of each room a large air conditioner poked through to the outside. Each struggled noisily with the afternoon sun streaming in through big bay windows. The north room was partitioned into editorial space at the front and the production equipment in back. The south room contained several small printing presses, a diminutive, enclosed photographic darkroom for the camera used in the newspaper processing, and bulk supplies of newsprint, ink, print shop paraphernalia and other assorted rummage. The entire complex of two rooms was perhaps fifty by seventy-five feet. There was a single toilet in a small room behind and attached to the main building.

Like most small weekly newspapers, it was neither neat nor tidy. But the familiar smell of ink and accompanying press chemicals was familiar and comforting. It gave me a brief respite: It would be hard to stay, but maybe not impossible.

There was great curiosity about me inside the little newspaper office. For weeks, the employees had wondered what was going to happen to them after the previous editor, Billy Bodden, had marched out of a board of director's meeting impetuously, leaving a letter of resignation in his wake. Even later, I never, ever, fully understood why Billy had carried so much anger with him when he walked out. He had started *The Caymanian Weekly*, the country's first and only weekly newspaper, in the mid-1960s upon returning to his island home after working in the composing room of the Miami News.

For several years, the little newspaper had been a cash cow. It had hit hard times. There was an argument at a board meeting and Billy stormed out. He thought the newspaper would quickly collapse.

The directors were in a quandary about what to do. There were many in the country who coveted the editor's position, but the board was cautious. They wanted their own man. It was a powerful position in the small politically sensitive country, since the newspaper was the sole source of news and editorial opinion.

Then, one day later, a letter of inquiry from an adventure-seeking reporter in Port Arthur, Texas, arrived on Dr. Roy's desk.

A devoutly religious man—as are most Caymanians—he saw my letter as the handiwork of none other than God Almighty. Port Arthur, Texas, was an American stronghold for the sea-faring Caymanians. It has been estimated that as many Caymanians live in and around the seaside municipality of Port Arthur as reside in The Cayman Islands.

"Praise be to God!" Dr. Roy said as he read my letter. "An American!"

The faces in the newspaper offices were, like the crowd at the airport, mostly various shades of brown. They offered me tentative smiles while I was given a brisk tour, but stayed as far away as possible without actually falling over the presses or cowering beneath the paste-up tables. A few even watched from inside the doorway of the photo darkroom.

Within minutes of our arrival, the other two owner/directors had arrived and had been introduced to me. Norberg Thompson was a big, all-business, former sea captain who had returned to Cayman to start a bakery. A balding Caucasian always in a hurry, he sold most of the bread eaten on the island and also dabbled in real estate. He was always more gruff in Dr. Roy's presence.

Arthur Bodden—"Mr. Arthur" as everyone in the country knew him—was an older gentleman who owned another small print shop and a tiny, oceanfront grocery store. He was immensely proud of his son Truman, who had graduated law school in England and returned to the islands where he worked as an assistant to The Cayman Islands

21

Attorney General. The Bodden name was one of the most common in the islands, like Smith or Jones in the U.S.

Mr. Arthur had also been a seafarer, and a radio operator—the first in The Cayman Islands. He spent most of his youth working for Cuba in a coastal radio station that served the shipping trade. Oddly enough, he had worked long enough to receive a small monthly retirement check from the Communist government.

But like most Caymanians he detested the government that had taken over the Cayman Island's larger neighbor less than 200 miles to the north. Still, they continued to pay him every month.

Mr. Arthur always wore a freshly pressed, starched, cotton "uniform" consisting of white shirt and pants. His white cap covering his shiny bald crown had a polished, black brim. I never saw him dressed otherwise. He was in his 60s then and, right from the start, was one of the warmest, friendliest souls I have ever met. Rarely did I ever meet this extremely thin, almost gaunt, gent without a smile on his face, and I never saw him without a sparkle in his eyes like he had just heard some joke and couldn't wait to share it.

Mr. Arthur owned 40 percent of the company, more than any other shareholder did. He would become my friend and closest ally in the years ahead, and never once failed to rally to my aid when I needed it. Dr. Roy owned 20 percent of the company, and Norberg 15. Another shareholder, Clifton Hunter, owned 5 percent.

Hunter was one of the most respected citizens in the Caymans. A lawyer of mixed-blood and member of the country's legislature, I never heard one bad thing said about him during the years I would live there. From the brief time I knew him, he was cordial, helpful, polite and conscientious. Unfortunately, he died of a heart attack within weeks of my arrival in Cayman.

Many times I have wondered how differently things might have turned out had he not died so early in my Cayman career. His mild-mannered courtesy, calm, even-handedness and clear thinking probably would have averted much of the ugliness that lay ahead for me. Ironically, his death brought a vacancy in the legislature. The elections surrounding the filling of that vacancy were to cause me untold professional grief and toss me right into the middle of one of the country's most ferocious political campaigns.

So who owned the remaining 20 percent of the company? Ah, yes, there's the rub—the former editor, Billy Bodden.

Billy had walked out on the newspaper, but had retained ownership of one-fifth of the corporation. Had my giddy mind not been in the clouds, I probably would have walked out on that salient point alone.

Through his partial ownership, Billy had the right to attend the

22

annual meetings and periodically examine the books. It always galled me to reveal to my predecessor the financial condition of the newspaper and printing company. He was not only my precursor, but became my fierce competitor. He started a competing newspaper within a year after my arrival, a move I believe he had been plotting long before he left *The Caymanian Weekly*. Billy was certain the paper would fold without him. It would, but not in the manner in which anyone at the time would have believed.

The meeting that first day was over almost as soon as it began. There were only a few brief questions. What did I think about the possibilities of the newspaper? I told them I was surprised there were no grocery advertisements.

"That's a source of most of the revenue of weekly newspapers in the United States," I said. "Don't grocery stores compete here?"

That brought a quick rise out of Dr. Roy. "You better believe we're competitive," he laughed. I then remembered he owned one of the major grocery stores.

They wanted to know how much I wanted in salary. I hadn't thought about it. For the Beaumont Journal, I was making about $650 a month. I told them I would take $1,000 a month. They accepted immediately.

In reality, $1,000 a month was a great salary for a newspaper editor in 1971. In Cayman, it was even better because that was my net take-home pay. There were no deductions in Cayman because there are no income taxes and no social programs like Social Security and unemployment insurance. Consequently, I would double my net salary if I took the job. In addition, I would have to pay no U.S. income taxes at all. As I would learn, freedom from all taxes was the lifeblood of this strange little country.

But I didn't immediately accept. It was still too new and strange. I told them I would take a few days and then give them my decision. Privately, I was still wondering if I wouldn't be much better off in Texas. It had its strange odors too, but the plumbing worked and there were amenities like radio, television, grocery stores that stayed open Sunday and didn't close at twilight, cheeseburgers and good drinking water right out of the tap.

By the time the brief meeting ended, it was a late Saturday afternoon. Norberg said he would pick me up on Sunday morning and drive me around the island before it was time for my afternoon flight back to Beaumont.

The Caymanian's shop foreman, David Parchment, a local boy who was born on the island and trained there by Billy, came forward and told Dr. Roy he would he happy to take me to my hotel, and Dr. Roy agreed. David was friendly enough, but was hesitant to open up to

23

me.

David spent most of his time keeping up with the commercial printing. With so much banking activity in Cayman and few printers available, commercial printing was a very lucrative part of the company's operation. He kept most of the records either in his head or in a small notebook permanently stored in his pocket.

David asked if there was anything I wanted before going to the hotel for the night. I asked him if he could take me where I could buy a bottle of vodka. This was the first time I saw him smile. He drove me back to the airport and we went behind the terminal building to an attached shed. He walked up to a back door and knocked. He saw my puzzled face and said, "Supposed to be closed for liquor by now, but I'll get you a bottle."

It was my first introduction to the way the Cayman economy functions. Rarely was there an official prohibition that couldn't be overcome by personal contact. As long as you knew somebody, you could get anything. The back door he had knocked upon was to a duty-free liquor store that fronted on the inside of the terminal. The door opened and the owner, David's cousin, asked him what he needed. I was introduced and in a few minutes we drove away with my bottle of vodka.

As he let me out at the swanky La Fontaine Hotel on Seven Mile Beach, he hesitated, then said cryptically, "I'll come back to talk to you later. There's something else you should know before you decide to come here."

I was puzzled, but nodded my head. If he wanted to talk, I would listen.

I finished about half the bottle before sundown. I took a short walk on the beach. There were very few people. The sunset was glorious, almost surreal. I was tipsy. I could hear the Jamaican band imported from Kingston tuning up for the hotel's Saturday night dance.

The sky darkened and I went back to my room. The reggae reverberated through the walls from the courtyard. A colorful crowd of tourists and local Caymanians swirled to the surging beat of the Caribbean night. I sipped on the bottle until it was almost empty.

I should have been enjoying the spectacle, but instead I had a nagging worry that something was amiss. David's parting words earlier sounded like a warning. I wondered if he would have trouble finding my room. The next thing I remember it was early morning and I had a horrible hangover.

It was almost 5 a.m. and I needed a cup of black coffee. I quickly showered and walked down to the lobby. There was no one in sight. I wandered outside looking for a staff member. There was simply no one up this early. Not anywhere. With nothing else to do, I took a stroll along the beach to clear my head. I had the entire island to myself. The sea was almost dead calm. Every few seconds, a small wave would lap onto the shore, but even the ocean was struggling to come to life this morning.

When I returned to the hotel, a few staff members were stirring in the kitchen. They gave me a cup of coffee, but said it was too early for breakfast. So, I began my day hungry.

Norberg arrived about 8 a.m. and we began our tour. Most of the activity centered near George Town and northward for a mile or so along pristine Seven Mile Beach, which is not really seven miles but more like six. The beach ends at the northern community of West Bay.

As we drove back to George Town and turned eastward toward East End, about 20 miles away, the houses dwindled and it was soon open countryside. There was little in the way of hardwood vegetation. Most of the island was brushy, low and swampy, with almost no agriculture or ranching visible. Cayman owed its existence and its character to the sea, not the land. The islands developed over millions of years from the coral reefs that slowly rose out of the Caribbean. The three small islands of the country were, geologically speaking, three outcroppings of coral and limestone barely visible above the surface.

The small, tin-roofed "Caymanian" houses were the dominant architecture. They were of block construction, colored in various pastels. Pink was the favored color. The tin roofs were functional. Except for a few poor quality ground wells, most of the island's drinking water came from cisterns that obtained their supply from the rain on the rooftops. Most islanders drank it right from the spigot. The idea of the rainfall washing all of the dirt, leaves and bird crap from my roof into my cistern prompted me to boil my family's drinking water.

The sea was captivating. Not far offshore the bottom plunges quickly from mere inches to more than 1,000 feet. Just south of Grand Cayman in the Cayman Trench, the bottom is more than five miles below. But above in the sunlight, the sea is blue and clear. Rarely is there a day that passes when the snorkeler or diver cannot see 100 feet or more in the clear water.

When Norberg dropped me off at the airport for the trip back to Port Arthur from George Town after that first interview, I still had mixed feelings. The island—at least the sea—was enchanting. The idea of running a newspaper on a small island was strongly appealing; especially to the romantic young man I was.

This was my big chance. I would be in complete charge of the office. I would be the editor AND publisher. Everyone, including the production people, the artists, the salesmen, writers—all of them—would report to ME. Never mind that I had never managed a production department before and I knew nothing about the business side of publishing, I would be the boss. Me.

But—and it was a huge but—there were no McDonald's here. No quart of milk and a Twinkie at 10 p.m. at the gas station. No TV. No radio. No mall. And when you are restless and need to drive there were few roads to roam. There was one main road that ran all the way from the northwestern tip 26 miles to East End. Cayman could be very confining. No bright city lights. If you went to downtown George Town at night it was dark and deserted. If you ventured out early there was no coffee before 8 a.m.

And, I had no idea what kind of staff I would have. The only one I had spoken to at any length had failed to appear after mysteriously warning me about getting the "full story."

As I bid Norberg goodbye and left Cayman that Sunday afternoon and the jet climbed back into the sky, I was relieved to be escaping the strange, backward, isolated country with its curious people. I was anxious to return to the abundance of foul-smelling, oil-rich air and bright lights of southeast Texas and my little family. I decided I would tell my wife Martha that this was not going to work after all. Martha would understand. Our lives together had been an adventure from the very beginning, but this was different. This was over the ocean, beyond Cuba. Way out there in the deep water.

I would trust my inner voice. It would have been a wonderful diversion from our very frustrating situation in Texas, but, no, I didn't think so. It did not feel "right." Martha would understand.

3

MARTHA TAKES CONTROL

Before I had shaken the Caribbean dust from my coat on my happy return to Port Arthur from George Town, Grand Cayman, Martha demanded to hear about my interview with Dr. Roy.

"They offered me the job," I said, "but we need to really think about this."

My doubts about moving away from my newly appreciated, secure home were reinforced by my arrival back in the U.S. The Cayman Islands were a planet away from the conveniences of south Texas. Now that I was back safely on my own turf the brief conversations I had with the newspaper's owners only fuelled my consternation. None of them had said very much at all about what they expected from me. They let me do all of the talking and then asked me how much money I wanted. I regretted having such a glib tongue and personal charm.

"This isn't another wild-goose chase like Hawaii," I told Martha, referring to one of our previous adventures. "Hawaii's out in the middle of the ocean, but it's still America. They've got restaurants, running water, streetlights, neon signs, newspapers, television, movies, radio...

"Down there, there's none of that. It's a backwater! It's so dark at night you don't dare go outside without a flashlight! And mosquitoes are so bad they strangle cows left outside the barn."

Actually a soft, full moon had bathed the islands the previous night, which would have made my stroll on the beach enchanting. Unfortunately, I was passed out in my room and never made it outside. And I never spotted a fly, much less a mosquito.

"What is there to think about?" she snapped. "You hate your job. You can't stand the people you work with. This entire state reeks with oil and gas fumes. It's dirty! It's humid! It stinks!"

My jaw dropped with surprise at the intensity of her rebuttal. And, it was a rebuttal. I hadn't said it outright, but she knew I was squirming away from the idea of moving as fast as I could churn out my doubts.

"So Hawaii didn't work," she said. "It wasn't a pipe dream. We could have done it. We were starting to make it work."

"But you got pregnant and wanted to run home to Mama," I reminded her. "Aloha, Tupelo!"

"And you've been miserable ever since," she snapped. "Never satisfied!

"Look," I reminded her, "it wasn't my fault what happened at Ole Miss. We had no choice but to leave and make some money. And New Mexico was great. We had a life and career there. I'll never forget looking back down that long hill when we crossed the tracks the last day. I was sad. We left friends there."

"It was a miserable place," she snapped back. "The wind never stopped screaming and you went as far as you could go. We hardly made enough money to eat. You wanted a chance to write in a real city newsroom, and you got what you wanted, as usual."

"Yeah, I did," I answered meekly. "But I thought the bigger newspaper in Beaumont meant better writers and a chance to improve my writing. Look at what happened to me. I almost bit the dust."

She looked at me. "Babe, there are no better newspaper reporters than you. Don't forget it!"

The thing about Martha was she meant every word. There were times when I had few fans, but I always knew I had at least one.

"A few weeks ago you were in the hospital believing you were dying," she said, bringing us abruptly back to the verdict. "You wanted a change in our lives. Another shot. What do you think this is? What would you be leaving behind here? You'll regret it all of your life if you don't go. It's the Caribbean!"

Our two kids, Alison and Stephen, watched the lively conversation with wild-eyed, childish enthusiasm. They were too young to fathom the idea of moving to another country, but, like all kids, they were excited about the prospect of moving anywhere. Both less than ten years old, they were seasoned travelers.

Martha, of course, was right. When something like this is offered, you take it or spend your miserable life wondering what might have been. Hawaii was over, a would-be dream now wrecked. My first boss in Artesia told me that if you ever settled along the Pecos River, you would never leave. Well, Artesia still sits there on the banks. I'm long gone.

The newspaper profession in the 1960s was an open travel invitation for reporters with an itch for adventure. Anyone with actual experience could land a job at any one of hundreds of tiny newspapers that published tenuously throughout the country. The going rate was $65 to $80 per week. It was hardly a living wage, which explains why an enterprising young writer, especially one with a family to support, hardly gave a second thought to yanking up roots when a $10 raise drifts across his bow.

Within two weeks, I shocked my fellow reporters with my resignation, packed my bags, and purchased a one-way ticket to Grand Cayman to take charge of the newspaper.

Martha would sell everything at a garage sale, including our car, and follow with Alison, Stephen and Smokey as soon as she could. She did not understand Smokey would be a condemned criminal as soon as he set paws in the country. It would take "James Bond action" to save him.

4

ME AND MARTHA ANN JENKINS

Before Martha Ann Jenkins and I met, we both grew up in Tupelo, Mississippi. Although my father delivered the mail to her house almost every day of her young life and she knew Skippy—his dog who faithfully trailed along behind him—she never met me until after I returned home from my Marine Corps enlistment and started junior college in nearby Fulton.

After our marriage—a full decade before we heard of The Cayman Islands or even thought it possible to escape from Mississippi and live in any faraway, exotic place—we prepared to settle down for small-town life. Martha began work for an insurance adjuster for $100 a month.

Our contentment lasted three months. We both ached to leave Tupelo. Impulsive to the point of recklessness, we were restless romantics, and extremely resourceful.

While other local couples of our era joined a church, started families and focused on their ambitions and their perfect house, Martha and I probed maps and travel magazines. Another young wife might have been terrified when I talked about moving to Mexico or Alaska. Martha was thrilled. My mother was doubtful. Southern folks must labor at the foot of the cross if they expect deliverance, she said.

We loved our families, but when we faced the prospect of spending our lives in Tupelo, it cast a shadow over the conversation. We couldn't wait the four years it would take for me to finish college. We wanted to get out, now.

One day in 1960, I cut classes at my Fulton school to attend a dove shoot in nearby Okolona, Mississippi at the invitation of Jack Bowles, a friend from both high school and the Marines. Martha wasn't particularly happy with my blasé attitude about college. The bills were mounting and money was in typical short supply.

"Haven't you been cutting too many classes?" she said. I didn't answer, but she was right.

"Well, if you can afford to go kill those poor birds, I can afford get my hair done," she said.

"I think that's a terrific idea," I said as I grabbed my shotgun and shuffled toward the front door.

It was a hell of a shoot, the type outdoor writers spin in hunting magazines. About 100 invited guests ringed a narrow, 100-acre hay field that had been freshly cut for the occasion. It attracted doves in droves. As the afternoon settled in, the air reverberated like old Ulysses S. Grant was trying to get in the back door at Vicksburg again. We must have killed a thousand birds and shot at ten times that many. Empty shells and empty bottles of Old Crow and Southern Comfort littered the ground as the October afternoon roared on.

Fortunately, no hunters were killed or maimed. Occasionally some inattentive shooter would be peppered with birdshot when a panicked dove streaked down the middle of the field, but the alert among us knew to duck when someone across the way aimed in our direction.

When it got too dark to shoot at anything, everyone jumped into the cars and pickups and raced to a small, neighborhood grocery store that doubled as a watering hole for the gentlemen shooters of Okolona. The birds were plucked, seasoned, powdered with white flour and fried over open fires in massive iron skillets full of hissing, bubbling lard. Ears of fresh corn were boiled in washtubs and dunked like Popsicles into vats of melted butter and there was Old Crow and Coca-Cola to wash it all down.

I was filthy dirty, covered with blood and feathers and scarcely able to navigate when I stumbled into our apartment late that night.

"Guess what I read today?" she said, ignoring my appearance. "There was a magazine at the hairdressers that had an article in it about going to college in Hawaii." she said. "I remember listening to a Honolulu radio station when I was a little girl. It's so far away but you could hear it late at night here. I fantasized about being there. Did you ever listen to it?"

"Your hair is absolutely majestic," I muttered.

"The best part is the tuition," she said. "It's only $80 a semester and they don't charge extra for out-of-state students."

We had talked of going to Mexico City College. The tuition was enormous, so we forgot the prospect. Besides, an American cannot work in Mexico and Martha must work if I went to college.

For weeks following that fateful day, we talked of nothing else but the sandy beaches of Hawaii. It began as daydreaming, but the days passed and we grew serious. After all, Hawaii was now a state. Sure, it was across 2,000 miles of ocean but it was part of America. You could

31

hold a job if you wanted. And, the university was dirt-cheap.

We discussed it with our parents. My mother in law Agnes thought it adventurous and gave her blessing. My parents weren't so sure. They had been born in Tupelo and planned to die there. My father went to Chicago as a young man but after that, and a wedding honeymoon to Chattanooga, my parents' travels were limited to Sunday drives around Tupelo.

Since we had limited funds we needed a plan. We had $800 in savings. It was enough to get us there and pay expenses for the first few months, but I was convinced we could make even more.

From the movies, I knew California had beaches and flashy cars. I suspected that cars were cheaper in Mississippi than in California so my plan was to invest our life's savings in a sharp Mississippi car and drive to California. There, I reasoned we could sell it to the surfers for a huge profit.

That became our strategy. I applied to the University of Hawaii and began the search for the perfect automobile. I found it at a local Oldsmobile dealer, a 1955 powder blue Ford Sunliner convertible. I handed over $550 cash and drove it home.

Martha was elated. It was a beautiful car. They were going to love it in Southern California. "I bet we double our money," she said. "Or triple it," I said. We were certain we had made an unbeatable deal.

At semester's end a few weeks later we packed our few belongings into the back of the Ford, said our good-byes to friends and our concerned families, and headed south. It would have been quicker to head west, but we wanted to drive through New Orleans and visit the French Quarter. It was part of the plan.

A week later, I called my father and asked him for a loan. We had spent most of our remaining $200 in savings on food and lodging in New Orleans and the trip was coming to a halt on the plains between Liberty and Hondo, Texas. My father agreed to lend me $200 to get to California. I promised to repay him with interest once I had sold the car.

On the first leg of our trip we had managed 250 miles before running out of money. There were only 4,000 miles to go.

I remained convinced I would make a profit, but doubt was creeping in that I would triple my investment. I had discovered that the brakes were in pitiful shape. The brake shoes scraped the drums almost as soon as the transaction was consummated. It became progressively worse as we followed the sun westward.

And there was the right front door. When you made a sharp left turn, it would swing open because the latch was worn out. It scared the hell out of Martha the first few times it happened. She rode leaning against it so she could face me and talk. I fixed it temporarily by slowing down whenever I made a left turn. She did less talking.

There was no insurance on the car. Martha and I had tried to buy liability insurance, but no agent would sell us a policy because we were leaving the state for good and naive enough to tell them so. I asked one agent about trip insurance:

"Can't you just buy enough for a few days?" I asked.

"That's only for life insurance," he said. "Do you want any?"

"No," I said.

"I didn't think so," he said.

Fortunately, we made it without an accident.

The engine also overheated. I never knew whether it was the blistering heat of the Southwestern desert or a faulty water pump, but on numerous occasions the engine plunged into the red line on the temp gauge and the engine would sputter to a halt. This always happened at least 50 miles from the nearest available water. Fortunately in the peaceful days of the early 1960s it was easy to find help. Usually it only took a few minutes after I raised the hood for someone to stop and offer assistance.

Mechanical problems couldn't stop us, but our own health was another matter. It was deep in the heart of Texas when I first realized Martha's complaints were serious. She had complained for weeks about headaches and pain in her neck and jaw. She refused to see a doctor in Tupelo for fear of delaying our start.

But with each day the pain increased. We stopped one late afternoon in Gonzales to find a doctor. He examined her and told her she had an abscessed tooth. He gave her a shot of penicillin and insisted she see a dentist as soon as possible.

"I think more than one is abscessed," he said. "Maybe as many as four."

A dentist in Seguine confirmed the gloomy diagnosis. He said he couldn't pull them until the infection cleared and we weren't willing, or able, to stick around for that. We were running out of money again and becoming desperate to reach California and sell the convertible. He gave Martha more antibiotics and painkillers and turned us loose on the road.

The medicine helped. We made a sweeping Southwestern arc across west Texas, up through New Mexico, across Arizona—pausing briefly to gaze at the Grand Canyon and the Petrified Forest—and then, two weeks after leaving Tupelo, entered the outskirts of Los Angeles, our jumping-off point.

I had $30 left. Martha was now in constant pain. She remembers little of the trip after Texas because of the codeine the doctor gave her.

We checked into a small motel and I tucked Martha into bed. There were a few hours of precious daylight left. I checked to make certain I had the registration for the Ford and headed downtown.

I was confident I would sell the car quickly. With the profits, I would move to a better motel, find another dentist for Martha, and all would be right with the world again.

About two hours later, I returned to the motel. Martha was sitting up in bed.

"Did you sell it?" she asked.

"Well, no," I said.

"Couldn't you find a dealer?"

"Honey, there's a car dealer on every corner of Los Angeles."

"So why didn't you sell it?"

"We don't have a title," I said. "They think it's stolen."

5

IT POURS, MAN IT POURS

Mississippi at the time didn't issue a car title. They issued a certificate called a Road and Bridge Privilege Tax. It was perfectly legal but not many were seen in California. None of the dealers wanted to talk to me. I tried half a dozen and had been rudely rejected. They hadn't even glanced at my cream puff, powder blue Ford Sunliner convertible.

The next day brought more rejection. No one would listen to me. I tried a dozen lots. No use. Every passing hour, I hated Los Angeles more.

On the third day, I was despondent. The motel was eating up my $30 at $8 per day. I was low on gas. There were no credit cards in 1961. Even if there had been I doubt that we would have owned one. You either had cash or you were out on the street, and stayed on empty.

"We have to check out soon," I told Martha. "I don't have enough money to pay another night."

She just nodded. Her teeth were aching and she was running a high fever. She was a trooper but it became worse by the hour and I knew she was despondent.

"I just want to get out of Los Angeles," I said. "I hate this goddamn place. We can drive north. We've got sleeping bags. We'll sleep on the beach. We'll be OK."

I didn't believe we would be OK. For the first time, I was afraid. We had no money, no gas and no food. California had become very repulsive. We knew no one within 2,000 miles. I was out of place in the most hostile town I have ever been in.

I opened my bags and grabbed the only suit I owned. I told Martha I would be back soon and set out walking to find a pawn shop. They weren't hard to find in Los Angeles.

I walked up to the clerk behind a glass window and placed the suit on the counter.

"How much you want?" he asked.

"$20," I said. I had paid $40 for the suit.

He looked at the label, Hinds Brothers, Tupelo, Miss., and then at me. Without a word, he tossed the suit back at my face like I had insulted him. I was shocked and stepped back.

"How about $5?" I asked.

The bastard didn't even look up at me. I slunk out of the shop and walked back to the motel. The clock was rushing toward checkout time.

"Let's get going," I told Martha.

All I wanted to do was to get out of that city. I didn't care where we ended up as long as we didn't let the sun set on us in Los Angeles.

"Do you think you can hock this?" Martha asked, slipping her wedding ring off of her finger for the first time since we had been married. It had been given to me by my mother for Martha when we were married. It had also been my grandmother's, a thin silver band encrusted with a half dozen small diamonds.

"I'll find another pawn shop," I said, "if you are sure about this?"

"There's nothing else we can do," she said. "And take our suitcase. It's a Samsonite. They might give you something for it. It's brand new."

Packing the ring and suitcase, I walked out again into late-afternoon Los Angeles. Another shop was a half block away. I entered and walked toward the cashier's cage in the rear of the building. Guns, television sets, musical instruments, clothing and other transitory paraphernalia decorated the dusty shelving.

The single clerk watched me indifferently as I approached the cage. He said nothing.

"I need to pawn this," I said, holding out the ring.

He examined it under a jeweler's light and put it down.

"A couple of bucks," he said.

"That's great," I said, trying to appear as pitiable and amicable as I could muster beneath the rising anger I harbored for this awful town.

"And I can throw this in, too," I said, placing the luggage on the edge of the counter so he could examine it. "It's brand new!" I said.

He looked at the ring, the luggage, me, and then back to the ring again.

"Three bucks!" he said.

"Could you make it $3.50?" I asked humbly.

He looked at me again and a slight hint of humanity tweaked the corners of his lips.

"OK, sure," he said, and handed me three crisp bills and two quarters.

I was ecstatic running back to get Martha. More than the money was

36

the benevolent treatment, finally, from someone in this stink hole.

It wasn't enough money to stay another night but it meant we could check out, buy food and get a gallon or two of gasoline.

"Let's get out of here!" I told Martha.

I had $3 and change in my pocket. That bought a loaf of bread, a jar of peanut butter and three gallons of gasoline. It filled the tank to a little over one-quarter. It was enough to get us moving again.

We drove north through Santa Monica toward Malibu on the Pacific Coast Highway. The farther we got from downtown Los Angeles the better I felt. I began looking for a spot along the beach around Malibu to spend the night and regroup.

I chose a lonely point absent of swimmers, parked, and walked down to the surf. It was so cold we couldn't bear touching the water with our toes. We dove in anyway, then came scrambling back. I looked around at the beach. It was gray and dreary, completely different from the beach-movie image of bright, sunny sands and happy, carefree surfers that had drawn us like a magnet. The water was full of seaweed and smelled like rotten cabbage. The day was rapidly slipping into evening and Martha began to cry.

"We can't stay here," she said. "This is dreadful!"

I looked at my map. If we hurried, we could make it to Oxnard by 5:30 p.m. If the used car lots were still open, I would make a deal. Any deal. I would sell the car for $100. All I wanted was to get Martha off this cold, windy, bleak beach into a warm room.

The trip that began with hope and promise stumbled into reality on that deserted beach. I was the complete fool. I had wasted all of my savings for nothing. Worse, we would probably have to return to Tupelo in disgrace—if we could get back.

I tried bravado with the first dealer I found.

"How would you like to own this beauty?" I said.

He looked at me, then at Martha. Her face was swollen and streaked with dried tears. She was still in her bathing suit from the aborted swimming adventure at Malibu 30 miles behind us. A few strands of seaweed clung to her bare legs.

"What do you want?" he said.

"$550. It's a real steal," I said.

"No thanks," he said. "Can't use it."

"Wanna make me an offer?"

"Nope," he said, and suggested I try another dealer about a half mile down the highway. Why didn't I just say $100 and get it over with?

"There's a guy about four blocks down on the right who might want it," the salesman said. "His name's Munyan. He might be looking for something like this."

I thanked him feebly and drove off. The light was fading. The gasoline gauge was touching the big "E". Martha wrapped her arms around her legs. Her head was bent to her knees. She looked small, cold and forlorn. The gas tank wasn't the only thing on empty.

This guy Munyan was our last chance. He didn't realize it, but he would get a beautiful 1955 powder blue Ford Sunliner convertible for the price of a motel room, dinner and aspirin.

The big deal, the plan, the ridiculous strategy, it was over. A sledgehammer would have had a problem beating me any lower emotionally.

I pulled into the lot and cut the ignition. There were about 15 cars for sale. To my right was a tiny office with large glass windows. Inside, I could see a very big man in a tan sports coat and tie sitting behind a desk. He was watching us and speaking on the telephone. He hung up, but was in no hurry to come out and see what I wanted. On any other occasion, I would have said to hell with his attitude and left. We just sat there looking at each other through the window pane. Finally, he got up and meandered to our car.

"I'm closed," he said curtly.

His blond hair was neatly combed. He looked clean. His neatness made me acutely aware that Martha and I were still in swimsuits with traces of sand and seaweed plastered to our skin.

"I really need to sell this car," I blurted. It wasn't the pitch I planned, but the finality in his voice terrified me.

"Why don't you come back tomorrow and we'll talk," he said, his tone softening just a bit. "I can't help you today."

With that, he turned and walked back into the small office. After a few minutes, he turned out the lights in the office and on his sales sign at the front of the lot. Night was coming down hard.

"What are we going to do?" Martha asked. Her voice startled me because she hadn't said anything since the beach disaster.

"I don't know," I said. And I didn't. I didn't even have a dollar left. The car was drained of gas and so was I.

Munyan hesitated after locking his office and slowly walked back to us again.

"You have to leave," he said firmly. "I'm closing for the night."

"I can't," I said, "I don't have any gas and I don't have any money to get any."

He looked over at Martha and sighed.

"You kids a little down on your luck?" he asked.   "Yeah."

"Just a minute," he said, and walked back into the office. I saw him pick up the telephone.

"I think he's calling the cops," I told Martha. She didn't say anything.

I suppose we were both relieved. At least in jail we would get something hot to eat and a warm bunk.

Munyan left his office and began walking to our car. I expected a warning that the police were on the way. He would be astounded when he learned how much I welcomed a night in a warm cell.

"Would you two like to baby-sit?" he asked.

"What?" I said.

"My wife and I have five daughters and we need a baby-sitter tonight," he said. "I've got a big house. You can spend the night if you like."

I was so astonished I was speechless. I tried to object, wondering if the guy might be a lunatic or one of those California perverts we had heard so much about. This was only an hour from downtown Los Angeles. I reached down to turn the key in the ignition. At least we could outrun him for a few blocks. He waived away my protestations.

"Relax," he said. "I'm serious. It's okay. I just talked to my wife. She and the girls are anxious to meet you."

So he had not called the police. He had called his wife.

I looked at Martha. She looked back. It was a snap decision, but perhaps we were due for a change of luck.

Munyan patiently gave directions to his house, just a few blocks away.

Then he turned and walked toward his own car. I wondered if he was hoping that we would reject his startling impromptu invitation and get the hell out of his life. I was wrong.

He stopped, almost as an afterthought, and walked back to my side of the car. He leaned over and slipped something into my hand. "Here," he whispered, "you might need to get her something on the way."

I looked down at a $20 bill he had placed into my palm.

"We're going to make it," I whispered to Martha.

She nodded her head.

*   *   *

We did make it to Honolulu, broke, and found jobs with a wealthy family who provided us food and board in exchange for Martha's housework as a maid and cook. I handled the yard work, and began attending the University of Hawaii part-time. We struggled, but were making progress in becoming Hawaiians. When we learned after a year that Martha was pregnant with our daughter Alison, we decided it was time to return to Mississippi for the blessed event.

39

After Alison was born, we moved to Oxford, Mississippi in order for me to attend the University of Mississippi. I was hoping to major in journalism. Before I could graduate, black student James Meredith was enrolled in the segregated university by U.S. Marshals and a riot erupted that almost closed down the university. I immediately sought permanent employment as a reporter, and was offered a job as sports editor in the dusty Southeastern New Mexico town of Artesia. I spent almost six years in Artesia, and we loved every minute of it.

When I began to yearn for more experience in a larger newspaper, I was offered the job of news editor of the Daily Journal in Beaumont, Texas. That's where the seminal event of my life occurred.

6

DEEP IN THE HEAT OF TEXAS

In spite of my high hopes when I rolled out of Artesia, the first months at the new job in Beaumont brought uneasy times. Learning the new role of news editor had its challenges, but that wasn't the problem. I just didn't fit. There was none of the fellowship you normally find in a news staff. What I could not know was that this move would profoundly change my life.

People performed their jobs and went home. I told one fellow editor who appeared friendly that maybe we could get together one weekend with our families. He looked at me like I had suggested a mugging.

Within weeks after I arrived an announcement was made that the ownership of the newspaper was changing. The bank that had held the newspaper in trust since the private owners had died had found a new corporate owner and we had been purchased.

The former owner had been generous. The new owner was different. They were a typical major newspaper operator. Tighten the screws, even if it meant screwing long-time employees. Necessary changes long ignored by the bankers were initiated. There was a conversion of the printing process from hot metal to the new offset process. Almost a hundred employees received notice they wouldn't be needed after the conversion.

A new publisher was appointed. The newspaper had separate staffs for the morning and evening editions. Everyone knew this arrangement was doomed under the new regime. There would be a combination of editorial staffs to save money. As news editor of the evening edition, the conversion to offset type affected me directly.

With hot metal, each edition began every morning like hot biscuits from the Ole Dixie Café, from scratch. Almost every item in the newspaper delivered to the customer that evening was a product of that day's effort. That meant every morning literally began a new day for me. All I had to do was to send enough stories to the composing room to fill that day's newspaper. It meant hard work but it also meant that I didn't have to plan anything for tomorrow's edition. Tomorrow would take care of itself. It always had.

Offset printing, or "cold type" as we called it, changed all of that. Cold type came to newspaper publishing not because it is faster but because it is cheaper. Newspapers across the nation were able in the 1960s and 1970s to rid themselves of thousands of linotype operators and other hot-metal workers by converting to offset printing. Typists—preferably women; preferably non-union women—took over the typesetting chores in the composing room.

Since the offset printing process took longer, I began preparing many inside pages several days ahead of the printing schedule. This meant planning and scheduling.

Today it has changed again. Pagination has replaced nimble layout and paste-up artists. QuarkXpress and InDesign have replaced the X-Acto knife. It's still offset but everything is produced electronically by computers. Labor at the speed of light—a world completely different than 40 years ago. The traditional composing room, as I knew it, has become an anachronism. It has become more of a writer's venue, with fewer shackles and handcuffs. If these wondrous instruments had come 40 years earlier, my life would have been simpler and more productive. I know it.

Where I perceived Artesia as high, dry and bright, Beaumont was low, sticky and gray. The refineries in the area gave it an odious, sugary smell. Almost immediately, I learned my life in Beaumont was going to be different than in Artesia. One policeman was evidently keeping an eye on my license plate and when I had not changed to Texas plates within the required 30 days, he pulled me over and wrote me a citation. Me! A reporter!

Not only was the newspaper different, with its much larger staff of dispassionate reporters, editors and photographers, Beaumont was a problematic city for me from the beginning. Both the town and the newspaper depressed me.

And I began to bleed. It began three or four or months after we moved from New Mexico. I saw no connection. The weeks went by. For a while, I could forget about it with the help of an old friend, booze. Every night I would rush home, hug my wife and kids and reach into the liquor cabinet for a reassuring bottle of vodka. By 9 p.m., I was a comfortable vegetable.

Martha and I began to argue over my behavior. Slowly, my confidence and self-esteem eroded. My home became as unhappy a place as my work environment.

For weeks, I clung to the belief the bleeding would stop in time. It got steadily worse. I confided in nobody, not even Martha. I was convinced cancer was eating my guts.

"How old are you?" the doctor asked. "Well, men 33 don't develop colon cancer."

By the time I returned to the newspaper office, I was elated. A doctor had personally assured me that I was too young to have cancer. I threw myself into the job with a vigor I had not known in months. I planned newspapers for the next day, the next week, and the next month for God's sake!

Within a few weeks, my old trouble returned. I made an appointment with a specialist, who propped me upside down on a special table and conducted an undignified probe of my complaint.

Dr. De los Reyes was a Cuban trained as a pediatrician in his native country. He studied internal medicine after fleeing from Castro.

"Are you looking for a tumor?" I asked him.

"When you hear hoof beats in Texas, you don't expect to see zebras," he said.

I wanted a better prognosis than that—which I inferred was meant to be hopeful—but he wouldn't give one. I suspected he must have realized I was dying but wouldn't tell me. I began to miss my family immediately. What would they do without me? Who would sit around every night staring at television drinking himself into a stupor? Who would grumble every morning and slink bleary-eyed and headachy to work?

Dr. De los Reyes did give me medication. My blood pressure was at a dangerous level and he was concerned about a stroke. He told me not to eat anything with salt in it.

Two days later, I was sitting at my desk fighting to get the final edition out when I forced myself make the dreaded call to the doctor's office to get my lab results.

"Mr. Gentry, we've had a hard time reaching you," said the nurse. "Your tests came back; they are very positive for occult blood. Dr. De los Reyes wants you to enter the hospital for a few days of tests."

I was dumbfounded. I had expected reassurance, not zebras!

I hung up and mumbled something to my managing editor, and walked out of the office. Martha picked me up and I rode silently home and started packing for the hospital stay.

Martha didn't say anything but I knew she was now alarmed. She called her sister, Risë (Ree-sa) who decided to come to Beaumont while I was in the hospital.

43

7

EXCUSE ME WHILE I STICK THIS INTO YOUR GUTS!

Dr. De los Reyes came by early the next morning to give me a short report. "We're going to look far up inside your colon," he said. "I don't want to stop until we find out what's behind this bleeding." I suppose he was trying to be reassuring. I could have told him exactly what was wrong. I was being devoured by cancer.

He led me to a small examination room nearby and began. "I have my diagnosis," he said almost immediately to no one in particular. He sounded elated, happy. So far, there had been no pain at all. He had barely begun.

"You have a disease called ulcerative colitis."

Since I didn't have cancer, I expected to be released to go home immediately. It didn't work that way. I learned that this was a potentially deadly disease and although mine had not progressed to the life-threatening stage, Dr. De los Reyes was taking no chances with a patient he had decided was not only a hypochondriac and impacted with anxieties, but decidedly flaky.

I didn't know then, but the newspaper was making a number of personnel changes. One of them concerned me. They realized that I wasn't the happiest of employees but rather than sack me so soon after my illness, they found another spot for me.

It was a decision that would change my career and my life profoundly. At the time of my hospitalization, Martha had found a larger house to rent. It was midway between Beaumont and Port Arthur—a distance of some 30 miles.

When I was released from the hospital after two weeks, I was forced by the doctor to spend a few days at home in bed. But I wasted no time getting back to the office when the restriction was up. I hated the environment at the newspaper but it beat the heck out of hanging around the house.

My first day back, I was called into the office of the executive editor, Don Boyette. Don had hired me when I had been editor in Artesia. He asked me how I might feel about running a small news operation. There was an opening for a bureau chief at the Port Arthur office and since I lived close to Port Arthur now, it might be just the tonic. I jumped at the chance.

The isolated bureau was in an old building in downtown Port Arthur and wired to the main office by an ancient Teletype machine. Stories were rarely filed by telephone because the Teletype machine was so handy. Therefore, the personal contact with the home office was rare. It suited me fine.

It was a three-person bureau cramped into a tiny basement office in a rambling, old boarding house, but it was comfortable. The two other staffers included an older man and a writer who had been a housewife until she had started submitting excellent articles on a freelance basis. When Janis Joplin returned to her hometown for an unhappy homecoming celebration, the freelancer's inspired one-on-one interviews with the singer earned her a full-time job. The man had a reputation for gambling, not with news articles but with cards. The woman was rarely in the office. It may have been the worst excuse for a newspaper operation in the country. For a few weeks, I tried to inspire the staff to hustle. It quickly became apparent they had neither the desire nor the training to function like an actual news-gathering operation. And it wasn't long before I understood I had not been reassigned, but exiled.

I received pressure in the beginning to fire the older man and replace him. Instead, I found myself covering up for him. Perhaps in him I saw what could happen to a guy who had once been so interested in everything until everything passed him by. Besides, I was rapidly losing interest myself.

But, there is a cure for me when I reach the point of maximum malaise. Writing is hard but stimulating and fulfilling. In desperation, I throw myself into writing. Not the reams of routine news from our daily beats. I mean the story you have to sift for, research, poke and chum and swirl and often track down from a few enticing scraps of cryptic comment.

You unearth them on your own initiative. Reporters, clever ones anyway, are always on the lookout for the tell-tale signals. They search like prospectors probing desert topsoil for buried baubles. They are the imaginative, creative, visionary boughs of journalism.

There are so many reporters better than I and countless superior writers, but I've never met a more inquisitive person than myself. I was, and am, a master at discovering the inconspicuous and putting flesh onto empty bones. Curiosity drives my life.

I was in that probing mode one day in Port Arthur when I turned to the old gambler, Graham. I needed an idea. He reflected a moment and said, "I know a ship's captain who's going to retire and move back home to The Cayman Islands. That might make an interesting story."

Instead of berating Graham for failing to pursue it himself—as a proper boss might have done—I asked him for names. It was a perfect idea. Ships and islands! It would get me out of the office and it might generate some copy.

The following Sunday, September 12, 1971, my short enterprise story ran on Page 2-D of the Beaumont Journal: "Port Neches Pair's Island Dream To Come True, In Grand Gaymans (sic)."

The headline writer in Beaumont had misspelled the name of the islands, which wasn't surprising since few people had heard of the tiny archipelago halfway between Cuba and Jamaica.

When the captain's wife had answered my initial telephone call, I told her I wanted to write a story on their retirement to "The Bahamas." I had forgotten where Graham said they were going.

My article reported Timothy and Gwen Bodden of nearby Port Neches, Texas were retiring to their birthplace in Grand Cayman, the largest of the three islands. Like many Cayman men, Timothy had chosen the sea for a career and had migrated to Port Arthur in 1936. He had recently retired as chief engineer of the transport SS Gulf Panther.

They were a congenial couple and delighted I was interested enough to write an article about their retirement and their beloved island home. As they described it, I imagined it to be paradise. Until 1955, there were only 5,000 Caymanians. Then tourists discovered it. The Boddens spoke lovingly of crystal-like water shattering against the dark coral shore. That dinged a memory cell buried in my mind. I recalled an oil-rich zoning commissioner in Artesia, just back from vacation, describing a group of obscure islands in the Caribbean where the beach was called "ironshore" because it rang like a bell when slammed with a hammer.

"That's it!" the Boddens said, "But it's not all ironshore. There's a beautiful sandy beach that's seven miles long. It's the prettiest white sand in the Caribbean."

The interview had the anticipated result. I felt the sun and breeze as we talked.

"Do they have a newspaper?" I asked.

Mrs. Bodden said there indeed is a newspaper. *The Caymanian Weekly* was published every Thursday and everybody read it cover to cover. It was the only news medium in the country.

She remembered the owner, a retired dentist in his 80s whom she considered to be the most powerful man in the country.

His name, she said, was Dr. Roy E. McTaggart.

8

AN ANSWER FROM ACROSS THE DEEP BLUE SEA

For days, I couldn't get the image of that little newspaper on that diminutive island in the Caribbean out of my mind. Impulsively, I wrote a short letter to Dr. R. E. McTaggart, c/o *The Caymanian Weekly*, Grand Cayman, BWI.

I inquired if an experienced newspaperman was needed by his company or if he had any interest in selling the newspaper? I had neither money nor any hope of getting any, but I hardly expected an answer anyway. With that action taken, I promptly dismissed the Caymans, giving them as much consideration as a lottery ticket.

The next day, I received a call from my executive editor, Don Boyette. He told me he was enjoying my writing and that I was doing a great job. The staff had enjoyed my article on Pleasure Island, he said.

"How did you find out about that?"

"I have my sources," I laughed. Actually, I spent so much time wandering around the secluded waterfront that I guiltily wrote the article to help justify my time. Pleasure Island was consistently on the improvement wish list of the Port Arthur Chamber of Commerce. It is a marshy hinterland pitted with piles of discarded refinery rubbish. Politicians, who probably never set foot on the backwater, talked of turning it into Disneyworld on the docks.

I was a horrible bureau chief, but if Boyette thought differently who was I to argue?

"I really called to tell you that I've approved a raise for you," he said. "Congratulations."

That was great news indeed. Whether I deserved it or not, more money wasn't something I was going to complain about. My salary was going to be increased to $175 a week. It wasn't Easy Street, but it was a respectable wage for a newspaper bureau chief. Martha always told me that I was far too hard on myself. Maybe she had a point.

I was also feeling a little better about the bureau. I had received another staff member, a photographer named Bob Parvin. Like me, Parvin had been "exiled" to Port Arthur. Like me, he was also a talented photographer and writer who fit into the main office in Beaumont like a pickle in the apple barrel.

Parvin was sometimes at odds with his supervisors in Beaumont for either shooting off his mouth about an assignment he didn't like or offering his advice when it wasn't wanted. Boyette warned me that Parvin might be problematical and I didn't have to take him. But I had seen his work and he was an excellent photographer.

The easy-going Parvin immediately adjusted to the Port Arthur bureau. His first purchase was a small catamaran and he spent much of his time sailing it around Pleasure Island.

Most of Bob's photos were of people who had nothing to do with his assignments. He just loved to use his camera to capture people, moods and events. One of his great candid photos was of a young, chunky, perpetually smiling black boy about 12 years old who cleaned our office for small change. Local merchants called him "The Hustler." It wasn't because he wanted something for nothing; it was because he was always hustling the downtown area for odd jobs.

He would do anything for a buck and we admired his spunk. He came by every few days and we were always happy to see him. It was a pleasure to see him so eager to make some money and since we never cleaned the office it was always filthy.

Not long after my feature on the Boddens moving back to Grand Cayman appeared, I was making a customary check at the cop shop. This was a daily routine: check the blotter to see if anything violent, ghastly or bloody was worth pursuing. I glanced at the bulletin board behind the sergeant's desk where personal notes or special interest items for the watch were posted. I saw one of Bob's photos of the Hustler hanging there but didn't give it a second thought. I suspected the Hustler hung it himself since he also did odd jobs around the station. The cops were as fond of him as we were.

Bob did a short photo series on him—not for the newspaper but for Bob's personal collection. The boy's mother was thrilled at the attention her son received and asked Bob for copies of the photos. He was happy to comply.

That evening, I mentioned it to Bob. He said the photo had been given to the police by the Hustler's mother. Hustler had been missing for several days and she was distressed. Neither of us was worried about him. He was the type of kid who could take care of himself. We thought.

The countryside surrounding Port Arthur is low and swampy. Some of these swamps are impenetrable except for temporary dirt trails in the dry summer. They are popular with fishermen and the off-road vehicle crowd because there are shallow sloughs throughout the area that are home to all kinds of fish and wildlife.

It was in one of these sloughs several days later, not far from a main highway, that a fisherman found the severed head of a small human. It was floating in the water and he snagged it with his hook. The Hustler wasn't missing any more.

For the next several days, police and sheriff's deputies dragged the sloughs looking for more pieces of the boy's body. Bob and I both spent time following the grim funereal search in the swamps. I remember them finding pieces of his intestines caught in the brambles of a partially submerged bush at the edge of the slough. I watched while the deputy slid on his rubber gloves and reached distastefully for the remains.

The entire community was outraged by the heinous crime.

I had never before been so angry about a story I was covering. I had known this child. He was not much older than my own children. He had been so trusting of grownups. The police tried but there were no leads.

Years later, young Adam Walsh disappeared in a Hollywood, Florida Sears store only to turn up several days later when his head was found floating in a drainage ditch along an interstate highway. It would stir memories of that awful discovery in Port Arthur. Unlike the Walsh case, where a disgusting subhuman named Otis Toole eventually claimed responsibility, the murderer of the Hustler remains a mystery.

The grisly discovery of The Hustler's body placed a pall over our office. We talked about ways to help catch the killer. We were journalists; we would solve this case ourselves. But talk was all we could do. We had absolutely no idea how to proceed. So we sat and talked about motives.

The only plausible one that made sense to us was that the Hustler had run afoul of one of Port Arthur's sexual deviants or a transient pervert.

Perhaps the child had other ways of making money other than hustling work. Each evening I would go home to my own small family. I stayed very close to my own youngsters. As I lay in my bed after everyone was asleep, I could imagine the anguish that the Hustler's mother would be feeling.

Years later, I called the retired detective who had worked the case. He said there had been a suspect "but it didn't check out." I tried to interest the local daily newspapers in Port Arthur and Beaumont about an update on the murder, but they were not interested. Even a letter to John Walsh of America's Most Wanted television show drew no response. I had hoped the similarities between the murders of The Hustler and Walsh's son Adam might draw his interest. It would be another 35 years after I left Port Arthur before I could revisit the scene and try to put the story to rest in my own mind. The police had long closed the case, and couldn't even find it in their files.

Several weeks after the 1971 murder, my complete focus on the case contributed to my astonishment when I drove to Beaumont to check the post office box I maintained there. In addition to the regular assortment of advertisements and bills was a small envelope with a colorful, foreign stamp. I returned to my car and opened the letter, still not sure what it was. I read in disbelief:

"Dear Sir," the letter began. "Your letter of the 10th inst received yesterday and I note that you are a newspaper Editor, having worked in that capacity for a number of years.

"You mentioned that at the moment you are bureau chief of the Port Arthur news bureau for *The Beaumont Enterprise-Journal.*

"We are operating *The Caymanian Weekly* here in Grand Cayman, a small paper but with a very good circulation considering the size of the Islands.

"At the moment we have an opening for a person of your experience, and would suggest that if possible you should come to the Island as early as possible. We would like to see you and talk over the various aspects of the position offered, and if satisfactory to both sides you may have a good job here with us.

"I would suggest that you bring along any references that you may have; this perhaps could help. Looking forward to hearing from you as to when you could arrange to come over."

The letter was signed, "Yours truly, R. E. McTaggart, Managing Director."

I read the letter over several times as the shock began to wear off. I telephoned Martha and she was just as surprised.

"What do they mean, 'Come to the island as soon as possible?'" she asked. "Who's paying for it?"

51

9

GOING SOUTH TO STAY

There had been little doubt about my returning to The Cayman Islands after my initial interview. Martha had quickly decided. We were going!

Dr. Roy was again on hand to meet me when I arrived the second time, this time to stay. I was pleased to know the newspaper owned the Dodge he had driven to pick me up the first trip and the keys were given to me on the spot.

Norberg, who had driven me around the island after my initial interview, had arranged for me to stay in one of his beachfront apartment houses on the south shore of the island. On my first day as an actual resident of The Cayman Islands, I was properly ensconced in a three-bedroom, luxury apartment about 50 feet away from the rolling Caribbean. Martha was to join me in a week or two.

Soon I was alone. I unpacked, explored the spacious apartment several times and sat down before a window to stare at the water and ponder the machine-gun rapidity of events. I walked to the Dodge but decided against exploring on this first day. I wasn't comfortable with driving on the wrong side of the road. And I was homesick and still a little panicky about what I had done.

Since it was late in the afternoon, I convinced myself the office could wait until morning. I wanted to walk along the beach. So, I went to the shore, tossed off my shoes and stuck a foot warily into the water.

I heard a friendly "Hello" spoken with a decidedly British accent and turned to see a mustached young man with thick glasses approaching. He introduced himself as Richard Graham-Taylor, my neighbor. He was an accountant whom I would learn to know, respect, and like very much during my years in Cayman. A member of the British upper class, he held none of the pretensions someone like me expected from that group. In a few years, Richard would be with me the day the walls came tumbling down.

I should explain that my Cayman woes would stem from the British colonial service, not from everyday British subjects. The latter are not jackasses. Not all of them. But I'm getting ahead of myself.

"Would you like a swim?" Graham-Taylor asked after I had explained who I was and why I was here.

"I've never known anyone from Mississippi," he said. "Don't you have a rather large river there?

"Yes, we do," I said, "and we also have Elvis."

"I know who Elvis Presley is. Of course," he said.

"Well, I'm from Elvis's home town. He was two grades ahead of me in Tupelo Junior High School. I heard him sing once in the school assembly."

"That was very nice, I'm sure," he said.

Now, I was speechless. I couldn't think of anything else about Mississippi to tell him.

"Do you have any gear?"

"Gear?" I said.

"Swimming material," he said.

"I have a swimming suit."

"Well, I have an extra set of fins and goggles," he said, "I'll get them for you."

Before I could protest, he had turned and dashed into his apartment. He was gone about five minutes and returned with swim fins, a facemask and a snorkel.

"Spit on the inside glass of the mask with your finger and wipe it around," he said. "Spit keeps it from fogging on you."

He moved into the water and, standing on the bottom about waist deep, cleared his tube by blowing water through it.

"Is there anything in there I need to watch out for?" I asked.

It had occurred to me that I had never plunged into the Caribbean Sea before. I wasn't new to the ocean's surf, but this was an operation that was going to penetrate the water, not skim it at some popular, crowded, safe beach. For all I knew there were sharks lurking offshore. He had said we were going to swim to the reef. It sounded like a perfect hiding place for lurking sea creatures.

The reef was about one hundred feet away from the shore. At bay beyond the reef the waves crashed and spit mammoth sprays into the air as they fought to overwhelm the rocky obstacle. Inside the reef the water was calm, alluring. It was like a lake. But I had no idea what was below those opaque, surface waters. Seaweed and other grassy plants swayed gently just beneath the crest.

"No," he answered, "just watch out for the sea eggs. Don't step on

53

one!"

"Wait a minute," I yelled, but he had pushed away, ducked his head and was swimming rapidly toward the reef. It was a moment of truth. I could either swim after him or feign sudden illness and wait for him to return.

I was a strong swimmer and I wouldn't have had trouble making the reef if it had been in a hotel pool, but then swimming pools don't have strange wiggling things all over the bottom and darting shadows just out of your range of vision.

It took several false starts before I figured out how to breathe through the snorkel and I didn't create much of a wake with my speed, but I did manage to get under way and was soon flopping and splashing my way toward the reef behind Richard, who was knifing through the water ahead of me.

Any minute I expected to be the center of attention in a feeding frenzy, and I kept wondering if some deadly sea egg was going to come hurtling through the water and take off an arm or leg.

Every few yards I would stop and gently probe a finned foot toward the bottom. Richard was about 20 feet away and appeared to be standing on a ledge of the reef.

I was unable to reach the bottom with my fins and I was running short of breath. Just before panic seized me a large boulder appeared miraculously and I clutched for it with my finned foot. It was about four feet below the surface and I was able to stand.

I stood unsteadily on the rock and removed the mask. Looking back I could see I was only about 75 feet from the beach. Richard was a few feet away from me standing on the edge of the reef. My trepidation slowly ebbed while I crouched on the rock.

The more I relaxed, the easier it got. I found I could lie perfectly still on my stomach on the surface and breath through the snorkel without strangling. With just the faintest movements keeping me afloat, I could remain stable on the surface and stare straight down.

I could even look toward the reef and see its dark outline ahead of me. There were huge rocks of assorted shapes along the bottom of the inlet that I would soon learn were living coral colonies.

Many kinds of small, colorful fish darted in and out of the protective shelter the rocks offered. When I looked closer I could see the floor and the approaching reef were not dark, drab, colorless objects one would find in a rock quarry, but held countless colors that ranged from subtle to gloriously brilliant. I could see Richard's legs and body before me. He was standing on a solid shelf of the reef, waiting for me, smiling.

"Seen any sea eggs?" I yelled.

He just smiled and nodded as if I had asked a rhetorical question.

"I've got my knife," he said when I was standing on the shelf by him, "I'll kill one for the fish."

"Where are you going to find one?"

"They're all over the place. Can't you see them?"

He disappeared beneath the water and I donned my mask and stuck my head under to watch him. He approached one of the hundreds of small, black "plants" that littered the sea floor.

It was one of these plants that Richard attacked with his knife. I heard a distinctive "crunch" as he stabbed it and then stirred it rapidly with the blade like an open coconut shell. Almost immediately, tiny fish darted in from all directions and began chomping the pink and white interior pieces of the "plant."

I wasn't wearing corrective lenses inside my mask or I would have realized earlier that these plants were not plants, but sea urchins— small, living creatures with a bony, black surface and huge spines that stuck out in all directions like a pin cushion on steroids.

Stepping on a "sea egg" could be a very painful experience. It's like stepping on an angry porcupine.

I shuddered when I thought how close I must have come to tramping on a needle-spined sea egg when I stood on the rock.

Few people visit the islands without an encounter with a sea egg. They dot the bottom like big, black golf balls at a driving range and cling to every conceivable surface. Caymanian fishermen say the quickest remedy for the pain of a stab by one of the spines is to "pull out your pecker and pee on the wound." The ammonia in the urine is supposed to be the best first aid possible.

My first and only sea egg wound came a few weeks later when I was swimming off a rock wall in front of the *Sea View Hotel*. There was an iron ladder from the water to a dock carved from the coral ironshore, but a wave knocked me off balance and, as I reached for the ladder, I rammed my palm into a sea egg attached to the dock.

I climbed out with 13 spines in my hand and fingers. Fortunately, we were able to pull out the spines immediately and I recovered without having to ask anyone to pee on me.

Afterwards, I had no qualms about tearing these sea urchins to pieces to feed the fish. I suppose the disgusting sea eggs deserve to live undisturbed, since they are completely passive creatures, but I tried my best to kill as many as I could in Cayman. They have no natural enemies there and they breed like, well, sea rabbits.

Following our swim, Richard invited me up for drinks. I had never turned down a drink in my life, so I accepted. His wife Sara was waiting for us with gin tonics with lime, almost on cue.

"This is Mr. Dick Gentry of Mississippi," he said. "He sang at the assembly with Mr. Elvis Presley."

"How nice," she said. "We know about Elvis."

"He's a very nice person," I mumbled. "I didn't actually sing with him. I was just there. I think it was him anyway. It was a long time ago."

"Yes, how nice for you," she said. "We've never known anyone from Mississippi."

The three of us sat and watched the sunset and drank gin tonics with crushed lime. "So, how do things work in Cayman," I asked, hoping they would understand my question. They did. "Differently," they said in unison. I would understand in the coming months that was something of a polite understatement.

I had arrived in a new land, I had battled sea eggs and won, I had a warm glow from the gin and I would soon fry myself a well-done steak, take a hot, stinking, sulphur-well-water shower and pour myself into bed.

On the morrow, I would go down and straighten out that newspaper.

Martha was right. Cayman could be one spectacular place!

10

MY FIRST BILLY BODDEN MYSTERY:

THE CARIB AD AGENCY

There were many island conundrums to disentangle in my new position, but an internal ambiguity discovered early goes a long way toward explaining the business atmosphere within the little country.

"David, where do we compose our ads?" I asked our shop foreman shortly after I arrived. David had never explained why he had not talked to me about "something you need to know" during my initial visit. Now, he probably felt it would be of no use. Here I was.

There was no area in our building where the advertisements were physically constructed. Yet they appeared miraculously ready to paste down on the composing room flats.

"The ad agency brings them up on Wednesday," he said.

"What ad agency?" I asked, surprised that there was actually an advertising agency in Cayman.

"Carib Ad Agency," he said.

"Where is it?" I asked, now intrigued.

"Just down the street," he said, pointing toward an office building down a narrow side street about half a block from us.

"Don't we make up any ads here in the office?" I asked.

"No."

"What do you mean, 'no,'" I said, puzzled. "We must create some ads here in the shop."

"Carib Ad Agency makes them all for us," he said.

There's nothing particularly unusual about an advertising agency producing camera-ready ads for newspapers, but I certainly didn't expect to find such a facility in George Town, Grand Cayman.

Advertising agencies usually have regular clients for whom they produce advertisements. They offer their expertise in marketing to the client, sell the client on an idea and/or a marketing strategy and charge them excessive fees for the service.

Newspapers usually give these agencies a 15 percent discount off of the newspaper's normal advertising rate. It's actually a bonus for newspapers because the ads are normally received camera-ready and there is very little production cost for the newspaper.

However, it is highly unusual for advertising agencies to handle 100 percent of a newspaper's advertisements.

"How many ad agencies are there here?" I asked David.

"One."

"Who owns it?" I asked.

"Billy."

"Billy Bodden?"

"Yes."

"You mean the editor I replaced?"

"Yes."

What a sweet covenant Billy had arranged. He had started an advertising agency to take advantage of his position as editor and publisher. He sold the advertising and produced the ads and charged the newspaper 15 percent when the newspaper collected the total bill. What would seem a conflict of interest in the United States was obviously business-as-usual in Cayman. I was surprised that the board of directors had allowed it. But obviously they had.

I asked our bookkeeper about the classified ads. Billy's agency sold them, too, and collected 15 percent.

I decided to have a look at this agency and our odd alliance.

It was a two-minute walk down the dirt road by our newspaper to a small, two-room office complex. The sign on the door read, Carib Ad Agency.

Without knocking, I opened the door and walked in. Three women, one of them Sandra Parchment—who had become my favorite in the office because of her cheerfulness and hard work—looked up in surprise. Sandra immediately brightened, "Hello, Mr. Gentry!" she said.

There was a tall, very thin, young black man seated at a drawing table at one wall.

"This is Robbie, our artist," Sandra said.

Robbie and I shook hands and he smiled. I asked him to tell me about himself. He said he had been in Cayman about a year and he was Jamaican. From the artwork I could see littered around his desk it was obvious that he was talented.

Sandra introduced the others, who were Caymanians, and they told me shyly they were paste-up artists and typists.

Sandra said she had come down to pick up advertisements that were needed to start constructing Thursday's newspaper.

I asked Robbie to tell me how the agency operated. He said advertisements were telephoned in—generally by the clients—and he drew them. The young women performed the necessary production work to make them camera-ready, and carried them to the newspaper.

I had a puzzling walk back to the office. The more I thought about it, the more it appeared Billy had built himself a honey pot.

He was selling all of the ads, including the classifieds, and getting 15 percent of the advertising revenue of the newspaper in addition to his own salary and dividends. Instead of giving him a 15 percent reduction on our book price for advertising, we gave Carib Ad Agency 15 percent, because we billed and collected for the clients' ads. But I soon discovered there was much, much more.

Mr. Arthur was waiting to see me when I walked back into our office.

"I've been down at Carib Ad Agency, Mr. Arthur," I said. "Billy's agency..."

There was no reaction other than a smile and a nod.

"How long has Billy had an advertising agency?" I asked.

He thought for a moment, and said, "I guess it's been several years. You know he had that Desmond working for him for a while—that bastard!"

I wasn't sure who the bastard was, but I suspected it wasn't Billy Mr. Arthur was talking about. He did not care for Desmond Seales, and never mentioned his name without showing some distaste. I had actually seen Desmond Seales on my first flight to Grand Cayman for the interview. Of course at the time I had no idea who he was. He appeared to be just another passenger as we took off.

The threat of being hijacked to Cuba on that first flight was serious. But it was 30 years before the World Trade Towers catastrophe of 9/11, and a hijack to Cuba was considered more of an inconvenience than a disaster. Martha and I had joked about whether or not I could call from Havana. Everyone checked out their fellow travelers. I was certain a hijacker was right across the isle from me. His skin was inky-jet black and his hair curled into a dozen pigtails. Instead of a regular jacket, he wore a colorful robe that hung to his knees and there were no socks beneath his sandals.

I had never seen a Jamaican, much less a Rastafarian. He was talking to himself obsessively and gesturing angrily. I avoided looking directly at him.

There was a young, rather distinguished looking black man with long, wooly sideburns and dark, intense eyes several rows ahead of me. He was also observing our colorful passenger. He got the attention of a stewardess and I could tell he was admonishing her to keep her eye on the Rastafarian. I felt better knowing someone else had discerned the odd behavior.

The potential "hijacker" didn't make another sound the entire trip. He looked out at the empty sky, transfixed. I had never seen anyone completely stoned before.

I did see the dark, young man with the intense eyes many times. He had once been employed by the company to which I was heading for an interview. He was starting a competing business, a magazine called the Nor'wester. Desmond Seales would become both my friend and my foe in the small, politically complicated country towards which we were both speeding.

But we didn't speak on that first flight and I quickly forgot about him. There would come a morning when just the two of us faced the challenge of saving one of Cayman's few historical treasures from deliberate destruction. What's left of it survives today as a tourist attraction only because of what we accomplished that still-to-come morning.

I never learned exactly why Mr. Arthur didn't like Desmond, although in later years Desmond himself raised questions about it. Desmond believed my friend Mr. Arthur Bodden was prejudiced against blacks, and, in a way, the old man was. But the prejudice didn't extend to all blacks.

This special type of discrimination was common among whites in Cayman. There were some blacks some of them disliked, and there were blacks some of them liked. There were many blacks and whites in business together, and mixed marriages were common. There were blacks that didn't like some whites, and blacks that didn't like some other blacks. The line was not clearly drawn.

Discrimination just because a person was black, however, was not overt in The Cayman Islands to the extent it was in America at the time. A huge majority of the local population, about 80 percent, was of mixed blood. Almost all of the old-line Caymanian white families had cousins of various shades of brown. Since there was no overt discrimination against them, the blacks themselves held no festering resentment against whites. There were few island-born Caymanians in positions of great power in the government, but there was no prevalent feeling of inferiority because of race.

Discrimination against foreign blacks was something else again. Caymanians, black and white, didn't care much for black Jamaicans or blacks from other Caribbean nations. Generally, a native Caymanian was a Caymanian, regardless of his or her color.

Mr. Arthur was not a bigot; he simply did not trust Desmond, who was a native of Trinidad.

Outsiders quickly learned not to say anything offensive about anyone because of the probability that you might unknowingly be talking to someone about his or her distant cousin. So thick was the blood between native Caymanians that very few of them could, or would, serve in the police department. The government was forced to turn to Jamaica to staff the constabulary. With few exceptions, the ranking officers of the force were British.

One of my staff, a racially mixed Caymanian, said to Martha once after a trip to Miami, "I've never seen so many red-headed niggers in my life!" Baffled, I asked Martha what she meant by such a shocking, derogatory remark. "I think she meant American blacks have a chip on their shoulders she can't relate to," she answered.

More than once I heard that blacks from Trinidad were particularly clever. Whether or not that's true is debatable, but political correctness suspended, it makes sense. In the eighteenth century, hard-to-manage slaves around the Caribbean were banished to Trinidad.

Over the years, these "troublemakers" raised families. The politically incorrect theory is that it was the more aggressive, more intelligent slaves who were expelled to Trinidad. Thus, thanks to genetics, their progeny were progressively bright and assertive.

Until recently, Desmond had worked at the Carib Ad Agency. He had, in fact, been its star salesman. He was disappointed that he had not been named editor instead of me when Billy walked out, and indubitably began planning his Nor'wester Magazine.

The knowledge that Desmond had been involved in the agency and was going to be a competitor to me with his magazine didn't help me feel comfortable about him. It was another little peculiarity added to a list that was giving me apprehension about every facet of my new job. Desmond probably would have made a fine editor.

I hadn't seen anything yet.

The next day was payday.

As I signed paychecks, I saw one made out to Robbie and the other two employees of the Carib Ad Agency. I asked the bookkeeper for an explanation.

"It's payday," she said.

"But these people work for Billy at the agency," I protested.

"We pay them," she said.

It took a moment for me to grasp what she said.

"How long have we paid them?"

"I don't know. As long as they been down there," she said.

61

So, it appeared our newspaper was paying the salaries of the people who worked for Billy. I knew the answer to the next question: "I guess we also pay his rent?"

She nodded.

"All his expenses?"

She nodded again.

I sat in the chair in front of her desk and looked intently at her eyes. Did she understand the implications of all this? I couldn't tell.

"Does that equipment down there belong to Billy or to us?" I asked.

"It all belongs to the newspaper," she said.

What had first appeared objectionable to me suddenly looked unethical.

How could my directors, all among the business elite of the islands, have allowed this? I was baffled.

I called Mr. Arthur, told him I had something important to discuss and asked him to come by the office. From the very beginning, I was drawn more to Mr. Arthur than to any other of the directors. Not only was he the largest stockholder, but also he was the one most willing to provide help.

As I explained the situation with Carib Ad Agency, he sat silently, nodding ever so slightly whenever I looked at his face. There was no indication of excitement or anger on his part, just patience as he listened to my story.

"Mr. Arthur," I said intently, "Billy has set up a dummy company and is taking 15 percent of our advertising revenue. Not only is he getting 15 percent, we're paying all of his bills. We're even paying the salaries of his employees! He's using our equipment! I want it back!"

He sat silently digesting my tirade. Finally, he spoke. "Now, friend Dick," he said, "this is something you shouldn't worry about. We'll take care of it."

"Aren't you angry?" I asked.

He reached over and patted my shoulder. "I'll call Dr. Roy and Norberg and we'll get this settled."

It struck me that he was more concerned that I might be upset than he was to learn that Billy had been skimming the newspaper for years.

"Don't you worry," he said again, "we'll take care of everything."

I walked with him to the door. "I'm going down there and get our equipment," I said.

"You do that," he said matter-of-factly, and walked to his car.

I picked up the telephone and called Carib Ad Agency. Robbie answered.

"Robbie," I said, "I'm moving all of you up to the Caymanian. We'll set up an advertising department in the newspaper office."

A few days later, the board met with Billy privately over the Carib Ad Agency scheme. Mr. Arthur never told me what was said and none of the directors ever mentioned it again. I did not bring it up. If there was more to it, I was never informed. Perhaps Billy had convinced them it was a great bargain for the newspaper. Billy was clever and resourceful. Perhaps he, too, thought he was providing a service to the Caymanian. In any event, I would not abide it.

I remained confounded for several weeks. But astonishment in The Cayman Islands was never in short supply. Every day something came along to wipe the slate for a fresh surprise.

The memory of Carib Ad Agency faded.

The darkroom had become my refuge the first week in Grand Cayman. Here was the only place where I could be completely alone. My office was nothing more than a desk in a corner. At any time one of the employees or a visitor could walk over, sit down, and start talking. Even if I was engaged with someone, no one had any qualms about interrupting.

It was a serious mistake in Cayman to show irritation with someone. They might have their feelings deeply hurt for weeks.

But everyone knew that the darkroom was for isolation. If you open the door unexpectedly, you can ruin hundreds of dollars worth of film and destroy its processing. Consequently, going into the darkroom was about the only ensured privacy I could find other than the bathroom, and that little fiefdom was never safe because there was no lock.

The darkroom was also black. With only the soft yellow glow of the Safelight burning, the room had a mellow, secure feeling. I could shut out the insanity of my new world.

There was a small creature of unknown variety hiding atop the roof of the darkroom. Every so often, it would let out a soft, almost purring sound. At first, I thought it might be a snake but there are few snakes in Cayman. It could have been a rat. It might have been a lizard driven inside by the rainstorm that had been raging outside for days. The weather only recently decided to clear up. A Caribbean tropical wave had arrived shortly after I did in Grand Cayman and had drenched the islands for days before moving on. Everything was soggy.

The darkroom was constructed within the large room we used as a combination pressroom and storage facility, and the space between the darkroom's ceiling and the main roof above it was stacked with an assortment of used chemical cans, dusty remnants of lumber and cardboard cartons containing God knows what. The roof of the darkroom was rimmed with wood and formed a natural catch-all for this assorted junk. It was about a foot deep inside this rim.

The darkroom's roof was composed of large panels of sheetrock painted with a sealant to protect the room below from any crack or crevice that might allow a single ray of light to sneak in and ruin whatever film you were processing.

From somewhere beneath this trash dump on the roof of the darkroom would seep the occasional "peep" from the unknown creature. It was familiar to me after a while and I no longer considered it a threat.

I was sitting in a chair in the middle of the darkroom when the peeping began again. In its own way it was comforting. I even thought it might somehow be telling me to maintain my cool: "You have not fallen down a rabbit hole. Things will stabilize. Your life is not over. This is the adventure of a lifetime!"

The peep became more rapid, more intense. I looked up. I could see nothing in the dim light. I stood and turned on the bright overhead light and was shocked to see the roof beginning to move. The peeping grew more desperate and changed its pitch. Now, it was more "creeeaaaak!" than "peeeeep." The ceiling began to sag.

With a shudder it gave way and hundreds of pounds of accumulated trash, wet sheetrock, ink cans and water plunged into the darkroom. Everything was awash and I was knocked to the concrete floor.

Unharmed but stunned, I looked around at the pieces of wood, paper and boxes floating around me. There was a half-foot of water moving sluggishly toward the bottom of the locked darkroom door.

The ceiling of the darkroom had collapsed and was now exposed to the main pressroom's ceiling.

Outside, I heard the press slowly roll to a stop. Footsteps approached the doorway.

There was a knock and I heard Sandra's voice.

"Mr. Gentry, can I come in?"

I brushed the trash off my head, shook the water off my hands, opened the door and looked at her.

"The roof leaks over the darkroom," she said looking me over from head to toe. "All that rain durin' the storm must'a leaked in and stayed on the roof. We could hear it creakin', you know. This whole building leaks every time it rains. I guess it just finally gave up."

"I guess it did, Sandra," I said.

"Did it ruin the camera?" she asked, looking beyond me into the darkroom. There was a 16-inch camera that we used to photograph the pages when they were finished and ready to go to the plate-making process. Without the camera we were out of business.

Beyond Sandra, I could see the faces of all of the employees now nervously gathering behind her.

I took some pleasure in realizing there was at least a little concern about my safety. Still, no one had asked me directly if I was hurt. They were looking rather solemn except for Jo Ann, my fastest typist and most valuable Caymanian typesetter. She looked confident. No, she looked smug; as if she knew a secret she couldn't wait to tell.

"Mr. Gentry," Sandra said, "Everyone has asked me to tell you somethin."

My stomach tightened.

"What now?" I asked, swiping at the water on my face.

"We're goin' on strike in the mornin'!" she beamed.

11

THE STRIKE DOESN'T DESTROY US,
BUT I ALMOST DO

"I knew they would probably do this," Mr. Arthur said when I called him later that night. "They are testing you, friend Dick," he said. "You are the new boss, so they want to see how far they can go."

"So, what do I do?" I asked. "We have a paper to print tomorrow."

"You call Dr. Roy and tell him," he said.

I placed a call to Dr. Roy and found him less than sympathetic. For some reason I inferred that Dr. Roy thought it was my fault a strike was imminent and that it was up to me to get it settled quickly without spending any money.

Dr. Roy didn't wish to be bothered by basics. He had done his job in hiring me. It was an appropriate reaction from an aging businessman who knew absolutely nothing about the core business of which he was managing director.

"They are trying to test you," he said. "I know, sir," I said, hoping for some additional recommendation. None was offered.

I was expected to deal with it myself. This was, after all, my job. I was the boss.

I hung up and drove to the office. It was just after 8 a.m. and everyone was sitting around the composing room waiting for me. My two new reporters greeted me with chagrin and embarrassment. Clearly they were not part of this, and wanted to help.

Marge met me outside and whispered privately, "You're the new man. They are testing you to see what they can get away with."

I nodded my appreciation. I understood. I also knew that if I didn't make a strong stand, I would be pushed around for my entire stay in Cayman.

I had two reporters. Marge was Marge Delello, an American who had moved to Grand Cayman with her retired husband Al. They had built a small, fashionable resort on Seven Mile Beach called Seascape. She had no formal training in journalism other than she liked people and thought she knew how to write. She saw the newspaper as a way of expressing herself.

The other reporter was Mary Lewis, the expatriate English wife of the crafts instructor at the island's high school. She was also a qualified elementary school teacher but again had no journalism training. They had seen an advertisement by Billy Bodden for reporters, and applied. Billy had hired both of them after he had decided to leave. Marge and Mary had both been inactive, awaiting my arrival for instructions. Though they were both energetic and eager to learn, I would have preferred some experience. Oh, that Billy.

I continued through the composing room without speaking to anyone. I tried to make my face appear grim and determined. Taking control of the newspaper meant taking control of the pressroom first. My strategy was to be firm with the head pressman and that would force everyone into line quickly.

I had fired only one person in my entire life, and that was a terrible mistake. For me, not him. Manny Marquez was probably the best sports editor the Artesia Daily Press ever had. I lost my temper one day when he didn't react fast enough to stop what he was doing and go take a stupid photo at the chamber of commerce. It was an overreaction and I've always regretted it. What a brainless, immature reaction. Manny moved on. I tried to hire him back, but by the time I asked he had moved on to a larger newspaper in Hobbs, N.M. as sports writer. Eventually he became executive editor. I now call my firing him as the best thing that ever happened to him.

I saw my newly appointed chief pressman as a target of opportunity. First of all he was a huge, surly, ink-black Jamaican who had been in Cayman about a year. I understood even in those early days that Jamaicans were not considered equal citizens by the Caymanians. They were given jobs only when they filled a need the Caymanians couldn't, or wouldn't, accept. These jobs ranged from technical executives to janitors. Mostly, however, it was the latter. Joseph had worked as a carpenter's helper in Jamaica and could be very useful around the shop when he was in the mood for it.

In spite of the obstacle, I planned to enjoy this because I knew Joseph was a sulking, resentful troublemaker who had spent most of his time since my arrival glaring at me as if to dare me to ask him to do something.

My dander was up and if he wanted a confrontation he was going to get it. Fortunately, I had an experienced manager in David Parchment and two other apprentice pressmen, Walwyn, another Jamaican, and

Raymond, an easygoing Caymanian who had been openly friendly toward me.

I planned to order Joseph to repair the darkroom. If he refused I would fire him on the spot. Donald Trump and Jack Welch had nothing on Little Dicky Gentry's executive skill and boldness this morning.

Everyone's eyes followed me as I approached him.

"Joseph," I said in the sternest voice I could summon, "I want you to get that roof repaired and when you finish it you can get to work and get some of these jobs printed. Just about everything here is overdue."

He glared fiercely at me and I pulled back just a bit.

"Well?" I said.

"Sir, I'm not your carpenter and I've got to have more money to run the presses!"

"Well, you're not going to get it here!" I snapped. "Either get to work or get the hell out!"

I could hear the gasps of delight from the others who were watching. They were enjoying the show and could not care less about Joseph.

The big Jamaican looked at me without expression and spun around; picked up the lunch he had packed and started to walk out. He paused and looked at me.

"You owe me money," he said evenly.

I turned and said to the bookkeeper loud enough for everyone to hear, "Pay him off and get him out of here!"

I was satisfied, invigorated. I had faced a serious challenge and come out victorious. I turned toward the others.

"OK," I said. "I am going to give everyone a raise."

They looked at each other.

"Now, it's only going to be a little bit and I expect everyone to work doubly hard from now on. We have a very serious situation in this company. The old boss man is gone and the directors are looking at me to bring this company out of the doldrums.

"I can't do it without your help. I know from what Mr. Arthur and the other directors have said you are all hard-working, loyal, dependable employees who are ready to pitch in and do your part. We're in this together and we'll pull together. We'll succeed. I promise you. Now, let's get to work!"

They stood silently in their tracks. Finally, Jo Ann raised her hand.

"Yes?" I responded.

"Mr. Gentry, how much money you gonna give us?"

"About 25 cents an hour," I said, feeling a little deflated by the fact they had not all turned and raced to their posts after my stirring little homily.

"Can't you give us more now that Joseph and David are gone?" she asked.

"David?" I asked, looking around for my indispensable shop foreman.

"He's gone," Sandra said.

"Gone? What do mean, he's gone?"

"David quit this morning, Mr. Gentry," Angela the bookkeeper said.

"What's he going to do?"

Once again, I was dumbfounded by a pronouncement that was perfectly obvious to everyone else.

"I don't know," she said.

David knew everything there was to know about the printing side of the business, and I knew nothing. All of our commercial printing orders were controlled by him. He kept track of every detail in a little notebook he carried in his back pocket: What jobs we had, where each one was in the process, when they were finished, how much they would be charged and who had paid.

The Caymanian Weekly was managed like most other businesses in the country. Everything was recorded either by memory or written in some individual's little notebook. There were bookkeeping records, but only superficial ones.

This was a country where there were no income taxes, no sales taxes, no workmen's compensation, and no unemployment insurance payments. Who needed records? Basic records were kept in corporations, but my experience with Carib Ad Agency had shown me how loosely business was conducted.

Generally, it was the FIFO method of accounting. First in; first out. First, you take your money in for your work. Then you go out and spend it.

Some businesses didn't even have bank accounts. Fortunately, we did.

The pronouncement about David hurt me in ways other than financial. He had tried to tell me something on my first night in Cayman. He had worried about me when I arrived, as if he knew some deep, dark horror that was lying in wait.

He sometimes drank too much and was barely functional when he did but he had a sense of humanity and dignity about him that I knew I was going to miss as much as his expertise.

The self-assurance I had recovered by firing Joseph vanished, and I was now dependent on two apprentice printers.

Things stabilized for almost an hour.

Sandra, who had assumed the role of spokesperson for the employees, came to my desk and said the Jamaican apprentice, Walwyn Clark, wanted to speak with me.

69

"Do you know what he wants?" I asked.

"Mo' money," she said. "With David and Joseph gone, they gonna test you."

"No shit," I mumbled.

When I walked into the pressroom, Walwyn and Raymond were standing by the idle presses, waiting.

I had a deep scowl on my face, which was my attempt to demonstrate I would put up with no more foolishness.

"OK, what do you want?"

Walwyn said quietly that he wanted to make $2 an hour, which was double what he was being paid. Raymond also wanted $2 an hour.

"That's what you were paying Joseph," Walwyn said.

"Well, you are not going to get it," I said. "I will give you both 50 cents more an hour. That's it. This company isn't making any money now."

"Then we'll quit," he said.

"No, you won't quit," I said, my anger rising, "because you are fired. Both of you. Get out! Collect your pay."

Walwyn's face was impassive, but I could see Raymond was taken aback. He hadn't wanted to go this far but he wouldn't lose face by backing off if Walwyn didn't. And Walwyn didn't.

After paying them off, I walked back to my desk and sat down.

My two reporters, Marge and Mary, sat quietly, anxiously, watching me.

"How are we going to get a paper out this week?" Marge asked.

I looked at her. "I don't know," I said, and I didn't.

"What kind of articles do you have?" I asked both of them.

They just looked back blankly.

"We don't have anything," said Mary. "We were waiting for you just like everyone else. We were hoping you would tell us what to do."

Billy had neither trained them nor told them what to expect. It was another favor he had invented to welcome me. But they were both willing to try. Better yet, they had no desire to test me. They only wanted to help. For that, I was grateful.

The immediate big problem was the pressroom. Our typesetting consisted of used Varitypers, old ones but still serviceable. Even if they were inexperienced, I knew I had enough staff to produce a newspaper. It wouldn't say much, but I would have one. My recurring nightmare from college of an approaching press day and nothing to publish stirred deep down in my stomach. I tried to ignore it. The immediate problem was printing it. I now had no one who could run a press and no prospects of finding a pressman.

I had been appointed by the journalism professors at Ole Miss to

70

edit the daily school newspaper for the summer my first year there. All I was required to do was to edit the copy that the summer students wrote for the paper. The department ended up canceling the summer classes, and I was stuck with a daily newspaper to publish almost by myself. It was a harrowing summer.

Finding a pressman to hire immediately in Grand Cayman would have been like finding a diamond in an oyster. And I couldn't fly one down from Miami even in my emergency because the government was extremely protective and hiring an expatriate worker is a long process.

In short, I was screwed big time.

As the day progressed it was obvious disaster approached, both professionally and personally. The probability loomed there would be no paper this week. It would be the first time in history that the Caymanian had not hit the street on Thursday. Billy Bodden would relish it. In fact, as I was later to learn, much of my discomfort was part of an organized effort on his part to send me packing back to America with my tail between my legs, the quicker the better.

Mr. Arthur was clearly worried when I told him of the latest predicament. To my amazement, the old man was unable to operate the main press at the Caymanian. In fact, he couldn't operate any of the presses. Although he himself was a printer, his equipment was as ancient as he was. It was all hand-operated with no electrical power.

I could tell that Dr. Roy was also concerned when I reported the news to him. Again, he had no suggestions on what to do, but I could tell that he was growing disappointed with the Almighty's choice as his new publisher.

Fortunately, I have always been resourceful in publishing. My methods are seldom heroic but rarely have I ever been completely stumped; even when the solution is embarrassing and normally beneath contempt, I usually persevere.

Such was the case with my lack of a pressman. By the middle of the afternoon it was clear that I only had one choice and I must truly hurry.

When I reached the airport, Joseph had purchased his ticket and was standing in line at the bottom of the ladder waiting to board his flight home to Kingston. If he was surprised to see me barging through the cluster of people toward him he didn't show it.

"OK," I said, breathless after my dash across the tarmac, "I have decided to give you a raise."

He looked, but didn't say anything. Several people in line were now watching us.

"I'm going home," he said. "I miss Jamaica. This place doesn't suit

71

me."

"Listen, Joseph," I said, my voice turning into a plea, "Walwyn and Raymond both quit right after you did. David quit, too. There are no other pressmen I can find."

He shook his head and started up the ladder. "I'm going home," he replied, "you will have to run it yourself, sir."

I moved away and watched as he reached the doorway.

"I don't know how to run the goddam thing," I yelled.

He paused at the top of the ladder and looked down at me, his dark face inscrutable in the bright sun.

"I apologize," I said to him. "I need your help!"

For a long time, he looked at me. People in the line were enjoying the spectacle but were growing impatient with us. The stewardess walked out onto the platform and looked down at me.

"OK, sir," Joseph shouted, "but you have to pay me $2.50 an hour!"

"Yes," I said, "$2.50 an hour!"

I suppose I should have been mortified at having to go to the airport and beg Joseph to come back to a job from which I had fired him just hours before. But I didn't feel mortified. I was exhilarated because I was going to publish a newspaper that week. It might never publish again, but, right now, nothing else mattered. Next week would take care of itself. *The Caymanian Weekly* was going to be printed. On time!

As we drove toward George Town, I unleashed a loud victory whoop.

Joseph might have smiled just a tiny bit but I really couldn't tell because I was watching the road ahead and he had insisted on sitting in the back.

The next week, I rehired Walwyn and Raymond and gave them a 50 cent raise. Little Dicky Gentry was beginning to learn the ways of The New World.

In spite of it all—the lack of enthusiasm for hard work, the tenuous supply line for materials from the United States, the aging equipment, the dearth of trained staff and the lack of competent leadership from management—I understood that *The Caymanian Weekly* was a potential gold mine.

CHAPTER 12

WHERE THERE'S SMOKEY, THERE'S IRE!

The Cayman Islands strictly prohibited importation of any dogs and cats, no matter how revered they might be. The authorities were terrified of importing rabies.

In fact, the shrinkage of the gene pool in The Cayman Islands over the years had contrived the "Cayman Cur," a rather sad-sack family of smallish mongrels with short hair and thin, rangy bodies. They were quite unattractive animals of various colors and dispositions.

Smokey the cat could have made a magnificent genetic contribution to the feline sperm bank of the islands had he been allowed to land and plunder like the Spanish explorers. But, there were no exceptions. Besides, Smokey had lost his ability to plunder at the vet's office when he was only a year old. Perhaps he could have given advice, or served as a role model. He was a magnificent animal, as kind and gentle as he was big and furry.

"I just can't do that!" Martha told me in astonishment when I telephoned and told her to find a home for him or drop him at the pound.

"You have to," I said. "There are no exceptions. They will put him on the next plane back to Miami and God only knows what will happen to him."

It was bad about Smokey, but we were undergoing a sea change in our lives. We had made the decision to move to the middle of the Caribbean, and the cat would have to be sacrificed. Or, a home found.

A few days later Martha telephoned to say that she was ready.

"Have you found him a home?" I asked.

"Yes," she said, "Your mother wants him."

I was greatly relieved because I was afraid she would try to bring him in spite of my warning.

Every day I waited for word that Martha and the children were on the way. I couldn't wait to show them our new home.

Dr. Roy had promised me a house overlooking the sea but it wasn't ready for us, so I found a temporary furnished home to rent. It was inland, but convenient with a screened porch. Everything was ready for my adventurous family to join me.

Back in Texas Martha had developed an ear infection that prevented her from flying. Day after day we waited for the illness to recede. It clung stubbornly for two weeks.

Finally, I got a wire that she would be arriving the next day.

I was at the airport well in advance of the flight and wandered around the facilities until I spotted the silver Costa Rican jet approaching. It rolled to a stop in front of the terminal and down the gangway came my two excited children followed by Martha. They were the first ones out. I grabbed them and hugged them and we headed for the terminal to wait for the baggage to pile up. In a few moments it was ready for plucking and we walked to the heap and began scrambling with the rest of the passengers. Rather sheepishly, Martha pointed to a large, gray, carrying cage with a wire front door.

"Don't forget that one," she said.

I looked at the cage, suddenly afraid of what was inside.

"Martha, it isn't? You didn't?"

"What was I to do?" she moaned, "I couldn't leave him with your mother. I couldn't leave him with anybody."

I looked inside the wire mesh. Smokey was resting calmly. He mewed a drowsy greeting.

"They won't let me bring him in," I said angrily. "They're going to put him right back on the plane!"

"They told me it was Okay at the airline in Miami," she said. "I gave him a tranquilizer...I asked and they said there would be no problem at this end."

"I don't know how they got that," I said. "They are very strict about it here. They'll send him back."

She started to cry and so did the children.

I looked toward the customs shed. The passengers were placing their bags on the long tables for inspection.

"Come on!" I said ruefully. "Let's see what happens."

I placed our bags on the counter. I threw a jacket over Smokey's cage hoping the officer might not notice him. I had no idea what the punishment was for smuggling a cat but I couldn't think of anything else. If I turned him in they would send him back. They might even lose him in Costa Rica, where most of the planes landed before returning to Miami.

The customs officer working his way down the line was the same one who had inspected me when I first came down to meet Dr. Roy and the board of directors.

He reached our bags. I looked at him and smiled engagingly but he didn't recognize me and started opening one of our suitcases.

From inside Smokey's cage I heard a sound. I froze. What a hell of a time for him to start springing out of his induced tranquility.

He cried again. Louder.

The inspector looked around.

"How are you doing today?" I asked loudly. He looked at me.

"I'm down here to work for Dr. Roy. Remember me?"

He looked at my face.

Smokey howled again. On the tarmac the BAC 1-11 revved its engines and began rolling heavily toward the runway for its takeoff dash. It stayed on the ground only long enough to offload the Cayman passengers and dump their luggage on the tarmac.

The inspector looked at me and said something, but I couldn't hear over the roar of the engines. I could also hear Smokey, screeching in tune with the engines.

I was weak. How could anyone miss the yowling?

The inspector smiled, closed my bag and stuck the little turtle sticker on each of our bags.

"That one too!" I yelled over the roar and pointed to the cage.

He obliged and quickly anointed the cage with a turtle.

I snatched the cage and a bag, told Martha to grab the rest and ran toward the open door. The immigration officer at the gate recognized me, glanced at the luggage with the lifesaving stickers and waved me through.

Outside, I raced toward the car. The jet and Smokey were both howling. Breathless and desperate, I flung open the back door of the car and pushed the illegal immigrant into the rear seat.

I was safe. There was an exhilaration that I hadn't known in weeks. I had managed to get my family onto Cayman soil safely—my entire family, including the beloved illegal alien.

Within minutes we were heading away from the airport and danger. Now if anyone asked I could say Smokey was an island cat. Who could challenge it?

"Martha," I said. "I can't believe you did that. I told you it wasn't possible."

"I just couldn't leave him," she said. "Every time I looked at him I started to cry."

Perhaps Smokey was destined to end up a Caribbean cat. At Miami International Airport the baggage crew lost his cage. Martha searched the entire airport. About to give up, she heard a "meow" from behind a metal post. A careless handler had placed Smokey out of sight. A few minutes more and he would have been lost from us forever. We never exposed Smokey. For all anyone knew, except for our family and very closest friends, he was a native cat-of-the-soil. It was the only Cayman law I ever intentionally violated and I never regretted it. Nor, I am sure, did Smokey.

Martha's boldness and impulsiveness had paid off again.

13

PRINT THE TRUTH
AND THE TRUTH MIGHT MAKE YOU FLEE

I was several months into my struggling stewardship of the newspaper in Grand Cayman when an incident occurred that became the anamnesis of my great adventure and established in granite the tone of the relationship I was forging with my newly adopted government.

Peter Thompkins, the president of The Cayman Mercantile Bank and Trust, was the first person who told me why I had been "invited" to Government House to see the Governor.

Thompkins, like me, was an expatriate. Unlike me, he was British. He had not been invited; he had been summoned. So had the other seven bank presidents I had interviewed for a particular story I had just published. It was my first real enterprise feature article as head of the newspaper.

An ominous sign began an otherwise beautiful day.

"I saw nothing wrong with the first article last week," Tompkins said, "but that second part this week when you talked about all the 'crap' the locals have to take from the English!'"

He shook his head at me disapprovingly and walked out into the morning sunshine in spite of my plea to remain and explain.

I had a feeling I had just been scolded.

There had been very little reaction to the first part of the series. The second installment had come off the press only yesterday.

"I suppose you'll be at H.E.'s office in the morning?" Tompkins had first remarked when he came in to buy an extra copy.

That surprised me. The Governor's secretary had called only moments before and said the Governor would like to see me at 8 a.m. tomorrow. I had no idea what he wanted but I was pleased and impressed. I dared hope things were changing.

Normally I would have been pleased that they were all talking about my articles, but then they had been talking about me and everything I had written since I had arrived. As far as the government was concerned I had done nothing right.

I was considering pursuing Tompkins when Sandra tugged at my sleeve. "Mr. Gentry," she said, "you're wanted on the telephone."

I asked her to take a number but she didn't budge.

"It's Mr. Doty," she said, and my discomfort level rose. Doty was Malcolm Everett Doty, The Cayman Islands Commissioner of Police.

Like most of the British Colonial professionals who made up the government's bureaucracy, Doty couldn't easily tolerate the idea of an American as editor of the only news medium in the country—even a very tiny one published once a week.

He was a powerful individual and not one to be ignored.

I grimaced and picked up the telephone.

"I've received a number of complaints about your article," he said in an angry, rapid-fire, public school, upper-class cadence. "We've all been talking about it and wondering what you are trying to do? Do you realize the damage you have done?"

I was at a loss to understand what I had done, and I was only beginning to understand the depth of the sensitivity the government had about everything I wrote. All of my perceptions about freedom of the press had come unglued in the past few months and I was beginning to understand I had been thrust into a role for which I was woefully unprepared.

It seemed mere months ago I had upset the Carlsbad High School football coach with a particularly mean-spirited cartoon character on my sports page. I had drawn that cartoon myself—Carlsbad, New Mexico's hated Caveman mascot with a flattened-out head to illustrate the club pounding given it by our Artesia Bulldogs in the bitter Eddy County playoff.

Of course, Carlsbad's coach was secretly thrilled that I had insulted his team with the cartoon because after the Artesia high school Bulldogs whipped the cross-county rival Cavemen 8 to 6—thanks to that controversial 2-point touchback on the opening kickoff—he nailed the cartoon to the locker room wall so that the juniors and sophomores would have to face it all year long—until next season.

Now, here I was with an entire—albeit small—country having a shit hemorrhage over what I had thought was a good banking story. And like the cartoon, it was a very clever concept too.

After all, this country had more banks than hotels even if they were, in my view, rather peculiar banks. But, there wasn't a chance the Commissioner of Police was secretly pleased. The man hated me even before the articles appeared.

I stammered a bit and told Doty I was defining a developing problem of communication between the Caymanian people and the growing population of expatriates.

"You are a very dangerous person," he said, cutting me off. "The government is much upset with you, particularly that part where you said the people were getting a lot of crap from us!"

The phrase, the single point in the second installment of my "offensive" banking series that galvanized the English civil servants against me and brought the order to report to the Governor's office, was a quote from one of the unidentified bankers that "the local Caymanians were getting tired of all the crap they get from the English."

"I wasn't talking about you or anyone else in particular," I said, "I was only..."

He slammed down the telephone abruptly after telling me there would be more to come about this. I walked over to my desk, shaken, and sat down.

I began to suspect some in the government thought I might be fomenting some kind of revolution—not a good idea in a foreign country.

With every edition I had published, the Caymanian government's tolerance level shrank. But being called in to face the Governor, and Doty's confrontation? This was special. I would explain to His Excellency that I did not mean the local people had to take a "lot of shit" from the English and "crap" in America meant "red tape." That should satisfy him and the event would be over. I felt better.

I did not believe crap meant red tape, of course, and I had meant it to mean "shit." But I was convinced I could explain my comment was an innocent misunderstanding. The Governor would nod his approval and I would be forgiven and order would return to paradise. Still, I wondered why he had ordered everyone I had interviewed to be present?

There was a problem with my spelling since taking over. Normally, I was pretty good. But, if I spelled "color" instead of "colour" or "program" instead of "programme," I would get a perfunctory call from Olive Miller, the British colonial import who served as Information Officer for the government, and its official critic of me.

She was a constant reminder that I was now in a British Colony and the newspaper was read by loyal British subjects. Mrs. Miller had already managed to let me know she had told Dr. Roy and Mr. Arthur before I had been hired that they should find a "nice English editor" for the newspaper because as the only publication, it played a crucial role in the country.

There was no mistaking that. It was a forceful tool for molding public opinion, as I would learn during the next several years.

It was the only medium for news and opinion—the only one in the country. There was no radio reception except from short wave abroad. I admit to a heady feeling in the beginning. Before things deteriorated, I fancied myself a Caribbean Lawrence of Arabia with notebook and typewriter. The only journalist in the entire country, and I had it all to myself.

In my initial enthusiasm I saw myself a blossoming media mogul, or, in my most light-headed moments, the brilliant publisher responsible for convincing the small nation to become the newest American state. At that point it didn't seem a far-fetched idea. After all, there were more Caymanians living in America than in Cayman. And they loved America didn't they? Like everyone else in the entire world?

Those were the first days, of course, before the roof started leaking, the air conditioner quit, the press broke and my shop foreman David walked out, before my first labor strike, before the boat failed to arrive with my supplies...before there was this "English shit" problem. And, there was a change at the pinnacle of government that coincided with my arrival.

The new Governor of The Cayman Islands had been an information officer in the colonial service in Africa prior to his appointment. At first I thought we might hit it off, his being a former information officer and all. No such luck. Kenneth Roy Crook was a pompous career civil servant who took his job and himself, like most colonial bureaucrats, far too seriously.

I had tried to make this tall, trim, elegantly gray appointee welcome when he was chosen. I believed it my responsibility and a good public relations move for the newspaper. In big headlines, I printed, "GOVERNOR NAMED," meaning, of course, that Queen Elizabeth had appointed a new Governor. I got a frantic call the next day from Sybil McLaughlin, Clerk of The Cayman Islands Parliament.

Sybil was not English but she was a native Caymanian and fervent British Subject who enjoyed her elevated status and understood she owed everything to the Crown. She was of vital importance to my little company because Sybil chose the printer who published all of the government's legal documents.

My company had always done that. Newspapers everywhere need to publish "legals" to survive financially. This is why there is always at least a weekly newspaper in any county seat. They overcharge for the service and get away with it because the law requires important documents and new rules to be printed in a "newspaper of general circulation."

I always dropped what I was doing when Sybil called. I discovered during my first few hours in command of the newspaper that we were in financial difficulty. The loss of government legal business could mean the end.

Sybil was incensed. She was an enormously tall black woman with livid eyes that could pierce solid rock. She was so intimidating in stature I would have been scared of her had she been only a grocery clerk.

"You have embarrassed and insulted His Excellency!" she shouted. Even the telephone in my hand was shaking.

Good God, I was bewildered! "Wh-wh-what?" I stuttered.

Sybil said being "named" in English parlay meant being "indicted."

"You have said His Excellency has been INDICTED!" she yelled.

She couldn't see me of course, but I was on my knees as I apologized to her, and begged forgiveness.

"I'm SOOOOOO sorry, Sybil," I whined. "I didn't know."

I explained how in the United States "named" was one of those highly overworked words in the vocabulary of headline writers who are always looking for a shorter way to say a-p-p-o-i-n-t-e-d or c-o-m-m-i-s-s-i-o-n-e-d. It saves space in the headline. If you use shorter words you can use larger type.

"Mr. Gentry," she said icily, "You are an embarrassment to our country."

"I am and I'm sorry," I said.

For the moment, she sounded mollified. After she hung up, I hoped it wasn't just the eye of the storm. I waited for her to ring back but the telephone was silent and I breathed easier.

I had not met the new Governor yet but he had already caused me enormous woe.

Mrs. Miller, the information officer, scolded me for calling the Governor "the governor." Any time I wrote about the Governor, I must call him His Excellency the Governor. On second reference, I may refer to him as His Excellency. I must set the right example for young Caymanians, she said.

Mr. A. C. E. Long, C.B.E., had been "Administrator" until the day before I arrived. On October 28, his title was changed and he became "His Excellency the Governor," for 10 days. He left on vacation October 29, the day I arrived, and I never met him.

In the month-long interim before Mr. Crook arrived, The Hon. D. V. Watler, O.B.E., J.P., whose title of "Deputy Administrator" was changed to "Chief Secretary" at the time the title of Administrator was changed to Governor, was sworn in as "Acting Governor" pending the imminent arrival of Mr. Crook.

Mr. Crook's name was without letters to place after his name when he arrived. Like all British bureaucrats, he wanted them badly and that certainly must have affected his personality. Had Her Majesty simply appointed The Hon. D. V. Watler, O.B.E, etc., to the new Governor's post—a natural thing to do since this older civil servant was the No. 2 man in the government and had lived in Grand Cayman all of his life—my life, and the future of The Cayman Islands might have taken a different turn. But that's not the way the English govern. They have a cadre of professional, political bureaucrats to shuffle around the world.

Watler was a kind, confident, well-respected member of the Cayman civil service. He was competent. He was local. He was, like most of the Caymanian people, of mixed ancestry.

Having grown up in the Deep South before segregation was banned, the restrictions placed on people of color were not unfamiliar to me. Nor did I find segregation particularly offensive in my youth. I did not understand, and it was the way that it was.

The English have a pecking order. Supposedly, the better job you do in service for your country, the bigger medal you get near the end of your career. Ordinary citizens can also receive these coveted awards. I have to admit I thought about it in the beginning. Those at the very top become peers. You then call them "Lord." Then there are knights. You call them "Sir". If they are women, "Dame." Dames are not knights but the honor is still up there, loftier even than America's Junior League.

Then there is the Knight Grand Cross, G.B.E., and its female equivalent, Dame Grand Cross, followed by the Knight Commander and Dame Commander, K.B.E, both of which admit an individual into knighthood or damehood immediately; next in order of seniority is the Commander of the British Empire or C.B.E., followed by the only-slightly-lesser O.B.E., or Most Excellent Officer of the British Empire. The lowest rank of the five classes is M.B.E. or Member of the British Empire.

The English love these awards, announced on the Queen's birthday, April 21, a day after my own. It's a sign of influential accomplishment in service to one's country. It's also a jump-start for the climb up the arduous ladder of social status. British subjects with one of these awards can list it after their signature on any legal document. It goes with them into the newspaper, too. If you leave their letters off or get them backward in the newspaper, they become very animated.

Like most Yanks, I have never been quite certain about these ranks, but whenever I saw a name like Sir Sam Jones or Dame Beulah Buckley, K.M.B.E., I knew I was not reading about white trash.

My initial editorial conflicts with the government were painful. Like most Americans, I was impressed in the beginning with the English and the elegance that surrounded them like a halo. The accent itself sounded worthy of respect. When an American hears any opinion spoken with an educated English accent, it carries a certain ring of truth even though it often sounds prissy.

I wanted to be like that. I wanted to spell like the English, write like the English, even sound like the English. I became an Anglophile wannabe. I told myself I could and would learn and eventually the government must accept and like me as I had been liked back in the high school gymnasium in Artesia when I gave a pep talk to the Bulldogs before a game.

I tried to make amends to the Governor and to Englishmen everywhere for some of my earlier spelling calamities—such as my "humor" column which Mrs. Miller reminded me should have been "humour" column (and was never really very funny again)—by inviting His Excellency the new Governor Mr. Crook to "tour" the newspaper office.

We scrubbed the floors and polished the press. Everyone wore their Sunday best. When his white limo arrived with the red Cayman flag flapping above the front bumper, we stood in line ready for inspection. Resplendent in his formal ice-cream suit and feathered pith helmet, he smiled graciously as I fawningly welcomed him. He was nice enough during the small talk but when I asked him what he thought of my newspaper he said, "You're very irresponsible."

Like most Americans I had been taught that the war the Colonials fought against the British was because of taxation without representation. I often thought during my years on the Cayman ironshore I could greatly simplify that. I would just say, "These people are all assholes."

With almost every edition I printed, I managed to offend somebody. If not the British, the Caymanians. There was a difference. I was learning just how different.

The Caymanians take their local elections very seriously and I introduced a new element into our political coverage: interpretation. One member of the local parliament clearly won an upset victory.

I reported an "upset victory." The morning after the newspaper hit the street I heard a pounding on the front desk. The winning candidate demanded to see me.

"What do you mean 'upset victory?'" he said angrily, "Nobody is upset!" I should have learned my lesson never to interpret anything political in The Cayman Islands.

The two-part banking series that resulted in my summons to Government House to meet the Governor ran one week apart in the spring of 1972. My purpose was to recognize the beginning of conflict and, by pointing it out, eliminate it. It was a "show the people the truth and it will make them free" approach.

Before the crap hit the fan I thought it a noble effort. The first part concerned real estate speculation. Before tax-haven bankers and tourists discovered the country local Caymanians saved for the future by buying land.

The speculators arrived first and talked the naive Caymanians into selling their land to buy better things—like washing machines and refrigerators. The Caymanians sold on easy, cheap terms. Before they realized it, most of the traditional family land was gone and the Caymanians had taken themselves out of the real estate business.

The new hustle would be between the new owners and developers, I suggested, which would lead to new problems. But the early 1970s were bringing recession and land prices were cooling.

The huge bucks were yet to be made in Grand Cayman so no one was upset that I was pointing this out. And even if it had upset the powers-that-be it wouldn't have bothered me. I was on familiar territory and could defend my stand. I was telling the truth.

One banker believed Cayman needed a condominium law.

"The condominium was the big thing in the Bahamas," the banker said. "The people who buy them are not looking for someone's job to take away, they just want to visit and spend money." Everyone loved that idea.

As the first installment concluded, it touched the fundamental problem: "To ensure political and economical stability, we have to ensure the Caymanian is getting the largest part of the action so they won't feel the economy is getting out of their hands." (Years later, I would point out in a different story in a different time and place that this is what happened in Hawaii, beginning shortly after Martha and I left to return to Mississippi in the early 1960s. The native Hawaiians were shut out of the progress).

Another banker said, "What I'm worried about is what the Caymanian (native) is going to think five years from now if we are overloaded and the ex-pats have all the top jobs?"

"We have two types of divisions here," another mused: "The haves and have-nots, and the foreigners and Caymanians. A lot of your have-nots are black and a lot of your North Side and East End are black, but it's not so much being black or white, or have or have-nots, as the have-nots just happen to be black," he said.

"Caymanians used to look after their people. Three years ago, we would always pick up anyone walking. Now, I'm not as nice as I was then. I don't know the people walking any more."

If I had stopped with those observations in Part One, my life as an American editor on a beautiful tropical island in the middle of the Caribbean Sea might have taken a different tack.

Some might even have seen the interpretation of the status quo as admirable. What I had authored was no surprise to anyone. It was the first time it had been in print. It had not angered anyone because everyone with any powers of observation understood Caymanians were on the short end of the stick and the expatriates the long.

The next morning, as instructed by the Governor's secretary, I walked over to Government House. It was a large wooden frame building that housed the administrative offices. The roof was tin. The Caymanians had yet to build the huge imposing structure which stands on the site today.

I wanted to clear my thoughts but it was impossible. I was on my way to a severe scolding.

The Governor's office was on the second floor. My heart sank as I walked into the foyer. Seven unsmiling faces swiveled toward me. They were all early. There was no warmth in any of their greetings.

There was Rodney Briggs of the Bank of Nova Scotia, Barry Phillips of the Canadian Imperial Bank of Commerce, Colin Whitelock of Barclays, Bob Eichfield of First National City Bank, Jean Doucet of Interbank and Sterling Bank, Ron Soley of the Royal Bank of Canada and Tompkins, the banker who had first alerted me.

These men controlled and manipulated billions and billions of dollars in financial transactions and the fate of individuals and companies around the world rested with their skill and judgment.

Probably for the first time in their successful careers they had been called on the carpet by a very temperamental government that had the power to shut them down and boot them off the island in a nanosecond.

If I had expected sympathy from this group, I was mistaken. They had agreed to my interview and not one questioned me on fact or accused me of taking their comments out of context. I did not attribute any of the quotes to any particular person. But I quoted each one's individual manner so accurately that the government had no problem identifying who said what.

Collectively we were in hot water but there was no camaraderie. Actually there was, but it was all on the other side of the room. The only thing we shared was our mutual fright.

As individuals, the banks tried to outdo each other by building huge concrete and glass buildings that were transforming the capital city of George Town into an architectural oddity. Wood frame buildings two stories high sat side by side with multi-story, glass and steel massifs twice as tall. They were also changing forever the lifestyles of the Caymanians and the character of The Cayman Islands.

At the time I didn't understand why the government was so politically sensitive. I was not aware that a few years earlier some of the more aggressive Caymanians had wanted to follow Jamaica and Grenada to full independence from Britain after a grand scheme to create a Caribbean Economic Community fell apart.

They had staged a rally. A rally in Cayman means a "march," which is a favorite Caymanian political tactic. A boisterous Caymanian crowd will gather and march harmlessly around the few downtown blocks of George Town.

That's how they make their political statements. They do the same thing on Christmas Eve except there is more alcohol involved and they sing carols while dancing from house to house in a giant conga line.

The independence movement has always been considered economic suicide by the majority of Caymanians, but the government, anticipating a crisis, overreacted, and asked England for help in preparing for the march.

Her Majesty dispatched a cruiser with a detachment of Royal Marines aboard and they sailed back and forth on the horizon for a few days "just within sight" of the jolly, bunny-hopping Caymanians.

It blew over quickly without incident and the ship sailed away, but reaction around the world in financial markets terrified the local government and the banks. The incident was reported in the world press and an enormous amount of offshore money was temporarily pulled out of Cayman by frightened depositors who thought a full-scale revolution was in progress.

The leadership in the Caymans sent a delegation to London and asked to be considered a Crown Colony, and not independent. That arrangement is the one that eventually prevailed.

I'm certain that all of those bank managers sitting there in that foyer that morning had already received telephone calls from their home offices about my first article. They were more frightened than I, but for different reasons. I'm certain every one of them was told the same thing: "Don't you remember what happened the last time the Caymans were mentioned in the press? What kind of fool are you for talking to that American person?"

Suddenly they were all staring directly at me.

Just then, the Governor's secretary opened the door to the inner office and motioned to us. She held the door open, which was her way of announcing that the Governor was ready.

Far off, there was the sound of distant thunder or maybe just my own heart pounding in my chest.

14

MY REBUKE BY THE GOVERNOR
BEGINS WITH A SURPRISE

I caught the Almighty's rare attention on another good day in Grand Cayman, the day of reckoning with His Excellency because of my banking article. My summons to the Governor's office for the anticipated reprimand and possible deportation caused me to prepare for the worst.

But the chief executive of The Cayman Islands who marched into the room where eight bank presidents and one anxious newspaper editor sweated that fateful morning was not the highly pompous, most frightening His Excellency the Governor Kenneth Crook, but the Most Honorable, Most Decent Chief Secretary, Desmond Watler.

The tall, dark, thin, graying indigenous Caymanian was the country's highest-ranking civil servant behind H.E. Mr. Crook and became acting Governor when H.E. was called away on Her Majesty's business. That, or H.E. had turned over the nasty assignment of dealing with the ugly American to his second in command, and was frolicking in nearby Jamaica.

The stoic expressions on my associates' faces did not change, but I could sense the enormous relief spreading around the room when Mr. Watler walked in.

"Good morning gentlemen," Mr. Watler said, sitting behind His Excellency's grand desk and smiling at everyone. Everyone, that is, but me. He avoided eye contact.

"Good morning, sir!" we answered in unison.

"His Excellency was called away and I was asked to bring you together for a brief discussion," he said.

I could see the Honorable Mr. Watler was uncomfortable with this assignment and I immediately experienced a sense of regret for bringing this problem down on his head as well as on ours.

"About this article in *The Caymanian Weekly*," Mr. Watler began, as the air quickly thickened in the office, "you all know what happened the last time this kind of publicity got out....."

He was referring to the celebrated march which resulted in the dispatch of an English warship to George Town and the resulting flurry of departing dollars from bank accounts. I listened as each bank manager explained that they had no idea that I was writing "this type" of article, and they would never have consented to an interview had they known what I was really up to.

I was perplexed and would have been outspoken had I been in my own country and certain of my rights. Here, I was not certain and a bit afraid of what could happen to me if the government decided to pounce on me.

Finally, the Honorable Chief Secretary looked directly at me. His face was stern, but not grim. "You know, we have enjoyed freedom of the press in this country forever..."

It was a veiled warning—which I interpreted as unofficially meant only for me and not the constitution—the kind that probably originated for this particular meeting in a hastily called committee meeting of government bureaucrats. I knew I must present something in my defense.

"I don't see anything wrong with the article I wrote," I began. There was complete silence in the room as everyone watched me. "It was accurate, and everyone here knew they were being interviewed by a reporter."

I was aware the mood among my comrades was turning to annoyance. I knew they wanted me to shut the hell up and try to get them out of this with no damage.

"But what good does an article like that do?" The Honorable Mr. Watler asked me.

"Well, I've always believed that the truth speaks best and I have heard so much of this—about the animosity; I mean unhappiness—between the locals and the British elite that I thought it should be brought up for public discussion," I said. That was the crux of the second part of my article, the local resentment against the all-governing hand of the English.

"I've not seen any of that!" Mr. Watler retorted. I didn't wish to dispute him on his own turf.

The other bankers looked at each other and nodded their assent. "Well, I can see how it might do some good," one of the bankers said, and everyone, including me, turned in shock. Someone had actually dared to speak up in my defense.

But when pressed to explain how it could possibly help an economy based on a tax haven industry to have an "article in the local press talking about unhappiness between the locals and the British," the culpable banker stammered, and couldn't come up with an appropriate answer.

But I appreciated the attempt and I never forgot the one man who attempted to help me in that horribly awkward situation. He was the only American banker on the island, Bob Eichfield of First National City Bank.

With that, the meeting abruptly ended and we all left quickly without speaking to each other. I did manage to stop Eichfield briefly, and thanked him. He acknowledged my gratitude, but pointed out he had already received a call from New York about his participation.

"Are you in trouble?" I asked, concerned.

"Aw, not really," he said.

As for me, it was a new low in my Cayman career. I wondered how many of my American colleagues had been called before the American government and chastised for an article? I would have enjoyed some satisfaction had this happened in my own country.

As it was, it became a defining moment in these islands, a reference point, which was a stumbling block for other articles I attempted to write about the offshore banking industry.

In the official Report on The Cayman Islands for the Year 1971, the year I landed in George Town, and printed in London by Her Majesty's Stationery Office, the stable population of the country was reported to be 10,249 persons, up from 8,511 ten years earlier. Tourism reached 24,354 visitors in 1971, according to the report, reflecting a steady increase. Under the caption, "Newspapers," there was the mention of a new "high quality glossy magazine, The Nor'wester," which had just been published for the first time by Desmond Seales. "This monthly publication was favorably received," the report drooled.

There was also the curt acknowledgment of the nation's only real news medium, my weekly newspaper:

"*The Caymanian Weekly*, which has been in existence since 1965 was published throughout the year maintaining a tradition of fair comment and unbiased presentation of views," the stodgy booklet reports.

"Management and Editorship was changed completely in October 1971 since which time there has been a noted difference in presentation and format consequent on the editorial staff coming mainly from the U.S.A."

Of course, when first I stepped off the jet on October 28, 1971 and gazed on the hot tin roof of Owen Roberts International Airport, I had no plans to become a prejudiced footnote in the official government handbook. I thought I was there to manage a newspaper, not threaten a nation's stability.

As for His Excellency's absence from the official scolding, I realized years later he could not possibly have attended. Had his admonishment of the editor and publisher of the only newspaper in the country ever reached the international press, the reaction could have been temporarily catastrophic for the offshore-banking industry.

At the time, I am surprised I did not cut and run. But I didn't.

15

WHAT IS A BIAMI ANYWAY?

I was anxious to improve our news-gathering methodology. The newspaper printed what the government handed down through Mrs. Miller, and I found that truly distasteful. I wanted "hard" news, from the source.

I needed to get into the local police records in George Town, just as I had as a journalist in Artesia and Port Arthur. We got very little police news in Cayman and the authorities watered that down. I saw no reason for this. Mrs. Miller protested when I suggested I be allowed to go through the action reports at the station, but agreed to set up a meeting with the police commissioner, Mr. Doty. There was no question I was nervous about a meeting with my fearsome nemesis, but it was something that had to be done if the newspaper sought to be taken seriously. At least in my view.

It would be my first face-to-face meeting with him and I knew he wasn't pleased that an American ruled the local press. And he did not hesitate to let everyone know what he thought about this particular American. My ears were still scorched from our telephone encounter following the banking articles. I'm certain that to him I was a subversive influence.

Our meeting was to be at 9 a.m. It was a gorgeous morning and I decided to walk to police headquarters. It was an easy stroll and I went by the harbor to see what new boats were calling. The harbor was one of the most interesting sights in the country. There were no fences, no guards and no restrictions. You could walk right up to any boat moored next to the bank and ask to visit. I was apprehensive and if anything would cheer me up, it was a stroll by the docks.

During my years in Grand Cayman I was never denied permission to board. The seafarers were of all types and varieties and their ships ranged from 20-foot sailboats to magnificent yachts hundreds of feet

91

long and worth millions.

There was a newcomer, a lobster boat named *Gulf Star*. It rode at anchor several hundred yards offshore and looked deserted.

I also wanted another look at the talk of the islands. The *MV Sharon Michelle* was a graceful, 70-foot motorboat once employed by the Royal Air Force. She had been in port several days while its owner, Englishman Eric Palmer, enjoyed a vacation ashore after his lengthy, solitary sea voyage.

The boat was unusual because of its look—it rode low in the water like a torpedo boat and was painted black and white with polished teak decks—and because of its electronic equipment. It was equipped with gear that allowed it to be operated by one man from anywhere on board by remote control. It was equipped with twin diesel engines and had a range of 3,500 miles.

The owner travelled the oceans alone on his ship and motored all the way from Plymouth, England to Grand Cayman. That earned him a measure of respect among the seafaring Caymanians.

I had not met him yet, but I was sure that he would invite me aboard if I asked. As I stopped to admire the vessel, I saw him climb into his dingy and head for shore.

I hesitated, thinking I might introduce myself when he stepped ashore, but a glance at my watch told me I had about 30 minutes before meeting with Doty. I had plenty of time but I wanted to be early. I didn't want to give Doty any chance to be a snotty Englishman and cancel.

I waved and Palmer waved back.

The morning continued clear and calm. Nothing was stirring. Seabirds high above wheeled lazily. I envied their grand view and their freedom.

The harbor at George Town—Hog Sty Bay—is a natural one. The sea's edge abruptly meets unyielding coral rock, or ironshore—not a sandy beach—and boats of shallow draft anchor a few feet offshore and extend a wooden gangplank to touch dry land. On the north side of the harbor, only a few hundred feet away, the water was deeper. This is where the larger merchant motor vessels docked to offload supplies.

For years, the government of The Cayman Islands had wanted to deepen the George Town harbor and build a rock jetty to protect the boats from any sudden shift in the weather. The harbor faced the open sea and there was no protection during storms.

Dr. Roy and a few of his friends owned property on the North Sound, a large, shallow, protected cove on the northern side of the island. He, with some justification, including legitimate engineering studies, thought that the government would be better off dredging a harbor on the North Sound rather than improving George Town harbor. He believed North Sound was a natural harbor.

It was an argument that I would support in the newspaper, not because I was an engineer, but I thought the idea made sense, at least in the beginning. Also, since Dr. Roy was the managing director of my company, I trusted his judgment and I had little confidence in the government. The public stance against the George Town harbor plan by the newspaper didn't make me any more popular with my government detractors.

In later years, the government's version would prevail and a jetty would be built to protect the anchorage. On December 23, 1971, however, as I walked slowly toward my meeting with Doty, there was nothing to protect the harbor from the open sea but fresh air and sunshine.

Mrs. Miller was waiting for me at the station. She greeted me formally. I had been disappointed with Mrs. Miller's treatment of me. I learned she had actually worked at the Caymanian before my arrival. When the government decided it needed an information officer, she was the logical choice. But she longed for an Englishman as editor.

"Hello, Mr. Gentry," she said. "I've just spoken to the commissioner and he'll be with us in just a moment."

We sat silently for a few moments, and the door to the commissioner's office opened. Doty stuck his head out and motioned us inside.

He shook my hand stiffly and seated himself behind his desk.

"What can I do for you, Mr. Gentry?" he asked.

"I was hoping I might be given permission to go through your police log each morning to see what events have occurred during the evening," I said.

He looked at me in astonishment.

"There's no way I can allow anyone to look at our police files," he stammered. "This isn't allowed."

"I don't see why I shouldn't," I said, "They are, after all, public records."

"Mr. Gentry," Mrs. Miller interjected, discerning that the conversation was not evolving well, "I know you told me that you have access to these records in the United States, but that is simply not done here, or in England..."

I was confident I could convince this anti-American pair to cooperate, given enough time and my infallible personal charm:

"Mr. Doty," I began. "I have great admiration for your English tradition, and even greater admiration for your own service to the Crown. I've heard many great things about you.

"My own personal genealogy is rooted in English history," I said, which was partially true. It would be hard to be named Gentry without some bond. "The collective Gentry family in America is directly linked to our common ancestor, Oliver Cromwell. The truth is, we are all related to soldiers of questionable character who may, or may not, have deserted to seek their fortunes in the West Indies.

"All we want is to have access so that we can report it in our newspaper," I said. "We don't plan to use all of the information and we'll certainly be judicious. I understand the laws of libel..."

"I cannot have this!" Doty snapped with an icy stamp of finality. "Besides," he added, "I've seen your editorial efforts."

"Well," I said, ignoring the sarcasm and struggling to remain diplomatic, "what can I do to get the police news? I think it's important to tell the country what's happening. I don't think that's ever been done here."

"Why don't we do this," Mrs. Miller interjected, trying to keep the conversation from deteriorating further, "why don't I make a point to call the police department every morning and...?"

Before she could finish there was a sharp knock on the door and a uniformed officer opened it and told the commissioner he was wanted on the telephone.

He picked up the telephone, listened for a few seconds, then stood and excused himself.

"I'm sorry," he said, "I must go."

He turned toward Mrs. Miller, "We'll work something out."

Mrs. Miller and I sat looking at one another and I realized my interview was over.

"Well, thank you," I told her. "You tried to help."

"We'll work on it," she said.

"Can I drive you back to the newspaper?" she asked.

"Thanks, but I need the walk," I said.

I noticed that the wind had freshened. In fact, the wind was quite strong and the sky, so clear minutes ago, was dark and ominous.

I was about to skip the view and go directly to my office when I became aware that people were running toward the harbor. A young man dashed by me and I yelled at him, "What's going on?"

He looked back and shouted, "Biami comin'!"

I had no idea what he meant but there was no doubt something was amiss. This probably had something to do with Doty's sudden departure. So much for better communication with the police chief.

Within minutes I was able to see the harbor. A crowd was gathered at the south shore where the beautiful, black *Sharon Michelle* was wallowing dangerously close to the ironshore. The waves were building up and I wondered why the owner was foolishly allowing her so close.

Because of the northwest wind's sudden strength, I had trouble running toward the harbor. I could see other vessels underway, making for open sea. The harbor, so peaceful earlier, was a caldron as the wind lashed its surface.

The *Sharon Michelle* began banging her beautifully crafted black hull against the ironshore. I watched in disbelief. I couldn't understand why she wasn't roaring away from the deadly rocks with those two powerful diesels. There was a loud screeching sound like someone scraping the side of an automobile with a dull knife. It was physically painful to hear it.

Unknown to me, owner Eric Palmer was approaching in a motor launch and watching helplessly as his beautiful ship began grinding herself to pieces. There was no one aboard *Sharon Michelle*. The wind was suddenly so severe that the ship had dragged her anchors and was fully engaged with the ironshore. It was no contest.

Farther out I could see a lobster boat struggling to get underway in the middle of the harbor. A few puffs of black smoke blew from her stacks and she moved a few feet forward, but then the puffs stopped and she lay dead in the water. Slowly, as the crowd ashore watched in horror, she began drifting toward the ironshore, relentlessly shoved by the wind.

The launch carrying Palmer suddenly veered away from the *Sharon Michelle* and headed toward the lobster boat, the *Gulf Star*. Palmer was aware of the possibility of sudden storms and had warmed his engines twice the previous night in case he might need an emergency break for open water. Both times, it had been a false alarm.

The older Caymanians called them "Biamis," the sudden appearance of nor'westers—strong cold fronts that occasionally blow through the islands. Cold fronts rarely make it as far south as Grand Cayman. But when they come the results often prove disastrous. The U.S. weather bureau had reported that the Caymans were on the southern boundary of a 400-mile-wide trough, but the violence of the storm wasn't predictable

A year later we experienced a Biami with freak winds clocked at almost 100 miles per hour. I made Martha and the children run and lie down on the kitchen floor when the terrifying winds struck. Fortunately, no one died and there was no damage.

This day, there would be tragedy.

When the storm struck, the captain of the lobster boat *Gulf Star*, Danny Martin, 47, of Saint Petersburg, was at Bob Soto's dive shop on Seven Mile Beach buying engine parts for his crippled boat. The owner of the *Sharon Michelle*, Palmer, was also there. A motor launch carrying the two frantic captains and driven by a brave young Caymanian, Fordie Bodden, raced to rescue the doomed ships.

There was an engineer on board the *Gulf Star* but he was having no luck starting the engine.

What happened next became the basis for the first-ever special "Extra" edition of *The Caymanian Weekly* published the day after the disaster.

Within the hour, I interviewed the shaken owner of the *Sharon Michelle* as we both stood on the edge of the ironshore looking down at the floating splinters of black and white planking and assorted debris that was all that remained of the sleek *Sharon Michelle*. He was wearing a borrowed jacket. Everything he owned was on the bottom of Hog Sty Bay.

"I went to Bob Soto's where a small motor boat was trying to carry the captain of the lobster boat to his ship, and was able to join them," he said.

When the terrible reality hit him that he could not make it to his ship before it was impaled on the rocks, he directed the launch to try to save the lobster boat.

"Its captain tried to board but could only get his hands on the scuppers," Palmer said. They proved too high and the captain, Martin, fell into the water. Palmer managed to climb aboard.

As his own ship was being disemboweled by the ironshore, Palmer located the engineer and told him to start the engines and he would steer.

"But by that time the rocks were approaching and I knew it was hopeless," he said.

The 80-foot lobster boat slammed into the ironshore. Fortunately, the boat's steel hull did not shatter. But, it was rolling dangerously in the high surf, and there were fears that it would capsize.

Someone threw a line from the shore and it was made fast. With the help of dozens on the ironshore creating a tightrope, including the shaken American editor of *The Caymanian Weekly*, the engineer and Palmer crawled hand over hand to safety.

We searched the shoreline for the missing captain. I spotted him in the water close to shore, but he appeared too exhausted to swim. He was right in front of me, and then he went under. Without thinking, I started toward the edge of the ironshore. Several husky Caymanians grabbed my arms and threw me backward. I sat on my butt and watched them create a human chain, reach down, grab him and drag him ashore. An examination indicated a large cut on his head from the lobster boat or a rock. He was dead even when I saw him go under.

With a low groan, the *Gulf Star* made a slow roll and capsized just offshore in front of us in eight to 10 feet of water. A more romantic writer might have thought the ship's final cry and rollover a tribute to her dead captain. I was too awestruck and shaken to think about anything but how quickly death can find you in the sea.

As suddenly as it arrived, the Biami left us.

Within an hour the sea was calm enough to see bits and pieces of the *Sharon Michelle* through the clear water on the bottom.

"Did you have insurance?" I asked Palmer.

He shook his head. "No, everything I owned was in that ship," he said.

"Is there anything I can do?"

"You might report that if anyone finds a little black bag I need my passport," he said. "It's down there."

The next day someone found his bag and his passport was intact. He left Cayman to find support to raise the valuable diesel engines. They had not been running when the ship sank so he was hopeful they would not be damaged by seawater. It later proved he was correct. Within a week he returned and was able to salvage them and ship them back to England. "I'm flat broke now," he said, "but I'm going to build another ship someday."

The overturned *Gulf Star* became a tourist attraction. She was heavy enough to be solidly anchored to the bottom.

It wasn't long before Caymanian mariners began scheming about ways to salvage the lobster boat. It might be legally tricky but if they could find a way to right the ship, they might be able to place a salvage claim on her, or at least put a hefty lien on their work that the owners would have to pay.

Almost every day, enterprising Caymanians attempted to right her. Most of them hooked heavy cables to the side of the ship facing the open sea, then attempted to roll her upright by tugging with their boats.

Every motor vessel of any size in Cayman gave it a shot. Even some of the small freighters that hauled supplies between Grand Cayman and the U.S. roared and strained and belched clouds of black diesel smoke, but the *Gulf Star* proved as solid and unmoving as a rock. She wouldn't budge. All the daily tug of war managed to do was to entertain the crowd that gathered to watch.

After about six days, a stranger appeared on the horizon and slowly closed in on the *Gulf Star*. I saw the newcomer, a large, sea-going tug flying an American flag. I walked down to watch what I expected would be an interesting attempt.

The big tug came very close to the sunken lobster boat and a crew quickly drew up to her in a small launch. They hooked several cables to her seaward side. They worked so swiftly I knew they were professionals.

As they moved back they signaled to the tug. It slowly revved up power and pulled until the cables were as tight as violin strings. The steel lines strained and the *Gulf Star's* lifeless bulk shuddered as the huge tug's props roiled the water. In a matter of seconds the lobster boat began to roll under the enormous strain of the cables.

A few more seconds and she rolled upright and floated again, bobbing from side to side as she righted herself. The men who had attached the cables sped to her side and climbed aboard. They loosened the cables from her side and hooked them to her bow.

The tug took up the slack in the cables and she began easing toward the open sea with her sluggish partner in tow behind. The *Gulf Star* rode low in the water because her hull remained heavy with seawater, but she appeared in no danger of foundering again.

As soon as it was evident she would ride safely under tow the tug turned up the power and the ungainly pair raced in a straight line toward the open sea.

I smiled, understanding that the tug's captain knew full well that he had to reach the territorial limit before The Cayman Islands custom officials could react and either demand that the boat be released or that a hefty salvage fee be paid to the country. But there was no reaction from any part of the harbor, and within a few minutes the tug and her charge had disappeared over the horizon.

Secretly, I was proud of how proficiently the tug flying the stars and stripes had snatched the lobster boat.

It was the last we saw of the *Gulf Star*. She's probably still sailing somewhere.

16

BUSINESS IS GOOD IN CAYMAN, BUT WHO WORKS?

Physically producing the newspaper in Cayman was vastly different from anything I had experienced. No one accepted responsibility for keeping business moving. Consequently, I was called at every point. If there were classified advertisements to type, I had to gather them and take them to the typist. If a customer wanted to insert a news item at the front desk, I was called to take it.

I didn't mind this. I believed I could train the staff the way I wanted and eventually I would be able to turn my attention to the greater events occurring on the island that should be reported.

What made me nervous was the tenuous stability of the printing department. I was unfamiliar with the presses, the cameras, the stripping department and the bookkeeping required. I was depending on a staff of workers who still eyed me suspiciously every time I walked into the production department. I worried that they were waiting for another opportunity to strike. That opportunity could have been anything—broken air conditioner, the daily loss of electricity, too much work, too many clouds.

Fortunately, we continued to make our press deadlines and had a Caymanian Weekly ready for the crowd that gathered outside our office each Thursday morning. Production of the newspaper never failed to draw that crowd. The Caymanians considered the newspaper THEIR weekly newspaper. Regardless of how little hard news it contained and how amateurish and provincial it appeared the readership remained loyal, at home and abroad.

Our readers cherished the tiny publication. Not only did our circulation list contain thousands of American customers, there were thousands more subscribers from all corners of the world—from Luxembourg and London to Johannesburg and Paris and anywhere and everywhere in between. Wherever there was an individual or a company interested in world banking, there would be a Caymanian Weekly around.

It wasn't long before my trepidation took form in the printing department. Without David and the accounting system he kept in his head it was impossible to know where anything was at any given time. If a customer wanted to check the progress of his order, the entire printing department would shut down and initiate a search.

More often than not the job would not be located and the customer would be told, "Don't worry; it will be ready tomorrow."

Since we were the main printing company and enjoyed most of the printing business, the customer had few options other than accept our promise, knowing it wouldn't be ready tomorrow.

The newspaper was profitable from its beginning because of its printing business. The previous year the company had made a tidy $20,000 profit and the directors had quickly declared themselves $20,000 in dividends. That was an annual occurrence for the directors and there was no puzzle why they were so happy with the operation. *The Caymanian* had been a cash cow.

I had been an appalling accounting student in college. However, it didn't take Alan Greenspan to understand the owners had milked the company and the equipment had reached the obsolete stage.

In addition, our cash flow was nonexistent. There were thousands of dollars owed to the company and no one had made any attempt to collect it. A few rare customers, most of them banks or law firms, paid on time and on schedule.

The British banking system provides customers with an overdraft. Customers can draw beyond the cash in their accounts up to an approved credit limit. We were constantly dipping into our overdraft. Fortunately, the directors were wealthy enough to cover any red ink and there was no pressure on me in the beginning, but money was a constant worry. There were so many improvements necessary and so much of the equipment needed to be repaired or replaced.

I saw the potential for increasing our business immediately. We were the leading printing company and remained well respected in spite of our foibles. The demand for our product was there if only we could deliver. Time after time, I saw clerks from the various banks appear at our printing desk inquiring about their orders. More often than not they would leave empty handed.

Still, they continued to bring more business. With offshore financial services, new bank accounts most often resulted from new company incorporation. There are letterheads and envelopes to be printed. The banks themselves required letterheads, envelopes, forms and ledgers of all types. There were more forms required by the government. We did it all.

But, I saw more and more customers slip away to our new competition, Billy Bodden's Instaprint, which he had started after deserting *The Caymanian Weekly*. Billy had purchased an Itek Camera that combines many of the labor-intensive processes we employed. He could turn out printing jobs in one day. When InstaPrint said, "Tomorrow," they meant it. What I needed more than anything was experienced help.

Caymanian businesses enjoy freedom from taxes. There is no sales tax, withholding tax, income tax, or tax of any kind to burden the bookkeeping operation. The government operates on fees collected from the offshore banking industry, from the duty on imports, arrival and departure fees and postage stamps. What the businessman does with his profit is his business alone.

The downside of doing business in Cayman is labor. Although warm, friendly people, the Caymanians did not deserve, nor enjoy, a reputation for hard work and efficiency. They put off until tomorrow that which should be done today. Generally, the response to any question of accountability was, "It's not my job." Fortunately for me, I had a few loyal Caymanians like Sandra Parchment who were smart, loyal and goal-oriented helpers.

In many ways, this predisposition toward work was so entrenched in the Caribbean society it worked in our favor. Businesses looking for rush jobs knew there was no such animal. Consequently they weren't particularly annoyed when the job they desperately needed yesterday wouldn't be ready until tomorrow.

Most composing room foremen were particularly foul, mean-spirited individuals. To make their deadline, they spend their careers detesting and resisting editors who constantly challenge their authority. Composing room foremen live and die by deadlines. Writers have a tough time with deadlines. If not for foremen, writers might spend their entire careers working on one story. There's always so much to say, too little space to say it and not enough time to make it perfect.

I thought longingly of Milt Houston in Artesia. He was six-foot-six and sat at his linotype machine studying his Masonic manual when he wasn't typing. It was Milt's job to get the paper out on time regardless of how much the writers procrastinated. He was severe at times. I remember days when I discovered "typographical mistakes" in articles about to be printed. More often than not, Milt would look at the corrections I had marked on tear sheets, sneer, and crumple them into a ball and drop them to the floor. "You're too late!" He would snarl. "It's past your deadline!"

"But Milt," I would beg. "This is gonna make me look like a fool." He didn't care. "It's past the deadline," he would repeat. "And it's not a typo anyway. You're trying to change your column again."

I would fume and pout until the next time, the next day, the next deadline.

I would have given anything in those early Cayman days to see Milt walk in the door and take over the composing room.

The biggest threat to business in The Cayman Islands was the protection the government gave to the Caymanian locals. In order to import labor, you must convince the immigration officials that there was no Caymanian available. This policy contributed to the Caymanian work ethic. Any Caymanian who wanted a job would get one because every business was anxious to show the authorities it employed its fair share of locals.

Importing labor was a matter of paper shuffling, plus the payment of an annual fee for a work permit. It cost less than $100 in those years. Still, it was a bureaucracy that prevented the importation of too many foreigners. The native Caymanians were terrified of being overrun by Jamaicans, Americans and British.

The local legislature continuously passed legislation to protect the natives. It became almost impossible for an outsider to start a business in Cayman without a Caymanian partner. The local partner must, by law, own 60 percent of the business.

As an American used to wide-open entrepreneurship, I was at first offended by these protective laws. Americans generally welcomed foreign investment and foreign ownership of property.

I would argue, "There are more Caymanians living in the United States than there are living in The Cayman Islands! What if they started imposing these restrictions against you?"

In later years, Cayman friends told me I, as an American, had no idea how hard it is for a foreigner to work legally in the U.S. And anyone with the money can buy all the property they want in the Caymans.

"You can also hold dual citizenships," I argued. "You can be an American and a Caymanian, with two passports!

"I can't vote here," I said, "and won't EVER be able to vote here unless I become a citizen of Cayman." That means a loss of U.S. citizenship.

Again, the smile and shrug. I could have added that even if I had wanted to become a citizen of Cayman, it was a torturous process. The Caymanians were even more protective of Cayman citizenship than they were of Cayman employment. There was a five-year wait before you could even apply. Until then, you had to reapply yearly for a work-permit and a visa.

It was quickly becoming an education for a naive American. I knew that anyone born on American soil, for whatever reason, was automatically an American citizen—even if the parents illegally crossed the border as the labor pains were just beginning. Well, that doesn't happen in Cayman, or any of the other Caribbean nations. Many things, I was learning, happened only in America.

America had struggled through the turbulent 1960s and was still mired in Vietnam. Everywhere in America resentment was building against the government. The Watergate Burglary brought a lot of confusion to the Caribbean nations, including The Cayman Islands. For me, and many of the other American expatriates, the Watergate aftermath was a personal family drama being played out before snobby neighbors, dirty laundry and all.

"Why are they doing this?" we would be asked as news reports that Richard Nixon might be impeached were received by short wave or read about in the Miami Herald. We were hard pressed to give an answer. We weren't sure ourselves. To us, America was still the rare beacon of freedom and opportunity. The prestige of the United States suffered greatly during the Watergate years in the Caribbean.

17

LOOKING FOR HELP IN ALL THE WRONG PLACES

I told Mr. Arthur that I must import expert help immediately and he was sympathetic and supportive. I explained my problem to Dr. Roy and obtained his approval. I knew I had to generate revenue to pay for my new help and I was dangerously close to having a permanent overdraft.

Martha and I talked about the possibilities. Lois Purvis, who had taken my place as editor of The Artesia Daily Press, was one of the possibilities I considered. When I wrote her, she immediately indicated an interest. Her husband, Jim, a retired Marine sergeant, even investigated the possibility of working in a print shop prior to coming down, because I had indicated I could use someone to take over as foreman and a retired Marine sergeant fit the image.

In the end, I couldn't offer them enough money. I even discouraged them from taking a chance because I knew they wouldn't be able to survive financially in the islands. It wouldn't have been fair to entice them. I was making a considerable amount of money and yet Martha and I were having trouble. Suitable accommodation was a common problem for expatiates in Cayman, sometimes a fatal one. During the summer months rentals were plentiful but as the tourist season approached, they disappeared. If you rented a resort home or apartment you were kicked out in the fall when the tourist season began.

I often thought about building an apartment house for my expatriate employees but the cost was always just out of reach. The problem with housing was also a problem for my first expatriate employees, my sister-in-law Risë Price and her husband Nolan. They were younger than Martha and I and had lived in a number of cities after Nolan graduated from Ole Miss with a marketing degree.

Both Risë and Nolan were exceptional people. Nolan, in addition to being a star basketball and football player at Tupelo High School—where he was "Mr. THS" his senior year—was one of the sharpest guys I knew. I had always been a writer and what little I knew about selling newspaper advertising could be told in 10 minutes. So when I eventually hired Nolan he started studying books about newspaper advertising and pursued it from the ground floor.

On a personal level, I knew it would be beneficial to have family members I could depend on. But, my conscience bothered me and I immediately wrote another letter discouraging them. I was aware that what I could offer—$500 a month—would put them in financial jeopardy. They accepted the risk and wouldn't be deterred, so I applied for a work permit for Nolan and told them to make plans to fly down.

It didn't take long for the Prices to become accepted members of the Cayman expatriate society. Nolan adapted immediately to the role of advertising salesman and I hired Risë as a typesetter. With both of them working they were able to eke out a living and they enjoyed the new laid-back lifestyle.

Nolan designed long-term contract forms for advertisers and together we created new, realistic advertising rates more in line with inflation and our increasing expenses. There was much to learn and many mistakes made but for the first time I began to feel order was being established.

Another fortunate hiring I made was of a young man from Oregon who had asked me for a job as an artist. His name was Mark Rice and he appeared so eager and had such an appealing manner I immediately offered him a minimum wage, about $40 a week.

Mark looked like a hippie with his beard and sandals and I'm sure he had done his share of pot-smoking, but he never gave me cause to regret hiring him. He was talented and hard-working, intensely loyal, and I never heard anyone say anything bad about him.

In spite of our progress, the printing department remained a problem. Orders were still coming in, but were very slow going out.

Then, I heard a chilling report.

Billy was planning to start his own newspaper.

I wasn't afraid of the competition from Billy. I was afraid of the limitations of my own crew. We were becoming a functioning unit but there was a large piece missing: a production foreman who could take us to a higher level.

I advertised in the Miami Herald for an experienced newsroom foreman. Among the numerous replies I received was a letter from Roy Kratt, a 48-year-old Navy retiree.

"From 1950 until 1967, I was a lithographer," he wrote. "I retired from the Navy as a Chief Lithographer. During my career I was in charge of four different print shops with four to 12 men under my supervision."

Since his retirement, he had worked for a printing company in Naples, Florida and at the Cape Coral Breeze, a weekly Florida newspaper. Before I had time to answer his letter he sent a telegram: "Most interested to see you personally February 25."

Although I had other applications, I waited on the enterprising retiree, Roy Kratt. I was impressed by his unilateral decision to fly down. When he walked in two weeks later, I immediately liked what I saw. Roy was a short, portly, blond, pipe-smoker who appeared easy-going and confident. Perhaps I was grasping at straws, but I was confident this mellow, unpretentious ex-Navy chief was going to help me salvage the floundering printing department. I hired him before he left the office.

I helped Roy locate an apartment and started the paperwork for his work permit. "Thanks be to God," as Mr. Arthur said, the process went smoothly, and Roy quickly moved his few belongings to Cayman.

One possession stood out. He brought with him a small, bright red, sporty convertible called a Mighty Mite. It was his pride and joy. He became a familiar sight driving around the island in that shiny little two-seater, puffing his pipe and scouting locations where he could enjoy a beer in his off hours. It was easy to locate Roy if I needed to track him down because of that car.

Roy was as good as his word. He began to sort out my production problems. He developed a schedule that would allow us to locate any job anywhere in the process, improved our camera skills and showed our pressmen how to implement short-cuts and improve proficiency. We were behind the curve in the production techniques and he began updating the shop. Instead of resenting him, the production personnel appreciated Roy's interest and expertise and I could feel morale surging.

Before long, production became nicely orchestrated. It was not yet a symphony, but we were striking harmonious cords. Business picked up, complaints fell off and I could walk about George Town with my chin up, no longer afraid of bumping into someone who would pull me aside and plead with me to check his printing job which was "desperately needed!"

With the mechanical world stabilizing, I began to dream of augmenting the editorial department. What I needed was a managing editor to handle the day-to-day news operations. I wanted more coverage of the parliament and the pressing social and economic problems. We also needed more space, especially if I bought a larger printing press. I planned to increase the physical size of the newspaper.

I was preparing for Billy, confident that in a few months my crew would be able to compete. I placed an advertisement in Editor and Publisher magazine for an editor. Replies came in by the dozens. The thought of a Caribbean adventure was beguiling. I corresponded with several of them and even asked for information for a possible work permit. Several received an offer but they turned me down with regret, they said, because of salary. I couldn't pay more than $500 a month and they were bright enough to understand they couldn't live on that pittance, even in paradise.

I also received a rare telephone call. It came from a printer in Oklahoma who had seen my older advertisement for a production foreman. He was so anxious to come down that I was sorry that I didn't have a spot for him. "I'll do anything," he said, "I've been looking for something like this all of my life. Let me just come talk to you!"

I told him the position had been filled, but I would keep him in mind.

"I don't care about the money," he said. "Whatever you pay, I'll accept."

"Maybe there will be another opening," I said. "Don't give up on your dream."

He pled with me not to forget him. Intrigued by his intense desire, I retained his telephone number for future reference. His name was George Heon and neither I, nor any of my friends and supporters, will ever forget him and what happened because of him.

As the time approached for Billy's first issue, I prepared my crew for the competition. I knew he had the advantage by being the local boy and I was still the outsider. When the announcement came that the Cayman Compass would have its first publication Tuesday, I gathered my staff for a pep talk.

"What we have to do," I said, "is to prepare to work harder, do our jobs, and never give in. "There's nothing wrong with a little competition. It sharpens you like nothing else. If you are the only business in a community, it's operating in a vacuum. Competition will keep us on our toes. We are going to have a fight with the competition, but I can assure you there's no one better than me in a newspaper battle. We're going to win this and *The Caymanian Weekly* is going to remain the No.1 newspaper in this country!

"We're not going to cheat. We're going to beat them because we're better, we're smarter, and we're more dedicated."

Secretly, I would have preferred to continue operating in a vacuum since I knew the last thing we needed right now was competition. I almost shouted, "Are you with me?" Thankfully, I didn't.

A few of my Caymanian workers came forward and told me nervously they planned to stick with me because they found me "entertaining."

They viewed the fight as a contest between Billy and me, but some of them knew "something else" was coming that I didn't.

I was seething over Billy's capture of our subscription list. Following Billy's instructions, a former bookkeeper took a copy of our subscriber list when she left us to work for him. I believed it a corporate crime. Those were 12,000 customers around the world who paid us $100,000 in annual subscription fees.

It was a priceless asset and I was angrier than usual because the board members had no interest in legal action against Billy. They refused to recognize it as theft and shrugged it off.

After my pep talk, my chief typesetter, Jo Anne, asked me for her vacation pay. I didn't see it as unusual because the Caymanians always asked for their pay in advance of vacations. She insisted I give her a check. I thought Jo Anne's nervousness was because I had recently stopped giving "vacation pay."

I thought it abusive. When I took over, the company allowed employees to receive vacation pay in addition to their normal wages if they decided to work instead of taking off. I put an immediate end to it and told them if they wanted vacation pay they had to take a vacation. It had amounted to double pay for two weeks.

After Jo Anne received her vacation check, about a half-dozen or so other employees approached Martha to give them their vacation pay, too. I had no idea what was coming, but since I had paid Jo Anne, I told Martha to go ahead this last time.

It was newspaper day and everyone's primary function was to get *The Caymanian Weekly* on the street. I was proud that with all of my problems we had never missed a publication.

The next morning, the Caymanian's office was quieter than usual when I arrived. It was Friday and Sandra was typing up the subscription-label list we used to mail the stacks of thousands of fresh Caymanians to our overseas readers. Each label had to be applied manually.

"Where is everyone?" I asked. It was unusual for the staff to come in so late on Friday, our busiest day.

She wouldn't look at me.

"Sandra?"

"They're down at Billy's newspaper," she said quietly.

I wasn't alarmed. They had Caymanian friends there and I saw no reason to prohibit a visit.

"Well, I hope they don't spend all day there," I said. "You need some help getting those labels out and pasted on."

I was joking, but she didn't laugh.

"They went to work for Billy," she said.

"They what?" I said.

"They all left you letters in your office," she said. "They're gone to work for Billy."

If I had not grown accustomed to Caymanian surprises, I might have reacted differently. I should have been shocked. I wasn't, but I was very disappointed.

Why not? I thought. Why not just up and quit and go to work for Billy. They worked for me until he got his operation running and then deserted me to go back to their old boss.

Sandra had stayed. Most of the others who had been at the Caymanian when I arrived were gone.

"Sandra," I asked, "Were they planning to do this all along. Wait until he started his newspaper and then leave?"

She nodded.

"Why didn't you go?" I was sorry I said it the minute it slipped out. She looked hurt.

"I'm glad you stayed with me," I mumbled.

It seemed to make everything OK and she smiled.

The loss of most of my staff was devastating but not as crippling as it could have been. I had a new printer who was putting some organization into the pressroom, I had Risë and Nolan, and I had Martha, Mark and Sandra. Walwyn and Joseph surprised me by staying, although their Jamaican citizenship probably played a part in their decision to stay. (They would have needed new work permits). And there were a few others with no allegiance to Billy.

I don't think the mass resignation was intended to cripple me. I think my skirmish with Billy was irrelevant to them. The newspapers were where they worked and going to work was something they did with their friends.

I realized then, of course, why they had asked for their vacation pay. They were going to leave when Billy was ready for them. They were willing to work for me, but now that other job was ready. Billy hired them all whether he needed them or not. Anyone he could hire from me helped him. Or so he thought.

I sat down and wrote a letter to the new publication. I congratulated them and wished them luck with their publishing venture. In the final analysis, I wrote, regardless of the competition that exists between our two companies, the Caymanian people will be the beneficiaries. I had the letter delivered with a dozen roses.

On Tuesday, The Compass was published with fanfare as planned. The immediate item that impressed me was its size. It was full tabloid, or about twice the physical size of *The Caymanian Weekly*. Beside it our little product looked puny. As for the editorial content there was nothing that scared me. I found the most interesting item was my letter, which they published in its entirety.

If we could maintain our course with no new surprises, I was sure we would survive. And then, with hard work and a little luck, we would prevail.

I had a surprise for Billyboy. I conducted no market study, nor consulted any of the directors. I just decided it would be tactically preferable to meet the new paper head-on rather than surrender the first part of the week.

I told my diminished staff we were changing the publication date of *The Caymanian Weekly* from Thursday to Tuesday. It proved to be a decisive tactic.

We were a smaller family now but here was a challenge and I wanted to show the other guy we weren't ready to rot on the ironshore.

It was no contest. The loyalty to *The Caymanian Weekly* surprised and thrilled me. We murdered the bums. According to the grapevine—which in Cayman is more efficient than any news medium—Billy was completely unprepared for our move. He was furious.

His advertising sales immediately dipped and his newspaper sales were less than a third of ours. Some of the curious advertisers who had given him business immediately retreated to the security of *The Caymanian Weekly*.

There were no newspaper house-to-house deliveries in Cayman. The intricate and complex structure of an operational circulation department would have been the straw that broke my back in Cayman had I tried it. It involves too much detail and too many people working in hectic harmony to have succeeded at that time.

Instead, there were deliveries to select retail outlets around the island. Every Thursday afternoon—now Tuesdays—the Caymanians would rush to buy their newspaper. Fortunately, they continued to buy *The Caymanian Weekly*.

Billy's brand new *Compass* did sell, but not as well as Billy had hoped. He blamed me for the stratagem and I never disputed the idea. Caymanians, for the most part, were open and above board with all of their business arrangements. Honesty was cherished. A handshake was still the way most Caymanians signed contracts in those years.

From the beginning, they didn't understand that Billy and I were staking out territory like two circling bulldogs. Billy thought there was room for two newspapers on Grand Cayman, but I didn't. We didn't have the unlimited resources necessary to recapitalize the company and purchase new equipment while fighting a robust competitor.

If the brawl had been successfully communicated to the locals that this was a desperate fight between a native son and a foreigner, I would have been in deep trouble.

Billy waited two weeks before moving his publication date to Wednesday. He believed I would not be willing to change my schedule a second time. Guess again.

Unknown to me, a subtle government conspiracy was developing which would have great consequences for both sides of the newspaper war. But at the time, all I could think of was putting the pressure on Billy.

Although Billy was upset when I kept changing my publication day to meet his, there was someone even more upset. The Cayman government was furious with my scheme. I heard rumbles coming from government house that I was being "unfair." Many members of the government, British appointees in particular, were delighted to see *The Caymanian Weekly* face a threat from a local Caymanian.

One afternoon soon after the newspaper war began, His Excellency the Governor Kenneth Crook, now sporting a newly awarded M.B.E. after his name, dedicated a new bank directly across the street from *The Caymanian Weekly*. He paused in his speech to mention the fine article that had been written about the new building in "Billy's newspaper." There had been a similar article in *The Caymanian Weekly*, but he made no mention of it.

Several members of the official crowd looked at me to see if the significance of the Governor's words had affected me. It had. The verbal slap turned my face crimson.

18

GOODBYE MIGHTY MITE,
IT'S BEEN GOOD TO KNOW YOU

After a few months, I began to notice subtle changes in my ex-navy chief. At first, it was the small things. Roy's personality underwent a change. His humour disappeared. He talked less. It began with our morning greetings. Every day a little more cheerfulness was missing. One morning he wouldn't smile at all. He gave me a silent nod. It worried me, but I hoped it was just a passing mood.

One night, I saw him at the *Sea View* bar. The *Sea View* was the island's oldest hotel. It had been built by Dr. Roy more than 40 years before. There was an early painful memory about the place. It was off the *Sea View*'s dock that I had lost my first battle with the sea eggs. It was only months ago, almost an eternity here. I waved to Roy and motioned him to join our group at my table but he brushed us off with a wave and left.

He became ever more reclusive, preferring to drink alone. It grew steadily worse. When I asked him what was bugging him, he would shrug, shake his head and walk away. Almost daily, I saw changes in my friend. He became quieter to the point he hardly spoke. He continued to perform his job but the vitality was slipping away. As much as I hated it, as much as it depressed me, I understood.

Cayman is so different from the nirvana of the travel brochures. It is just as beautiful as they say, but travel posters don't aim at those who exchange their comfortable lives in a thriving, efficient economy for the slower pace of the West Indies. After dark the island closes down. Unless you go to a bar or restaurant there is nothing to do. Seeking comfort night after night in a bar is lonesome for a single person, even when the bar sits on the ironshore. Alarmed, I tried to counsel Roy. I told him I understood the depression that can strike so quickly in Cayman. Roy was a treasure and I hated to see him so miserable.

I was afraid I was losing him and the thought made me sick. All the same, I knew it was inevitable. One night to try to cheer him, I took him to the *Sea View* bar. Roy sipped his drink and slipped further into the funk that had taken control of his life. I tried to boost him by telling him I was sending him to Miami for supplies and a little rest and relaxation. He shook his head.

"Nothing for me there," he said.

"What does that mean?" I asked.

"My wife," he said.

"You got a wife? I didn't know you had a wife."

"I don't," he said, "not any more."

The knot tightened in my stomach.

"You mean right before you came down here?"

"Yea."

This was big trouble. Roy's wife tossed him out. He saw my advertisement and answered it. He wanted to get away, put distance between himself and the source of his unhappiness. Now, he missed her. He wanted her back. He knew he could not get her back.

The disheartening portion of the revelation was my realization that Roy had taken the job at the Caymanian to run away. Here I was, on the verge of having a successful newspaper and printing company, and the possibility was imminent that my right arm was about to be sliced off.

My concentration and energy centered on Roy even as he grew more withdrawn. I sent him to Miami with the hope that the bright lights would revitalize him. It was a tactic most businesses employed in the islands when their valuable expatriate workers experienced island fever. Expatriates start feeling "closed in" and "confined" after a few months on the island. Usually, a trip to Miami cures the "fever." But when Roy returned nothing had changed.

I continued to press him about the job. Was everything OK? He assured me that he was planning to stay "for the duration" and wouldn't even think of leaving me. He said he had a responsibility to the company and a loyalty to me.

I was reassured but unconvinced.

I made a telephone call to George Heon, the printer who had begged me to bring him to Cayman months earlier. Heon was so excited to get my call I had to keep reminding him the call was very preliminary and that I wasn't certain I would have an actual opening. As far as George was concerned he was ready to pack his bags as soon as we hung up.

I informed Roy that I was bringing another experienced printer and pressman aboard. I hoped it would cheer him to know that more professional help was coming.

Roy's unhappiness did not go unnoticed in the production department. He began to lose the respect of his workers. The constant threat of running out of supplies with no place to quickly replace them, pressmen not showing up for work, shipments getting lost and the return to malaise in his department did not help Roy's disposition.

"That's good," he said when I told him I had called George Heon; "you need him." He said it without emotion and I knew my news did not bring the desired result.

Since George Heon and Roy were both experienced printers, I could promise the directors enough additional income to justify the added expense. My main concern was the immigration department. I knew if I brought in too many of my own countrymen I would initiate a backlash.

There was also the prospect of Billy Bodden complaining about the "competition from foreign workers." It was a genuine threat and I had to be careful to offend no one in the government more than I already had. The immigration department did not care about skill and job experience. If there was a warm Caymanian body on the island that wanted the job and had half a chance of performing it, I had by-God better offer it to that Caymanian before recruiting offshore help.

Fortunately, there was normally zero unemployment among the Caymanians who wanted to work, so professional help could usually be imported by navigating the bureaucratic process.

I often mused that if I could go to Miami, buy up any quick-print shop and bring it lock, stock and barrel to The Cayman Islands, complete with its industrious American workers, I could put everyone else out of business and make a fortune. The government also understood this and took strong steps to thwart it.

Soon after my chat with Roy about George, a shipping agent for one of the vessels that transported cargo to and from Florida stopped me on the street and asked me why Roy was leaving. "What do you mean?" I blurted. I was disturbed but certain he was making a terrible mistake.

"I just wondered why he's leaving," he said.

"What do you mean leaving?" I said.

"He's shipped all of his goods back to Tampa," he said.

I immediately turned and ran back to the office. Roy wasn't there. No one had seen him for several hours.

I telephoned Mr. Arthur. He had become close to Roy during the recent months.

I told him I thought Roy was running out on us.

"Oh no," he said, reassuringly. "Roy wouldn't leave without telling us."

I told Mr. Arthur I would pick him up and we would go together to

Roy's apartment to talk to him. He agreed.

We rushed to Roy's small apartment in West Bay and found the front door wide open. The apartment was bare. The closets were empty. All of Roy's clothing and personal belongings were gone. There wasn't a trace of him left.

"Let's go to the *Sea View* bar," Mr. Arthur said. "Maybe he's there. Roy wouldn't just leave..."

This time, I didn't know who he was trying to reassure.

We drove to the bar. Roy's little red car was nowhere to be seen but we parked and went inside. And there he was, sitting at the bar talking to the bartender and sipping a drink. I was weakened with the relief that flooded over me.

He greeted us warmly and cheerfully with no trace of guile. He was in a great mood.

"Hi guys, what are you'all doing here?"

"We need to talk to you, friend Roy," Mr. Arthur said.

The three of us sat down at a table and we confronted him.

"Are you leaving, Roy?" I asked.

"Leaving?" he responded, trying to sound surprised, "Of course I'm not leaving!"

"Roy," I said quietly, "we've just come from your apartment. There's nothing there. It's empty."

He feigned shock.

"It had better not be empty," he said. "Everything I own is there!"

"Roy, it's gone," I said. "What's going on?"

"Nothing's going on," he said.

"You're not running out on me are you, Roy?" I asked.

"I wouldn't do that," he said, "You guys know that."

"OK Roy," Mr. Arthur said, "it just scared us for a minute. We'll go now."

"I'll see you in the morning," he said.

"Okay, Roy," I said.

We didn't say much on the way back to the office. We were both confused but not yet ready to accept the inevitable.

"Well, maybe I was wrong," I said. Mr. Arthur just nodded his head.

As we passed the dock at George Town on the way back to the office, I saw Roy's little red Mighty Mite. It was about 40 feet in the air being hoisted aboard the transport ship MV Kirk Pride by a giant loading crane. I pointed it out to Mr. Arthur. He nodded, but said nothing.

I saw Roy once more. It's a funny thing with me. I seem to run into people from my past a lot. More often than not, there's no acknowledgment, or recognition. "I know them," I think silently as I pass by. I wonder if they too are thinking, "I know him."

115

It happened several years later. I was driving back to Miami from Naples on the highway they call Alligator Alley. I saw the little red convertible approaching from the opposite direction. Roy was driving. He was puffing on that pipe. He didn't look withdrawn any more. He looked happy. He was alone. I didn't have time to wave.

19

THE SUBMARINE MOUNTAINS

What I had discovered at the Port Arthur Library about The Cayman Islands before my very first trip for my interview had been intriguing and enlightening. The Caymans are three little islands that are hilltops of the Cayman Ridge, a range of submarine mountains continuous with the Sierra Maestra Range of Cuba. They continue west in the direction of British Honduras to the Misteriosa Bank.

Grand Cayman, 180 miles west-northwest of the westernmost point of Jamaica and 150 miles south of Cuba, is 22 miles long from east to west with a maximum width of eight miles.

Cayman Brac, about 90 miles east-northeast of Grand Cayman, is 12 miles long and a mile wide. Little Cayman, five miles west of Cayman Brac, is 10 miles long and about two miles wide. Grand Cayman, with the capital city, and virtually all of the commerce, is by far the most populous. About 1,200 lived on "The Brac" in the 1970s and only 20 or less, most of whom would eventually become my friends, lived on isolated Little Cayman.

All of the islands are low-lying with no elevations above 60 feet except for the eastern end of Cayman Brac, which rises to about 160 feet. In hurricane season it's Nervous Nellie time everywhere in the islands.

Very little of the Cayman soil is fit for agriculture and in spite of an excellent climate there was, and is, very little to support a Caymanian population. So for most of their history, the inhabitants depended on the sea for sustenance.

As the pirate era declined in numbers, The Cayman Islands slowly began to develop a stable population. Since there is no corroboration, who knows if those early settlers were really "groups of shipwrecked sailors, marooned mariners, debtors and buccaneers" as official history suggests.

Just as likely, a large number of the early inhabitants were slaves, since slave trading was one of the earliest forms of commerce in the islands. At one point, slave trading was the number one business in all the West Indies, eclipsing the combined revenues of all other endeavors. Records even show that some former slaves in Cayman went into the slave biz themselves after being freed.

Cayman historian/Administrator Hirst wrote the Caymanians made a living by fishing, planting, raising pigs, buying and selling slaves, selling turtle to passing ships of war and merchantmen, and ship wrecking. Also, "The frequent finding of piratical hoards of money shows us the island was made great use of by the sea robbers." But he gives no documentation for such enticing remarks.

I am not the first who has trouble swallowing the pirate legends. Hirst says: "I have abstained from making use of tradition where the tradition was unsupported by other evidence. This accounts for the omission of so many stories of bravery told in connection with the attacks of pirates.

"Again, tales are told so differently by each person that the foundation of truth is very difficult to detect, as each story starts from a different base, though referring to exactly the same incident."

Yet early Caymanians often had their hands full.

"The most exciting times the inhabitants must have had were driving off foreign privateers for which forts were erected in certain parts of the island," Hirst writes.

"None of these forts, with the possible exception of Fort George in George Town, would now appear to remain, those now visible being of a later date. That hand-to-hand fights with marauders frequently took place we have every reason to believe, tradition recording many such encounters in which of course it is unnecessary to add the Caymanian always came off victorious."

The fort in George Town was constructed toward the end of the eighteenth century, according to historian Hirst's speculations. It was made of earth and was originally circular with an entrance from the landside. It was about four feet high and three feet thick with openings at intervals for several canons. Exactly who built it is not known.

The English were fort builders whenever they settled and like most of these installations Fort George was constructed and manned by private enterprise.

20

DEFENDING OLD FORT GEORGE

Old Fort George, which once guarded George Town Harbor, wasn't much of a historical monument when I arrived in Cayman, but it was part of the long-ago, foggy past and therefore valued.

Developer and political activist Jim Bodden owned the fort and had plans to use a portion of the costly, seafront property for a new office building. He said he would save the fort and immediate property surrounding it, but he ran afoul of the government planning office, which refused to grant him a building permit for an office, thus setting the stage for a confrontation that almost obliterated the relic.

One morning, I was enjoying my second cup of coffee and reading the front page of the Caymanian when Desmond Seales rushed into my office shouting for me. Desmond had gained favor with the government with his new magazine, the Nor'wester, which he created after leaving the Caymanian. The government approved of the way he promoted tourism and stuck close to the government line that everything was perfect in the islands.

Even though it was a monthly publication, I felt competitive with him and mistrusted his motives after learning of his involvement with the ad agency I had dismantled. We had very limited cordial conversations in the beginning.

"They're tearing down old Fort George!" he yelled in obvious distress. There was a pained look on his face, unusual for Desmond. I was still having a hard time trusting anyone, especially anyone who had been connected to the newspaper prior to my arrival.

Desmond's office was located next to Fort George. When he heard the bulldozer, he ran outside and tried to flag it down before it destroyed the fort completely, and was almost run down by the tractor.

"Who is?" I asked. All I knew of the fort was that it was constructed in the late 1700s to protect George Town residents from Spanish marauders sailing out of Cuba—or at least that was what local legend purported.

It had only one or two cannon and a small earth and stone rampart when it was new and I doubted it would have lasted long against an authentic pirate ship with heavy ordinance. There were stories that a raider had once sailed into the harbor and had been chased away with a warning shot. In spite of its questionable past, Fort George was a beloved symbol of Caymanian heritage. I assumed it was public property.

"Jim Bodden is tearing it down!" he said, "We've got to stop him!"

I had no idea how we would handle the belligerent, hot-headed Bodden. The stocky, tough-talking ex-seaman was a controversial figure in the islands, often accused of being the ringleader for the disturbing goal of full, internal self-government for the Caymans.

Jim Bodden was born in the Caymans on October 5, 1930. His father was an American citizen. He began his American career as a cook for the Sabine Transportation Company in Port Arthur and worked there until 1953.

He had also owned a taxi business in nearby Port Neches and a novelty shop in Nederland. At nights he worked as a private detective in Port Arthur. He moved to Houston in 1954 to manage a detective agency. He returned to sea eventually and had been working on the ill-fated Sulphur Queen, but missed the fatal voyage that claimed all hands in 1963 when the ship sailed out of Port Arthur never to be seen again.

Following that providential episode he returned to his birthplace to enter the real estate business and politics. He was elected to the legislature but was unseated because of impassioned arguments that in spite of being a native Caymanian he was also an American citizen. Indeed he was, having worked for many years in my old neighborhood around Port Arthur.

To satisfy Cayman law he would eventually denounce his American allegiance, as required by the Cayman constitution. God forbid that anyone linked officially to Uncle Sam be seated in the Caymanian assembly. The government's refusal to seat him because of his dual citizenship was one of our front-page stories not long after I arrived in Cayman. The issue also played a role in my own future in Grand Cayman.

He told me later during an interview that he indeed wanted full internal self-government for The Cayman Islands but he also wanted closer ties with the United States. I suspect that it was Bodden's fondness for the United States that made him something of a pariah with the colonial government.

His efforts were honorable and neither of us liked the British bureaucracy, but we never were able to form an alliance until the final days of my island adventure. By that time, it was too late.

There was a college in the Caymans where it was possible to earn a bachelor's degree. Jim Bodden had given it invaluable help. It was The International College of The Cayman Islands and it had 46 students from throughout the Caribbean, Latin Americas and the U.S. ICCI had ties with Pacific University in Oregon which provided educational and emotional support.

Since it was an American school, it was beloved by the English bureaucracy almost as much as I was.

ICCI began in 1966 when a Caymanian teacher beseeched a visiting American Methodist minister, Dr. Hugh Cummings, to start a college in Cayman. Cummings, whose wife was of Caymanian descent, was a well-meaning, mild-mannered native of Oregon.

Stimulated by the dream of bringing a college to the void that composed the soul of intellectual pursuit in Cayman, he convinced other members of the Portland community to support him. The Cayman's favorite rogue, Jim Bodden, was persuaded to donate a couple of acres for a small campus.

At every opportunity, Dr. Cummings sought professorial help. When he found out that my advertising director, Nolan, held a marketing degree from Ole Miss, he enlisted him to teach a class at ICCI. Visiting professors from the University of London, Warner Pacific College in the U.S. and the University of Oregon also lectured there.

I tried at every opportunity to encourage ICCI because I knew that it was reaching students, even if only a few. More important, I knew that it annoyed the English elite that Americans were keeping the school ball rolling on the turf of the Brits. In fairness to the Cayman government, I think it felt the school was not up to par academically.

With his background as a private detective in Texas, Jim Bodden once had me investigated by some of his former associates. But that would come later as I became unwittingly embroiled in the country's politics.

I told Desmond to sit down a minute, try to relax, and we would do something. Reluctantly, he pulled up a chair. I telephoned the government's information officer, Olive Miller, and asked about the impending danger to Fort George. "I know," she said softly. "We can't do anything about it."

I was beginning to understand Desmond's desperation. We left the newspaper and sprinted to Bodden's office, about a block and a half away.

We dashed past his startled secretary and entered his office, disrupting a telephone call. He was startled, but hung up and offered no resistance

121

as Desmond pled with him to stop smashing the fort.

"Let's take a few days and cool off and maybe something can be worked out," I offered, not certain of what to say in such a delicate, odd circumstance.

Instead of raging and throwing us out of his office for interfering, Bodden leaned back in his chair, looked at us quietly for a moment, and then stood up. "Okay," he said.

We were both surprised at his mild acquiescence. I wondered if he had his own doubts about his impetuous decision and we were catalysts who enabled him to save face for the catastrophic action.

He agreed to go to the site with us and suddenly appeared to be in an urgent hurry to get there. We piled into his car and raced the short distance to the harbor. When we got close enough, he leaned out of the window and began waving and shouting for the operator of a huge bulldozer to stop.

The operator immediately cut the engine and silence descended over the site, but tremendous damage had been done to the structure. Only about a quarter of the small fort remained visible above the rubble.

Bodden was wrong to bulldoze the fort, but who among the locals could blame him? Money was pouring into the islands and there were quick fortunes to be made.

Bodden told me he had seen government plans for a road to be widened in front of the fort, taking 30 feet of his property.

"I offered to give the government the fort," he said, "if they would let me build a two-story office building where I have a smaller store. They wouldn't allow it."

He owned a small building with a bookstore adjacent to the fort and wanted to increase its size. He offered to rebuild the fort and improve it himself, but the government wouldn't hear of it.

When I returned to my office, Olive Miller had been by to leave the official comment for the newspaper. "Government wishes to make it clear that Fort George ruins on Church Street which were demolished on the morning of 11th January were privately owned by Mr. Jim Bodden.

"The Land Development Law expired on the 31st December and the new law passed by the assembly at the December sitting is not yet in effect. Government, therefore, had no legal means of preventing the destruction of the fort.

"Mr. J. Bodden applied to the Land Development Control Board for permission to build an office block on a section of the property on Church Street and offered to hand the Fort over to Government if permission were given.

"Due to the shape and size of the piece of property, the board could not grant permission inasmuch as the regulations state that any piece of land on the seaward side on which a building can be erected in this area must be 150 feet from the road to the sea at all points.

"Mr. Bodden was advised that the board had no authority to break the regulations but he should appeal to the executive council. This appeal is pending."

The incident illustrated the great pettiness to which both the government and its citizens would go to settle a personal dispute. In any event, only two people, Desmond Seales and Dick Gentry, both foreigners, can claim credit for whatever original bones remain today of old Fort George.

The site has been tidied up a bit in recent years. The government also moved a watchtower from WWII to the property (For a time, Caymanians called it Cockroach Castle) and put up a plaque. Today, tourists can visit and wonder about the pirates and German submarines it may have discouraged.

There is an official plaque on the site, proclaiming the ruins of Old Fort George were preserved when destruction was halted. No mention of Desmond or me. It's especially appalling that Desmond isn't mentioned.

21

WHY CAN'T WE JUST GET ALONG?
(BECAUSE WE CAN'T STAND YOU!)

Beneath the warm sun, as pirates and privateers sailed into oblivion, the Caymanians slowly developed a homogeneous population at peace with itself as well as the rest of the Caribbean. Jamaica took over the reins of government, and although Cayman was self-governing up to a point, whenever there were serious problems, Jamaica, and its colonial bureaucracy appointed by His or Her Majesties, was always there to make the appropriate ruling.

The country remained happily isolated until the 1940s and the start of international air flights. But before the tourist trade would become a real contributor to the economy, the number one pest in the West Indies had to be controlled. And no, it wasn't the Spanish or French this time, it was the mosquito. Stories that mosquitoes were so thick and fierce they choked farm animals were only slightly exaggerated.

When modern chemicals such as DDT took back control from this worrisome annoyance in the 1960s, visitors to the islands, now able to spend as much time as they liked out of doors, began to take notice of the beautiful beaches, the nice people, and water so clear you could see for 100 feet or more beneath the waves.

More and more tourists wanted to see for themselves the lonely island with the beautiful white beaches that wouldn't burn your feet even in the most blistering sunshine, and the clear waters full of brilliantly colored, mostly harmless, critters.

And since it was an alleged pirate stronghold, there was always the possibility of stumbling over buried treasure.

But something else was in the wind in those formative years of the 1960s and 1970s, something that would make The Cayman Islands a household word in very exclusive, affluent circles around the globe. But first, a circuitous path had to be navigated.

124

The Great Experiment in the Caribbean in the middle of the 20th century was the political move for independence by most of the populated islands. For many of the small island nations, independence was a euphemism for freedom. Their darker-skinned populations, the result of the import of so many thousands and thousands of slaves in the 18th century, wanted to stand alone, without supervision and interference from any of the major powers, usually Britain, which had controlled and denigrated them for centuries.

For the purpose of explaining Cayman politics, the actions of Jamaica and the Bahamas are particularly important.

When it designed a new constitution in 1959 – approved of course by Her Majesty—The Cayman Islands ceased to be a dependency of the then-Colony of Jamaica, and got its own legislature—although the white Governor of Jamaica continued to be Governor of The Cayman Islands.

*   *   *

A Federation of The West Indies was created in the early 1960s—the heart of The Great Experiment which would supposedly unite all independent Caribbean islands. Jamaica and The Cayman Islands were both participants in the early rounds. But as talk began to concentrate on "independence," the Caymanians became nervous. They were, and perhaps still are, the Queen's most loyal subjects. Most of the local Caymanian gentry wanted no part of independence and a strong union with Jamaica and the Bahamas—if the British were not part of it. The times were just not right for this as far as the Caymanians were concerned.

There was some serious unrest in the Caribbean as the 1960s began. Fidel Castro, the bearded, wild-man attorney who in 1957 began raising havoc in mountainous western Cuba, was talking—ridiculously it appeared at the time—of overthrowing the dictatorship of Fulgencio Batista. He managed to pull it off two years later.

First embraced as the new-age Toussaint L'Overture, the black slave who led a successful revolt against the French in 1791 resulting in the creation of the Republic of Haiti, Castro cast a chill over the West by responding to a question from the press during a New York visit: "I am a Communist..."

As things happen, Napoleon, with an eye toward increasing his American assets—some say even taking over—was considering landing French troops in Louisiana about the time of Toussaint's Haitian shenanigans. Napoleon had to postpone this adventure and export troops to Haiti, where he was trounced by the impish revolutionary, who was said to look something like a frog. The expense obligated him to negotiate with the young United States for the sale of all of France's American possessions—the Louisiana Purchase.

The Cayman Islands is not the closest free country to Cuba but the ties between the two island nations go back generations. Turtle hunters from Cayman scouted the deserted beaches of Cuba searching for new killing grounds hundreds of years before the communists hatched. There are entire small towns in Cuba settled by Cayman Islanders.

It isn't unusual for Cayman ships to pull into Castro's isolated southern ports for refuge (and some rowdy, memorable parties with the Cubans) during hurricanes. Even today, an American can fly to Cuba from Grand Cayman and enjoy a visit without the American or British authorities knowing anything about it. Upon request, the Cuban authorities won't stamp your passport and you can wander at will in most areas of the forbidden country.

When Cuba became more and more isolated from its neighbors under Castro in the 1960s and 1970s some of the oppressed—perhaps "out of work" is a better definition—residents looked longingly at the three little islands south of them.

During my three years in Cayman several hundred Cubans fled to the islands and were welcomed as refugees.

I spoke to a Cayman police officer a few hours after a "hijacked" Cuban fishing boat landed. He just smiled. "That wasn't any hijack," he said, "The pistol they used was so rusty it wouldn't fire even with bullets. It was a cover for the crew members who still have families in Cuba and must go back. But don't put that in your newspaper or you'll get them arrested."

I didn't.

A poignant international incident a few months later gave me the brief opportunity to question Cuban Communist officials face to face.

Martica and Raulito Fagundo were children who had lived in Grand Cayman since their father escaped with them from Cuba three years earlier. The father found work in Miami and began saving money to send for the kids, who remained in Cayman with West Bay's postmistress, Pat Ebanks.

The mother chose to stay in Cuba, and filed suit there and in Cayman to reclaim the toddlers. In a most unpopular decision with the Caymanians and me, she won.

A twin-engine Russian Ilyushin of Cabana Aviacion came to pick up the children. There was only an hour's notice it was on the way.

The Cubans anticipated only a short visit, but the kids disappeared. A cat and mouse game began that lasted hours as the police were ordered to locate the children and turn them over to the Cubans. At noon, three hours after the search started, the police were baffled. An inspector at the airport told me, "This is embarrassing."

A crowd gathered at the airport and stood in the blazing sun glaring at the Ilyushin and its passengers, who deplaned and were inside a small, air-conditioned building.

There was a stir when the guardian, Mrs. Ebanks, arrived with some clothing for the children to take with them.

"I don't know where they are," she said sweetly. "I thought they were here."

The police gave her a stern warning. "If you give them up now it will be easier on them and you. We'll find them eventually and they will have to stay in custody until the plane comes back for them."

But a female Communist official at the airport, a lawyer in the Cuban Ministry, said the plane would not leave without the children on board. Reports began to circulate that the children's mother was now a bureaucrat in Havana and was exerting her power.

The government offered the officials and aircrew a room at the local Royal Palms hotel to spend the night. They accepted.

I attempted to interview the captain of the Cuban airliner, Roberto Abreu. My introduction as the editor of the local newspaper was greeted by stony silence.

"How do you like living in Cuba?" I asked.

He tensed and scowled at me.

"I am not a selfish man," he replied in perfect Americanized English. I followed his comment with, "What's it like in Cuba today?"

"It's different," he snapped.

"Different from what?" I asked.

"Different from the way you are thinking."

"Most of the latest refugees from Cuba say that your sugar crop is a complete flop. Is that true?"

At this point, he stopped his slow walk toward the hangar and narrowed his eyes at me.

"You get only one side of the story," he said. "There is another side."

I agreed that I only got one side and invited him to give me the other side. I wanted to hear it. But he walked away, leaving me sweating on the tarmac under the afternoon sun.

Cuba is a gorgeous country. I was there for a few weeks at Guantanamo Bay shortly after Castro announced his allegiance to the feared Soviets. Our Marine detachment conducted a series of maneuvers in the hills beyond the base. I still remember the beauty of the isolated, sun-drenched beaches and translucent water.

The next morning, police had not located the children and filed a writ of habeas corpus against Mrs. Ebanks demanding the children be turned over immediately.

Shortly after, police received a call and left for Mrs. Ebanks home. The children were waiting for them. Mrs. Ebanks insisted the children be taken to a hospital for a quick health check before they left. This was done. She was not charged.

About 26 hours after it first landed, the Ilyushin took off for Cuba with little Martica and Raulito aboard. They were laughing and smiling as they climbed aboard.

22

ANY AMERICAN WHO KNOWS
THE WEST INDIES, STAND UP

The West Indies has a marvelous history which most Americans know absolutely nothing about. It isn't pretty, but it is captivating. Like America, the Indians were there first. Some were nice; others wanted you to join them for dinner. Most of the Caribbean tribes have been annihilated, although a few remnants remain.

The Caribbean population is what it is today because the Indians made poor slaves. So, Africans were imported by the hundreds of thousands to satisfy the demands of European settlers. There have been countless civil wars, but none actually freed the slaves.

Not all of the slaves put up with it. I mean no disrespect, but the West Indies has produced civil-rights pioneers, such as Jamaica's Marcus Garvey, who make American civil rights hero Martin Luther King Jr. almost look like a rebel at a PTA meeting.

Hundreds disappeared beneath the waves trying desperately to reach the shores of the U.S. Still they come. They had rather die trying than exist in the "beautiful tropical paradise that is the West Indies." Had history been kinder, and men been bolder, they wouldn't have to leave home. Right or wrong, the U.S. could easily have owned every nation in the West Indies, including Central America and northern South America. But, that boat has sailed. Not PC today. We had presidents, not emperors.

There was one early history book written about The Cayman Islands circa 1910. The second, a magnificent book by Michael Craton with the cooperation of the government called "Founded upon the Seas" was published in 2003. There's an acknowledgement in the foreword that says, "No country can understand its own character or fully appreciate its unique identity without an accurate knowledge of its past. It was in this spirit that the Honorable McKeeva Bush brought to the Legislative Assembly in 1988 a motion urging government to prepare a new history

129

of The Cayman Islands..."

The first record of a European sighting of The Cayman Islands came in 1503. Fernando Columbus, teenage son of Christopher, recorded the moment. It came on the fourth and final trip Columbus made to the New World: "Upon Wednesday the 10th of May we were in sight of two very low islands called Tortugas, or The Tortoises, on account of the prodigious multitudes of these animals which so swarmed about these islands and in the sea around them that they resembled rocks."

Hirst claims this is not a true discovery, since it didn't include the main island. Since Grand Cayman is 90 miles away and would not be visible, "It is obvious the account of the discovery refers solely to the Lesser Caymans (Little Cayman and Cayman Brac)."

The official Cayman Islands handbook says a Spanish chart drawn by Alberto Cantino in 1502 shows the Caymans. It is arguably the earliest positively dated map showing with considerable precision the islands of the Caribbean and the Florida coastline, as well as Africa, Europe and Asia. I don't challenge the experts, but I've looked at a poor copy of the map and still wonder. The first map I could find specifically identifying the Caymans was one drawn in 1548 by Giacomo Gastaldi.

The 1971 Handbook reports no evidence of occupation by aboriginal tribes, although a few stone axes found in caves suggested that wandering Carib Indians might have visited from time to time looking for some poor soul to have dinner with. No ancient settlement has been archeologically identified in the islands, but from the earliest times, the numbers of turtles found around the islands attracted ships of all nations.

Turtles were perfect because of one strength. There was no refrigeration but a turtle could be kept alive in a ship's hold for weeks, sometimes months, before starving to death. When it was time for soup, the cook could grab a gentle turtle, slit its throat, boil it up and serve it to the crew.

Records indicate no country was particularly interested in owning the Caymans until Jamaica was taken from the Spanish in 1655 and ceded to England by the Treaty of Madrid in 1670.

History, although sketchy, indicates there were semi-permanent Cayman settlements in the late 17th century. The settlers were perhaps groups of shipwrecked and marooned sailors, debtors and buccaneers. Possibly, some were deserters from Oliver Cromwell's army. There were some soldiers in Cromwell's army named Gentry. In my mind, I'm thinking one of them was one of my ancestors. Some genetic memory may explain why I have such an affinity for The Caymans and at times felt at home there.

It took the first settlers only a few short years to exploit the turtles into extinction. By the end of the 18th century, inhabitants were compelled to leave the islands in large numbers to seek other sources of revenue. They straggled north to Cuba where they supplemented their fishing with shipwrecking.

By 1850, the Cuban turtles were exterminated and Caymanians turned south to the Central American coast where many settled.

The Caymanians are proud of their buccaneer legacy and each year conduct an annual Pirate's Day Celebration to flaunt their history. There's not a Caymanian around who doesn't like to believe there's a bloodthirsty pirate somewhere in his or her background—Edward "Blackbeard" Teach, or the most romantic cutthroat himself, Henry Morgan.

Truth be told, the origins of the earliest Caymanians are unknown. The discovery of the West Indies began in the late 15th and early 16th century much like a bag of popcorn simmering on a sizzling stove. A few early kernels pop and soon it's a crescendo. After a frantic series of little explosions it is over.

The Arawak and the Carib Indians had already arrived. They came up from the Amazon basin hundreds of years before the first European explorers.

The Arawaks were a friendly, farming people, but they had no written language and are today gone with the wind. (With apologies to Margaret Mitchell, but she didn't coin that. She also happens to be my daughter-in-law's third cousin; my daughter-in-law's says that herself sometimes, as did my own Southern mother).

The most that we know about the Arawaks is from sources dating back to Spanish explorers. They grew food crops and tobacco. They settled in the larger islands, but by the time Columbus arrived, they had already begun to face a very dangerous foe—the people-eating Caribs. These Indians were so mean and hateful that the first Spanish explorers learned to avoid their territories.

Neither tribe assimilated with the other, and only a very few Caribs remain today in the West Indies and they eat at McDonalds like most of us. That refusal to mingle was a generic trend that continues even today: Caribbean nations rarely associate with one another.

The Spanish tried everything they could to capture and enslave the Indians, but they would not work, so they killed or abandoned them. When the Indians failed as a labor force or died off because of imported diseases, the conquerors turned to Africa for enlistees. There were many African tribes willing to sell their enemies into slavery. The Indians might have numbered 15 million in the West Indies and Mexico when Columbus arrived. One hundred years later, they were down to about 2 million.

131

The Europeans who came to the Caribbean wanted to get rich and go home. In fact, that's generally still true today. Few ever have plans to settle. The Spanish wanted to live lives of ease and luxury by growing sugar and tobacco with slaves and Indians doing the work.

It proved easy to sail across the Atlantic and into the West Indies because the prevailing wind is your friend. Going home, you had better be a good navigator. Take for example the Spanish treasure fleets. The Spanish mined fabulous quantities of silver in Mexico and Peru. They toted it by pack-mule train to the sea, loaded it on ships and sailed to Cuba to wait for the best winds to race home. Once a year, they formed a silver armada convoy. Many floundered in the Florida Straights. Those wrecks made many contemporary treasure hunters—like Mel Fisher and Robert Marx—wealthy.

Sooner or later, most of the expatriate exploiters went home. The slaves had nowhere to go. That's why the Caribbean is mostly black and brown today.

Of course Europe was in trouble at the time the discoveries began. It was mainly because of religious differences. Catholic vs. Muslim. Really.

May 30, 1453 is an important date for the West Indies. My history books tell me this is when Constantinople fell to the Ottoman Turks (Muslims) and the surviving intelligencia fled westward toward Italy and Spain. This keyed a gargantuan change of thought. The staid ideas of the Pope in Rome began to be questioned, new ideas about exploration began. Free thinking flourished and the march to The Reformation began.

By 1492, the popcorn pot is blistering! Ferdinand and Isabella—a bigoted pair—have expelled 200,000 Jews from Spain by initiating the dreadful Inquisition. This meant if you were not a good Catholic, or were a—God forbid!—non-Catholic heretic, they tried to light a fire under you. This practice was transported to the West Indies by the Catholic Church, but instead of gathering converts, it inspired hatred. The priests burned almost everyone they could get their hands on— even the British—if they were heretics.

Grenada, the stronghold of the Muslims at the southern end of Spain, fell to the Spanish rulers Ferdinand and Isabella. It ended Muslim power and influence in Spain and provided the confidence needed for exploration. This is Columbus's big day. He tells the sovereigns he can find a new trade route to India. They approve. Part of their logic was the fear that the Muslims, now out of Spain but entrenched in Turkey, might go after that new trade route themselves.

Spices were THE hot item of the day. They were imported from the East, which was expensive. The trip took forever. With a new, shorter

132

trade route west to India, every Spaniard would be able to sprinkle exotic condiments on the barbeque.

Within a few years, Henry VIII of England approached Ferdinand and Isabella about an alliance. Thrilled, they pack off their daughter, Catherine of Aragon, to wed Henry.

Henry VIII's failure to obtain an annulment for his marriage to Catherine led him to separate The Church of England from the Pope and dissolve his marriage. Not only was he despised by the Spanish for dumping the princess bride—Catherine—the English King's action made many of his subjects qualify as heretics, and eligible for persecution by the Spanish Inquisition in the New World.

On October 12, 1492, Columbus landed in the Bahamas. He proceeded to explore the coast of Cuba and Hispaniola (Haiti and The Dominican Republic) and returned home with his report. He didn't know it, but there were about 50 inhabited Caribbean islands yet to explore.

Ferdinand and Isabella were quick to respond. They had maneuvered the election of Alexander VI to the Papacy, and he rewarded them with the Bull of 1493, which gave Spain the exclusive right to explore and claim the West Indies. Obviously, that didn't sit well with the English, French and Dutch.

Columbus made four trips to the West Indies. He suffered severe and numerous setbacks on all of the trips. On his fourth and final trip, he was returning to Cuba when he sailed somewhere between the three Cayman Islands. He was 51 years old, and his 13-year-old son Fernando was with him, and spotted Cayman Brac's 165-foot bluff.

There were some Indian attacks and another shipwreck in Jamaica, but on Nov. 7, 1504, Columbus staggered into his home port. Two years later, he died in poverty, without a clue about what he had discovered. Until the end, he thought he was sailing around islands off the east coast of India.

The door to the West Indies was now wide open. Other Spaniards began encroaching on the West Indies. Gonzalo Jiménez de Quesada, Francisco Pizarro, Cortez, Balboa and Ponce de Leon quickly followed Columbus and vanquished four flourishing dynasties: Central America, Mexico, Peru and Columbia.

The Spanish held reasonably tight control over the Caribbean for the 40 years following Columbus. Their successes in mining silver and agriculture attracted the attention of the English, French and even the Dutch. These countries began encroaching on the Spanish Main, as it was called, and were treated as enemies. Soon, it was the Spanish and Portuguese against everyone else. And so the Caribbean evolved with bloodshed, slavery, piracy and greed.

When Columbus passed by the lesser Caymanians it was still early in terms of recorded history. It would be three decades before De Soto trekked across the Southeast U.S. to discover the Mississippi River. The Pilgrims who would land on Plymouth Rock were yet to be born.

23

DEATH PERHAPS, BUT NO TAXES IN CAYMAN

By 1962, the high hopes of the Federation of the West Indies were in shambles. Jamaica was granted independence; the British hauled down their flag and sent their colonial bureaucracy packing and the Jamaicans elected their own government. Crime, inflation and rampant unemployment were off to the races.

My own managing director, Dr. Roy, played a historical role in the development of the islands at that point. According to a Letter to the Editor I received from the local Rev. George Hicks, "Dr. Roy led the fight to keep Cayman independent of Jamaica's move to independence. In the beginning, the majority of members of the assembly were ready to vote for the link with Jamaica," the minister wrote.

"It was only through the efforts of Dr. Roy McTaggart that the course of history of the islands was changed. Dr. Roy carried his ideas to the people of the Caymans, convinced them of the advantages of remaining a Crown Colony, and then returned to the assembly with the mandate of the people."

The Cayman Islands wisely chose to become a British Colony to be headed by its own Administrator, appointed by Her Majesty. With the assistance of a legislative assembly of 12 elected members and four to six members appointed by the administrator, the Caymans entered the modern world as an English colony with local self-government. God Save the Queen!

Exactly when and where in those formative years the genesis of the colony's present prosperity occurred, I don't know. What happened was that instead of becoming another remote former dependency with beautiful beaches, great diving, and opulent resort hotels with armed guards facing a despondent citizenry enviously hostile toward visitors, The Cayman Islands flowered into a small, secure nation where unemployment is virtually unknown and the flourishing tourist industry broke records year after year.

In the 1970s, The Caymans were among the few islands in the entire Caribbean where begging for money from visitors on the streets was unheard of.

Why this happened is much easier to determine. The Cayman Islands' good fortune is because of the government's decisions at the outset: There would be a country, it would be a Crown Colony, there would be a local government, it would do the best it could for the people with what it had and what it could beg from England, and, most importantly, there would be no taxes.

In the late 1960s, the international banking community became interested in finding a safe haven for its offshore banking operations. Geneva was, and remains, the capital for those secretive banking operations. However, there was plenty of room in the Western Hemisphere for concealed bank accounts.

The hub of offshore banking in the West had been The Bahamas, a nation of some 700 islands not far from Florida's friendly east coast. In addition to more than 300 banks there were thousands of expatriate banking employees—most of them white British subjects—who had learned to love the tropical shores of the small island nation so close to the reassuring American coast.

Like The Cayman Islands, The Bahamas were discovered by Columbus and had spent their entire modern career as British possessions. Internal self-government was established in 1964 and The Bahamas headed for full independence in 1973.

In 1967, the black Prime Minister, Lynden O. Pindling, narrowly ousted the white, old-guard merchants and gave a menacing victory speech where he spelled out his dream for a "Bahamas for the Bahamians." It sent a shudder through the expatriate crowd. The country was different but the complaint was familiar.

Prime Minister Pindling immediately began tightening the screws against his former bosses. He pulled in the reins on vital work permits making it harder for the bankers to retain, and virtually impossible to recruit, the expert staff international banking required. When it was suggested that tourism would suffer under Pindling's fist and the country could revert to a nation of fishing villages, one Bahamian cabinet minister was widely quoted, "That might not be a bad idea."

Pindling, perhaps taking his cue from Fidel, began talking about nationalizing big business. International banking panicked. The building boom on Grand Bahama screeched to a halt. Real estate values, which five years previously had been soaring, began falling off. Immediately, the banking community looked for safe harbor.

Within a matter of months, Pindling's government had lost the confidence of the banking community. Worse, the offshore investors themselves were frightened about what they read in the newspapers and began withdrawing funds. It doesn't take a genius to understand that without funds, banks can't bank.

As the bankers searched for a haven for their precious billions, their eyes fell on three tiny coral pimples smack in the middle of the ocean. They were self-governing, had a passive, racially mixed population and real estate was available. There were no radicals rattling about racial prejudice, a new jet runway was being built, the government was stable and determined to remain loyal to Her Majesty the Queen, and, best of all—no taxes! In fact, there were few restrictions at all imposed on business or anything else.

The most popular local legend in the Caymans, The Wreck of the 10 Sails, concerns the birth of the tax-haven status. Like a lot of Cayman history, its roots are entwined in sea lore and local heroism. A controversial visit to Grand Cayman by Penthouse magazine for a nude photo shoot at a popular beach gave me a rare opportunity to mix and mock legends and would-be legends.

One thing I'll say about those Caymanians. They may have rejected taxes, but not their puritanical mores. Even in the late 1990s, the Caymanians maintained their reputation for priggishness by refusing to allow a cruise ship to land its passengers for a one-day visit. Even when Her Majesty's government in London asked the country to stop being so prejudiced and allow the tourists to land and spend their respectable, straight money, the Caymanians flatly refused. The ship sailed away with its rejected, dejected cargo of 1,500 gay and lesbian couples.

However, back to "The Legend of the 10 Sails." The fable claims 10 sailing ships piled into the reefs near East End—one after the other— hundreds of years ago. That alone, if true, would have been the worst navigational blunder of the millennium. Aboard one of the wrecks was a prince. Caymanians braved the rough seas, rescued the prince, and were given tax-haven status forever by the grateful king.

The legend was the perfect foil for a column I wrote offering advice to the Turks and Caicos Islands, which was looking into the alarming possibility of establishing a competing Caribbean tax haven:

"I don't know everything you must do to create a tax haven, but I understand you should first get 10 ships, one carrying a person whose rank should not be less than a prince, and run aground, preferably on a stormy night. Get the locals to display rare courage and save the crews— especially the prince—and you have completed the first requirement. Full tax-free status and draft exemption may be expected to follow.

"Legend says that is what happened here, but I am not convinced of the date. I think the sailors ran aground about the time Penthouse's naked Avril Lund was nymphing around Smith's Cove a few weeks ago for a photo shoot: "'Watch where you are going, Captain! The reef! The reef!'"

When Penthouse's Cayman photo shoot was published in March 1973, I was surprised to see plenty of the nude Avril Lund, cavorting on the beach for a photo shoot, but nowhere in the magazine was Grand Cayman even mentioned. It could have been photographed in Miami Beach for all the tourism benefit it provided. The contentious issue sold out anyway as soon as it reached Cayman's shores.

The wife of a high government official confronted all of the storeowners who sold the nudie magazine, offering me a chance to further provoke the situation:

"Censorship is a dirty word to most journalists and publishers and I am certainly not going to be drawn into the fight on either side," I wrote, then promptly joined the fray.

"...the freedom to talk, to write, and to read whatever you choose should be left up to the individual. I certainly don't want anyone telling ME what I should read, or see. But then, isn't that the way everyone really feels?" I asked.

"They don't want anyone telling THEM what to read but they don't mind telling someone else what they should or shouldn't read."

Under that guise, I managed to let everyone in the government know I rejected their provincial, protectionist attitude.

Like all legends, "something" probably happened as far as the 10-sail wreck is concerned. Who really knows?

24

MAYBE A REFRESHER NAVIGATION CLASS?

The Wreck of the 10 Sails had its genesis in an incident that allegedly occurred about the time Fort George was built in the 1780s. At the eastern end of the island is a reef, offshore from the site of an old fort called Gun Bluff. There, remnants of several modern-day shipwrecks are still present.

According to historian Hirst, in November of an unknown year in the late 1700s a fleet of Jamaican merchantmen under the convoy of HMS Cordelia struck the reef at 9 p.m. The Cordelia saw the dangerous reef and fired cannon alerting the remaining vessels to avoid it. But the other captains mistook this for an order to close ranks and they did: "Splat!"

Hirst wrote that Caymanians took to canoes and rescued the crews. In payment for the heroics, the British Parliament passed a bill not to impress Caymanians into service during time of war. But Hirst acknowledges he was unable to trace any authority for this idea either.

His own details are sketchy about what happened: No lives were lost except for one captain and his wife who abandoned his vessel in favor of a raft. It isn't clear how many vessels, if any, remained stuck on the reef. Most were refloated to continue their journey to England.

My family enjoyed a number of outings in the shallow waters off East End beneath the Gun Bluffs. You could swim to the reef to picnic in the shadow of a merchant ship that had run aground and was abandoned in the 1950s.

Except for the thousands of sea eggs that littered the bottom, it was a wonderful spot to snorkel and observe the colorful wildlife frolicking in the waving turtle grass. Just by accident, I discovered an ancient cannon half buried in the shallow, sandy bottom. It was halfway from the beach to the reef, a distance of several hundred yards. There was another one lying on the beach with only the top of the barrel exposed.

They had lain there for years, perhaps centuries, and, surprisingly, no one had disturbed their rusty repose.

In his book, Hirst disputes the story that the cannon lying around Gun Bluff were from an old fort.

"...It was exactly on this spot the 'wreck of the 10 sails' took place," he writes.

I think the cannons probably had a far less interesting chronicle. Forts and cannons were owned, manned and deployed by civilians 200 years ago. When modern civilization rendered these defenses unnecessary, the burdensome barrels were jettisoned into the ocean during routine spring cleaning to get them out of the yard. The emotional ties to such romantic debris were still many years away.

25

LET US GET DOWN TO BUSINESS

If the wealthy banking elite of the Western World had tried to conjure up the consummate business climate they couldn't have done better than The Cayman Islands.

By 1971, the tax haven business in the Caymans was bubbling. By the end of the year there were over 3,100 offshore companies registered, and 324 trusts—all of which were paying registration and license fees of about $1,000 per year. These were companies that existed, for the most part, on paper in the files of bankers and attorneys.

The offshore trade could do anything it wanted for its clients with few restrictions. One restriction, however, was that it couldn't do any business within The Cayman Islands. But if a wealthy American wanted to establish a trust for his grandchildren with no interference from the United States authorities, or establish an untraceable bank trust account for his or her own private reasons, there was no problem.

The Cayman Islands had no tax laws for the American to break. In its infancy as a colony with a measure of self-government, the Caymans shunned tax treaties with all other nations to protect its tax haven status. If an American, or a Canadian, or a Belgian, a Russian, or even an Englishman for that matter, broke his own country's tax laws, that was his particular country's problem. The Caymans could not care less. No Cayman laws were being broken. That secrecy was reduced in the early 21st century.

If the IRS wanted to investigate a private American citizen in the 1970s, the Cayman banks would not help. In fact, the inquiry usually went into the trash bin.

In the early 1970s, the transfer of offshore money from The Bahamas to The Cayman Islands was a trickle. It quickly became a tsunami. Over the next two decades, The Cayman Islands became one of the premiere offshore havens in the world.

141

According to the New York Times—one of the few media giants aware of tax havens and the existence of one so close to American shores—the financial district of tiny George Town, Grand Cayman in the early 1990s boasted the highest density of banks and fax machines in the world.

For individuals, said the Times, virtually anyone can still establish his or her own shell company for a few thousand dollars, open a local bank account, and, because the disclosure is minimal and business operates behind a legal wall of strict secrecy, "no one need know about the company or what funds are stashed here. The few slips of paper that constitute the company records may be held in the office of a Cayman lawyer."

There are some in the United States aware of the internal workings of The Cayman Islands, but their numbers remain few, I wrote in 1973.

First, most Americans don't have the funds to interest them in offshore banking. They don't understand it, they think it's illegal, they are afraid of authorities and they are frightened of losing their money because there is no federal banking examiner and no Federal Depositors Insurance Corporation.

Occasionally, The Cayman Islands surfaces as an item in some huge financial-disclosure article—usually where concentrated pressure causes a breach in the normally impenetrable amour. Oliver North needed a front for the arms-for-hostages negotiations in the infamous Iran-Contra affair. The press discovered the company was incorporated in Grand Cayman.

The islands were also involved in the biggest "scam" in financial history. Agha Hasan Abedi, the founder of the Bank of Credit and Commerce International (B.C.C.I.), channeled many of his bank's illegal transactions through its Cayman subsidiaries.

As the Caymans began the new millennium its population approached 34,000, and its offshore banks and financial industries were also booming. There are more than 550 banks, almost 2,500 mutual funds and in excess of 500 insurance companies registered or licensed in The Cayman Islands. Deposits may have been as much as $1 trillion. Today, who knows?

The number of non-resident companies registered by individuals for whatever purpose—secret bank accounts hidden from spouses, family members and creditors; trust funds; tax evasion—is not publicized, but must number in the hundreds of thousands. An estimated 3,000 new offshore companies are registered per year. In recent years, more regulations have been added to avoid fraud and suspicious transactions.

There are still no taxes whatsoever today on income or profits, capital or wealth, or capital gains. There is little official communication with the taxing authorities of other nations, although concern that dirty money from the increasing drug trade and resulting money laundering in the 1980s would find its way into George Town and spoil a good thing, compelled the government to sign a treaty in 1986 with America and Britain that they would assist each other in the investigation, prosecution and suppression of criminal offences.

It's uncertain how much the government combats the flow of illegal money because the nation is so secretive about its offshore industry. It's illegal for any bank employee to disclose any information about any client's private account. The U.S. State Department still considers it "attractive" for persons wishing to launder money from drugs and other criminal activity.

"Much of the misconception about the islands' financial industry is due to a lack of information about the effort by the government and private sector to ensure we protect our financial industry from criminal misuse," Cayman Islands Financial Secretary George McCarthy told a USA Today writer in 1997. By mid-2002, in an effort to combat money laundering, the government began requiring banks and other financial companies to keep information on file on all of their customers and clients.

Tourists see almost none of this banking activity, since the offshore business is literally that—somewhere else, listed only on computer paper in some out-of-the-way bank office in George Town.

And if you ask the average American today what he knows about The Cayman Islands, he or she will still answer, if they recognize the name, "Isn't that the place where the scuba divers feed the stingrays by hand?"

Presidential candidate Mike Huckabee visited George Town in February 2008 to make a speech for the Young Caymanian Leadership Awards. Huckabee had complained during his campaign about the "$12 trillion" packed in offshore tax havens like The Cayman Islands, which he called a burden on the American economy. He also joked before he left the U.S., "I may go down there and visit one of those post office boxes where some of the other candidates have their money..."

The stingray-petting business temporarily collapsed after the death of Steve Irvin, the television Crocodile Hunter, and there were other woes ahead in the new century.

26

THE CAVALRY ARRIVES; THE INDIANS CHEER TOO

George Heon was an enigma from the get-go. Before I hired him, he held some impressive positions, according to his resume. But, by this time I understood that the Caymans don't lure people who hold steady, reputable jobs for Sears or General Electric or Bank of America for 20 years. As a result, I depended on insight and limited background investigation on job candidates.

Communication by telephone was possible but expensive. Personal references were checked by letter and that took weeks. Dr. Roy never talked to me by telephone when they were considering me.

George's resume indicated that he had 28 years of experience ranging from editor to pressman, and, even though I wasn't impressed with his skills as a writer, I never had any reason to doubt him. After leaving the Navy in 1945, he joined the St. Petersburg Times and Independent working in the composing room, a job he said he held for more than 10 years.

From there, he had worked in Oklahoma City as a composing room superintendent and as managing editor of the Washita Valley Herald in Chickasha, Oklahoma. In the mid-1960s, he had moved to Sausalito and then Walnut Creek, California.

Since 1968, he had been a consultant with the Oklahoma Press Association, serving as a troubleshooter on production problems for association members. I couldn't have found a better-looking applicant on paper if God had personally sent me another savior.

His resume said he had graduated high school in Nashua, New Hampshire in 1939. Like thousands of other ambitious young Americans that year, George faced a world that was already burning. The Japanese were in China, Germany had invaded Czechoslovakia and the Spanish Nationalists under Franco had taken Barcelona. The Big Show was only a few months away and everyone except the completely wacky knew it was coming. He enlisted in the Navy.

George arrived at the newspaper just like the cavalry when the troop was down to the last man, the ammunition was spent and the hostiles were a block away.

He was short, solidly built with a thick chest and muscular arms, gray hair and thick glasses that gave his eyes an added glint of wide-eyed, almost boyish enthusiasm. On his first day he said repeatedly, "I've been looking for this all of my life."

I thought that on my first day too, but I planned to make sure George's pathway was easier than mine had been.

I rented a room for George at a boarding house owned by one of the island's justices of the peace, Miss Frances Bodden, M.B.E., who also wrote a column for *The Caymanian Weekly*.

George arrived in the morning and insisted on working a full day before taking off and inspecting his room. By the time he got there, he was so tired he flung himself across the bed, asleep before he settled into the sheets.

George impressed everyone with his drive and energy. He was 50 years old, but tireless. I found him out of tune just a little when it came to operating the presses, but it didn't take him long to learn to operate them all. He quickly became a force in the operation of the newspaper and was just as quickly becoming a close friend of mine.

Then one day he questioned me about the possibility of bringing his fiancée to the island. As a child, I remember my dad telling me one time: "Sonny boy, women are just no damn good." Occasionally, he was right.

I was surprised that George was engaged but immediately decided that in this case I was not going to lose another valuable employee for lack of female companionship. Not only would I fly his fiancée down to Cayman, I would give her a job in the printing department.

George showed his appreciation by beaming that huge smile and then rushing into the printing department to keep production spinning along at its new whirlwind gait.

It was the first upbeat day I had experienced in months. Once again, I felt encouraged.

Erleen was plump, forty-ish, with an annoying, whiney, nasal voice and bright-red, dyed hair. She was not educated, pretty, nor sociable but she was madly in love with George, so we were all glad when she arrived and we were determined to like her.

George treated her badly, which surprised us. He often berated her in front of other employees. "If you don't like the way you're treated you can take the next plane back to Miami!" It was a side of him we hadn't seen. But she thrived in spite of the verbal abuse and within weeks the

145

two were talking of marriage. I encouraged the idea, believing that if George and Erleen were to marry, they could settle down in Cayman and I would have no worries about their skipping town.

George was proving invaluable to me, and Erleen, although ready to complain at a moment's notice, wasn't lazy, and pitched in at the print shop to help keep things moving.

Someone with a great amount of insight might have seen the trouble brewing in my little would-be paradise in Cayman. But the paper was now going to press on time, its appearance was more professional and our printing clients were picking up their orders as promised. Once more, life scurried along with sunny days and no particular panic.

We had established a practice, following the last visit of Martha's mother, Agnes, of exchanging tape recordings by mail. These were expanded versions of routine greetings, and we continued the practice for several months before tiring of it.

We started one last tape during a dinner party at Risë's, where much of the staff gathered and the rum flowed freely. I pulled out the recorder to let everyone say "Hello" to Agnes. When the recorder got around to me, I thought it might be fun to irk Agnes' husband Tom by pretending I was Dr. Roy, who had certainly been taken with her during a recent visit. We all knew that this had incensed Tom, who was possessive, often annoying and offensive, and jealous of my mother-in-law.

Agnes and Tom, Martha's stepfather whom Agnes had married during our life in Hawaii, had been anxious to come to Cayman on vacation ever since Martha and I had moved here. Their trip coincided with the recent marriage of Dr. Roy to an American from Mobile. She was a gracious lady and we were happy that the old man had found someone to share his life.

When I told Dr. Roy that Martha's mother was in town with her husband for a visit, he immediately asked me to bring them over to his home for dinner. He wanted to meet her and introduce her to his bride.

I was flattered by the offer and that night we all arrived at Dr. Roy's front door about sundown. I knocked and through the curtains in the living room, I saw the old gentleman rise and walk across to open the door followed by his wife, a portly, pleasant-looking woman, obviously much younger than the elderly dentist.

Smiling broadly, he welcomed us into his home. Martha and I went first, and I turned to introduce Agnes and Tom.

Agnes was still in the doorway when Dr. Roy brushed by me roughly and said loudly, "Well, who is this?"

I could see that he was instantaneously smitten, much to the displeasure of Tom, and Dr. Roy's brand-new wife.

The impromptu infatuation continued throughout dinner, and Martha and I grew increasingly uncomfortable while Tom fumed. Dr. Roy was oblivious to everyone else. He barely took his eyes off of Agnes. When we departed several hours later he told me to be sure to bring my mother-in-law again, "Soon!"

Martha and I had a lot of fun later that evening, kidding Agnes about her unexpected opportunity.

"Here's your big chance," I joked. "He's one of the wealthiest men in the country. It wouldn't take much for you to steal him away."

Tom remained annoyed but Agnes thought it was amusing. We didn't speak of it again, since it was meaningless. But at Risë's party, I couldn't contain myself once I thought of it. We were making another tape to send to Tom and Agnes back in Tupelo.

"Hello, Agnes!" I rasped in a deep, gravelly voice, trying to imitate the Caymanian drawl of Dr. Roy, "I've been thinking about you lately..."

Everyone sitting around enjoyed a good chuckle over it. George and Erleen were also present. They laughed.

And that was it. There was nothing serious, and nothing more intended. In fact, we never even mailed the tape.

27

ERLEEN BECOMES OVERLY AMBITIOUS

Within a matter of weeks, George had mastered most of the presses and taken over the operation and administration of the printing department.

He said he was expert at running large, multi-unit printing presses. I believed him, particularly since he was unfamiliar with the smaller presses in our company, but had learned to operate them successfully by trial and error. His impressive resume included press supervisor for the Lesher media corporation out of Walnut Creek, California, where he had operated a five-unit Hoe press and, at the same time, conducted seminars for the staff because the newspaper was converting from hot type to offset.

I was certain I had discovered a jewel. He pioneered the use of process color on our cantankerous English-made Rotoprint press by completing four separate press runs in the primary colors. It produced our first color photograph in the Caymanian.

I didn't pressure him about his background although I was curious. Occasionally, he would offer bits and pieces of his past. George told me he had been married previously and had a grown son who was an attorney. He had not been a very good father to his son and they were not close.

Since we both had military backgrounds, I was fascinated by his stories of war in the South Pacific. He served as a gunner's mate in the Navy and claimed he was captured by the Japanese on some South Pacific island and spent several years as a prisoner. He did not provide much information but I believed him. I asked how he was captured.

He waved it off saying, "I really don't like to talk about that," and I dropped it. Many W.W.II veterans will not discuss their war experiences and I saw nothing unusual in his reserve.

George appeared contented and continued his indefatigable habits.

He told me again and again, "This is what I have always been looking for!" It was reassuring.

The only time I had the slightest concern was when he dealt with an unhappy or complaining customer.

One afternoon I heard yelling in the production department and walked over just as George threw an order sheet at the face of a startled bank clerk.

When he saw me George backed off, but not all the way. I could see he was furious and I made a mental note that George was not to wait on impatient customers any more. It was one of many compromises that I made to keep my company alive.

"If there's someone with a bitch about something, just come and get me," I said, patting him on the shoulder for reassurance. I was certain that it had been the customer's fault.

There was something else about George. It was something he said that lacked the ring of truth—his lawsuit against Coke.

He told me when he first arrived that he was suing the Coca-Cola Company because he found a dead mouse in his Coke bottle.

Several times I overheard him on the telephone talking to someone he described as his attorney in Oklahoma. I didn't complain about the cost because it sounded important and I considered it a perk for his outstanding performance.

The case was scheduled for trial and George told me one day that he must return to Oklahoma. I had no problem with that and I wasn't worried he was going to run out on me. As it turned out, it worked out well for both of us.

Following the trial, George told me gleefully how he had testified on the stand that he had found this mouse in his Coke and how it had led to chronic indigestion.

"In fact," he told me with a wide grin, "as I was testifying, I got sick at my stomach and had to run out of the courtroom to puke in the bath room.

"My lawyer told me later that they could hear me 'gagging' in the bathroom and the judge said to the opposing lawyers, 'It really does make him sick, doesn't it?'"

The memory tickled George and he demonstrated his ability in front of me to appear sick at his stomach. I suspect George could have eaten cat shit with an agreeable smile if he found it necessary. His feigned sickness was an act designed to dupe Coke into paying.

"They really fight these things. They get a lot of them and they've never lost," he said. "But they lost to me. I won $22,000!" he said, and clapped his hands. I never saw the check but the incident could have been the truth.

149

He called me from Oklahoma with the good news of the award. There was another purpose for his call, too. He had met an old friend who was an equipment dealer who had a Compugraphic typesetter and supporting equipment he would sell me for $3,000.

As George described it, this would allow me to junk the old, trouble-making Varitypers we had been using and speed up our typesetting considerably. I conferred with Mr. Arthur and we went with George's recommendation.

When it arrived and George installed it, the computerized typesetting equipment did indeed revolutionize our little company's editorial department. Not only was it was quicker but the end product was cleaner and more aesthetic. I couldn't praise George enough for finding it.

When George returned he had another surprise. He and Erleen were going to marry the coming weekend and he wanted me for his Best Man. At that moment, I thought of him more like a brother than an employee.

The wedding was held in my living room and I happily paid for everything right out of my own pocket, even the preacher when it was apparent George wasn't going to.

Following the ceremony, George got roaring drunk and took me aside to tell me of his capture by the Japanese.

"You know how kids behave," he said. "We were marching along this path on this island in the South Pacific and grab-assing. We were told to 'shut up' but what the hell; we were cutting up and yelling at each other..."

George said the young swabbies ran smack into a Japanese patrol that had heard them coming and waited in ambush.

"The Japs jumped out of the bushes and pointed their rifles at us and started shouting in that gibberish. I thought we were dead meat. Everyone threw up their hands and surrendered. They shoved us around a little and then marched us off to a POW camp."

The worst part of that, he said, was the punishment meted out by the guards. Prisoners who misbehaved even slightly were shoved into open latrines, and forced to stand in the filth until the acid from the feces blistered their skin. He recalled standing in feces up to his neck. "It burned like hell," he laughed, rubbing his hands rapidly across his chest.

Later, Erleen called me aside and told me I should feel honored because George had never before told anyone about his war experiences.

He was a whirlwind. In her own way, so would be his blushing bride, Erleen.

Martha and Risë weren't so happy. They saw Erleen as a whiner and complainer at work. Their intuitions suggested there was hidden cunning.

Although she didn't voice it to me, Risë was especially concerned. She wrote to her mother, Agnes.

"There were stormy scenes between the newlyweds before the wedding and two or three good ones a week since," she wrote. "George was never a darling but he's a total S.O.B. now!

"I can barely stomach either but as long as they keep the presses rolling, guess we'll tolerate them. They stayed in an apartment upstairs from us only three weeks or so before moving in next to our layout artist Mark Rice—poor Mark.

"Anyway, they are both certifiable fruitcakes in my opinion, but they stay in the press room and I stay in composing and see as little of them as possible. George still takes the S.O.B. award in everyone's book, but has been behaving much better lately.

"He thought for a while that he was going to be able to replace Dick but was told by Mr. Arthur that Dick was the boss, and would be as long as he (Mr. Arthur) had anything to do with it. Since Mr. Arthur is the majority stockholder, it is safe to assume Dick's job is safe.

"Actually, the root of 90 percent of George's trouble is that he is married to an insane woman. Erleen is absolutely the most pathetic person I have ever met running around loose.

"Perhaps you don't recall her 'Okie' whine, which goes something in this vein: 'George, everyone else has gone home. Why do you have to stay?' Nag, nag, nag. She is really a case.

"In spite of it all, George continues to do his job and on this island you continue to employ Jack the Ripper if he is competent and will work. Finding replacements for anyone is no easy task. To find anyone worth a damn you always have to import labor and they are expensive and the protection board is getting stickier. At the paper, we only employ three native Caymanians out of our present complement of 12.

If my workers were frightened at the prospect of George replacing me, I was oblivious to the idea. I was confident I had the complete support of all of the directors and couldn't imagine they would ever entertain the idea of dumping me.

George continued to confound me with his offbeat comments.

I heard from our director—Norberg—one morning that the ex-president of the Teamsters, Jimmy Hoffa, was staying in one of Norberg's rental cottages and had told Norberg to send me over and he would give me an interview.

Thrilled about the prospect of an exclusive interview with such a famous ex-con, I grabbed my camera and notebook and ran for the door.

"Tell him I said 'hello'," George said. As I laughed and shrugged it off, he said, "I'm serious. He knows me."

Whether he did or not, I'll never know. I forgot all about George on the drive to see Hoffa. Later, George told me that he had been a notorious strike-breaker. It was something else in his background that I accepted as the truth simply because he had told me it was true.

In the end, the only solid facts I ever knew about George was that he came to The Cayman Islands and brought Erleen. And that he was a hard worker, and he may have been my friend.

Jimmy Hoffa was shorter than I imagined. I expected to find some fierce giant, a man who had physically whipped the mighty Teamsters Union into subservience before being jailed. When I arrived at Winter Haven, Norberg's apartments on South Sound where I had stayed my first week in Cayman, Hoffa was in the yard talking on the telephone. I brought along my new local reporter, Mary Lawrence, to sit in on the interview. Mary would become a significant player in my fight to strengthen my editorial staff.

There was only one telephone and it was attached to a telephone pole in a field in front of the apartments. I waited patiently, not caring to be thought eavesdropping while he finished his conversation, and then I approached him.

This was the ex-president of the International Brotherhood of Teamsters, the man many thought the most powerful union chief in the world. President Nixon had just pardoned him after almost six years in prison. Nixon had commuted his sentence for jury tampering on the condition that Hoffa remain out of any union affairs.

We shook hands and I could feel the strength in those huge hands. He might have been short of stature but the man's skin was wrapped around iron.

He and has wife had chosen Grand Cayman because of the press the island was getting.

"There's been more publicity about Cayman in the last six weeks in the States than in the last six years," he said. We talked about the islands and its tax haven status, but he wasn't sure it was as safe as the local government presented it.

"The U.S. can put the squeeze on anyone, anywhere they want to," he said. It was a comment I used in my article, which annoyed the government appreciably. As for his conviction, he was certain it would be reversed on appeal.

"I haven't done anything illegal," he insisted. "I'm going to run for union president again as soon as the court gives me the okay. And I'll win hands down! I did a lot for the Teamsters. Those guys don't forget these things. They don't forget..."

152

We sat at a picnic table by the sea for several hours in the afternoon, sipping Coke as he talked openly about everything I asked. I would have enjoyed a little rum in my Coke, but he didn't have any around. Hoffa didn't smoke or drink alcohol, nor did his wife.

He told me about his youth. About organizing his first union for the Teamsters in Detroit at age 16 and going to Texas in the 1930s as an organizer. They really hated him there.

"The Texas Rangers were ordered to shoot us on sight," he said.

"There were only 32,000 Teamsters then; I built it in to 2 million!" he said proudly.

I left as the day grew late. I can still picture them sitting there, Mr. and Mrs. James Hoffa, tourists, watching the clouds transform from purple and pink to red as another lovely day ended.

Within two years, Hoffa would disappear mysteriously after a meeting at a Detroit restaurant. The authorities never found his body or made any arrests. There is little doubt, however, that mobsters killed him to keep him from regaining control over the union.

I wrote a straightforward interview about my visit with the Hoffas and used my photograph of them on the cover of the Caymanian.

It didn't take long for the government to react. I received a scathing letter from Olive Miller chiding me for featuring this American felon in the newspaper.

This time, however, I was able to turn the tables. I was aware that there was a law prohibiting convicted felons of foreign nationality from staying in The Cayman Islands. Technically, the immigration authorities should never have allowed Hoffa to remain.

I printed the government's complaint against the newspaper, and then added an editor's note, which pointed out that it was the government that erred, not the press. I was simply doing my job and informing the people.

It was temporarily satisfying to goad the dragon, but it did nothing except to further alienate me and add another black mark by my name.

Spending an afternoon with Hoffa was an exhilarating experience as a journalist. I could ask him anything I desired and he responded. There was no timetable, and no other pesky reporters horning in on my interview.

That was one of the positive elements of working in such an exotic location. Island reporters presented little threat to visiting dignitaries and celebrities who were usually amenable to spending as much time with us as we wanted.

I spent an hour or two with the late sports hero Bob Hays, "the fastest man in the world," talking about the prospects for the coming season with his team, the Dallas Cowboys.

Actress Patrice Wymore, on her way home to Jamaica, stopped by the office one afternoon and chatted with us about life with husband Errol Flynn.

Astronaut Frank Borman brought his family to Cayman on vacation and I spent an hour sitting with him on a wooden bench at the airport talking about his Apollo 11 space flight when he read from Genesis on Christmas Eve as his craft slowly circled the desolate surface. He would soon be working for Eastern Airlines, and he wanted my thoughts on the possibilities of Eastern gaining a route to Grand Cayman.

My competitor Billy Bodden even had a celebrity of sorts working for him. Mitch Miller, the American bandleader and television network orchestra leader who had a popular television show in the 1960s called "Sing Along With Mitch," owned a home in Cayman and occasionally visited.

Miller's wife, who lived in Cayman year-round, worked for Billy as a photographer.

There were any number of celebrities on the island any given day, and I don't recall any of them rejecting our requests for interviews. Except one.

28

I WASN'T IN HIS WILL,
BUT I MIGHT HAVE SEEN HIS SHADOW

I first heard the rumor that Howard Hughes was in George Town when we got a telephone call from WQAM radio in Miami. UPI reported that Hughes was headed for the island to talk with Florida land promoter and financier George Davis about an upcoming business venture in Hawaii.

Davis, a multi-millionaire who owned the International Monetary Bank in Grand Cayman and other banks in the Bahamas, had allegedly suggested the meeting in Grand Cayman to avoid publicity.

As we tried to determine how we should check out this report, a man claiming to be a correspondent for TIME magazine, Bob Sherman, came walking into our office asking for assistance.

Sherman said he had caught the first plane out of Miami after a press conference had been cancelled the previous day in Miami. Sherman believed Hughes and Davis were scheduled to announce a huge land development in Hawaii from Miami but they had abruptly cancelled the conference and the word was that they were instead going to meet in Grand Cayman.

Sherman was so convinced that Hughes was here, or on his way, that he left Miami with only a credit card and his camera.

"He's here! I know he is," Sherman said, and he immediately infected me with his enthusiasm.

The legend of Howard Hughes was not new to me: He was, and is, one of the most enigmatic men of the Twentieth Century. Here was a college dropout who had made the first around-the-world aircraft flight in 1938. He became one of the richest men in the world through his ownership of Hughes Tool Co. and Hughes Aircraft. He had invented not only the famous Spruce Goose flying boat that flew only once, but also the twin-hulled, Lockheed Lightning, or P-38 fighter that had raised havoc with the Germans during W.W.II. (One of its pilots was Lt. Dan Wylie of Tupelo, Mississippi, my first cousin. Dan was shot down by a German fighter over occupied Belgium and spent months in a hospital. The ME-109 pilot who shot him down came by the hospital to make sure he was getting the proper care.)

Howard's real wealth came from the inheritance of a gadget his father invented for use in the oil patches of Texas, Oklahoma, Louisiana and eastern New Mexico. That is where I first heard of the Hughes family. Before Howard Sr. invented the Hughes rock bit, drillers could not tap the gargantuan reserves of oil beneath a protective granite shelf 2,000 feet beneath the Western prairie.

The rock bit, with 166 cone-shaped drill bits whirring independently, could chew through the stone like so much peanut butter. The bit has been responsible for at least half of all the oil sucked out of the ground in the world.

But that wasn't the end of Howard Sr.'s genius. Instead of selling his bits to oil companies, he leased them. A normal inventor would have reveled in the sale of his products while he counted his millions. Howard Sr. would only lease the bits for $30,000 per well, then reclaim and refurbish them once the drillers were finished and then lease them again. This made him even more millions and founded a financial legacy that provided fodder for all of his son's peculiar, pecuniary escapades.

Howard produced about 40 movies after taking control of RKO studios in 1948, including such classics as The Outlaw with Jane Russell, Flying Leathernecks with his buddy John Wayne, and Hell's Angels with Jean Harlow, his discovery. His best friend was Cary Grant.

But that wasn't why he was so in demand by the world press. Howard Hughes began to slip away in the early 1960s. He became reclusive, then phantasmal. Hughes managed his affairs in the dead of night. He spoke to almost no one face to face. He would make station-to-station, untraceable telephone calls. He traveled for business but never left his aircraft. A few trusted associates acted for him. He disappeared, living in hotel suites in Las Vegas and the Bahamas.

People began to wonder if he was even alive. A current photograph of him was considered not only a trophy for a photographer, but priceless.

Just the possibility of making that shot drove Sherman to rush to George Town. I called my small news staff together and we decided to join Sherman in the search for Hughes. I thought it quite possible that the reclusive billionaire would choose Grand Cayman to conduct his business.

Calls to our police and immigration service sources only whetted our appetite. They refused to confirm or deny that Hughes was on the island. It was very suspicious since they never played games with the press. Something was afoot.

There was a "stranger" at the airport, a small, private jet we couldn't identify. It added to the excitement and mystery. It made sense that a financial meeting of huge proportions might be held in isolated Grand Cayman. We knew that Hughes had spent time in the Bahamas. Why not Grand Cayman?

We knew the local manager of Davis's International Monetary Bank in Grand Cayman well. His name was Paul Harris and I got him on the telephone with no trouble. He refused to confirm or deny the rumor. "Come on, Paul," I pleaded. "This could be huge!"

It wasn't above Harris to put us on a bit but his hesitancy added to the intrigue, especially after we received another telephone call from the Miami radio station telling us Davis and Hughes had met in the Four Ambassadors hotel in Miami, which was owned by Davis.

By now, the excitement was infectious. We got an anonymous tip about 30 minutes later reporting Hughes, Davis and Paul Harris were holding a private party at the popular Lobster Pot restaurant. While Sherman bolted for the restaurant, I set up a little ploy to try to snare Hughes.

Susan Roy telephoned the Lobster Pot, and with her best Scottish accent, tried to convince whoever answered the telephone that she was an international telephone operator with an emergency message for Mr. Howard Hughes.

Susan, one of my prized office workers whose husband Roy had been a contractor in the Bahamas prior to the banking change, performed her assignment perfectly. We waited breathlessly beside her as she insisted her caller wanted to wait while the message was delivered.

Nothing stirred in the office while we listened.

"Hello!" Susan said when someone finally picked up the telephone again. "Mr. Hughes?"

A long silence.

She hung up and turned to us.

"It was Paul Harris. He wanted to know if he could deliver a message for the operator."

We were disappointed, but not defeated.

"The only thing we can do is stake out the airport," I said. Sherman, who had returned without a Hughes sighting, agreed.

All afternoon, we waited. And waited. And waited.

About an hour passed and there was absolutely no activity at the airport. None.

I stood for a long time looking at the small jet. It looked as if there was someone peering out of a window, but the bright sunlight made it

157

impossible to see anything more than a shadowy outline.

I walked quickly inside the terminal to relieve myself. About halfway through the process, I heard the startup scream of small jet engines.

I arrived outside it just in time to see a small group climbing aboard.

A single customs official was standing by the rail watching the plane moving slowly across the tarmac toward the runway.

"Who was on that jet?" I asked.

"I don't know. Four men," he replied.

"Was it Howard Hughes?" I demanded.

"I don't know him. I didn't know any of them," he said.

Later, Sherman said, "A recent photo of Howard Hughes would be worth $50,000, easy."

Dejectedly, he boarded the next jet for Miami and we never saw him again.

I never learned if Hughes visited Grand Cayman. But he could have. A check on his whereabouts years later indicated he was close enough to visit. No official would say. I think they enjoyed my consternation. Did I risk the photo opportunity of my life by taking a pee?

Hughes died in April 1976, about three years after the Cayman stakeout, gripped by the madness that tortured him physically and robbed his sensibility. He weighed less than 95 pounds and was kept in a perpetual stupor by codeine, Valium and Librium. He was being transported by jet to his home, Houston, from Acapulco for emergency treatment when he breathed his last.

Hughes was a popular topic of discussion for a few days around our office after the incident, but our chatter soon returned to the world-shaking events outside of our isolated little country; the Yom Kippur War was raging, and there were increasing calls for the resignation of Richard Nixon.

Could that obscure figure at the window have been him? It was said he never left his plane. Did Howard Hughes and I once stare at each other face to shadowy face?

I guess anything's possible. Ask Melvin Dummar.

29

DOWN TO THE SEA

Almost every day some new character or exotic craft sailed into our lives to merge one news adventure into another.

The Argonaut, formerly Hitler's private yacht, visited the island in January 1972. It was built in 1928, was 330 feet long with a 47-foot beam, and displaced 4,500 tons. It was a beautiful ship, now privately owned. You had to wonder what schemes and treacherous plots were devised forty years previously on those polished teak decks.

Not quite as mysterious, but still shadowy in its own stately way, was the See Drache (Sea Dragon), which slipped quietly into George Town harbor late one evening not long after the Argonaut departed.

I saw it far offshore and watched it for an hour as it drew closer. I told Martha and Risë we should walk down to the berth and get a closer look.

By the time we reached the ship it was early evening and we could barely make out anything but the shape of the 60-foot vessel. We could see that it was completely black and quite ominous looking.

We walked beside her, making our way carefully along the rough, rocky edge of the dock. We couldn't contain our enthusiastic comments about how we would love to board the vessel. It was anchored directly over the MV *Sharon Michelle*'s grave.

"Hi there!" a voice boomed over the side and we looked up to see a tall, deeply tanned young man looking down at us.

"Hello!" we answered.

"You want to come aboard?" he asked, pointing to a ladder over the side a few feet down the dock. Thrilled, we climbed aboard the vessel and introduced ourselves.

To our surprise, the young man was the captain and owner. He explained that we were aboard a yacht that was built in 1937 for Herman Goering. It was taken to England as a war prize after WWII.

159

The Sea Dragon had seen a number of owners before being purchased by the young man, who used it as a floating tourist attraction around the Caribbean. He was in Cayman hoping to get a franchise at one of the hotels to allow him to operate his boat as a business.

We were invited below, and followed him to a lush, wooden-paneled cabin, his living room and office. Soft electric lights bathed the polished wood with golden light.

He said he grew up aboard boats, was now 25, and was an ex-Marine lieutenant who had served in Vietnam. As we were talking, there was a noise from the stern cabin and a young woman emerged through a hatch.

"This is my wife Carline," he said, "My name is King."

We were so taken with King and Carline and their hospitality I felt I should offer King advice about working with tourists.

"I'm not that knowledgeable," I began, "but it's not easy for a foreigner."

"You mean it's expensive?" he asked.

"Not so much expensive as political," I said. "The Caymanians are rather jealous of outsiders coming down and opening businesses. It's hard to do without a Caymanian partner. Although it's not impossible, it is rare to find a business owned by an outsider unless there is a majority Caymanian partner."

"I know that,'" he said, "it's like that in most of the Caribbean countries but I've usually found a way."

"If you're talking about paying someone some money, King, that won't work so well here," I said. "Cayman is not corrupt like most of the Caribbean islands."

He looked at Carline and then at us: "Well, we're going to try."

"That's great," I said. "Others have done it. It's just harder these days."

"I have an idea," Martha chimed in.

"Why don't we invite King and Carline for dinner and I'll ask Ralph and Olivia to come. They not only own a sailboat but they are Americans who sail tourists around the island. If anyone knows the ropes, they do."

And so within the scope of a half hour we made new friends—interesting ones at that—and embarked on a political quest we hoped would end favorably.

"You guys will have to come for a sail with us," King said.

As it turned out, the only one who would get to sail would be me, and only at the end of a harrowing experience that came close to costing me my life.

Ralph and Olivia Davis had lived aboard their 36-foot trimaran

Windchime for three years, the last year in Grand Cayman. They met at American University and Ralph built the boat himself at a small boat factory in Hyde Park N.Y. One of their early passengers was Norman Rockwell and he had rewarded each with a pencil portrait, now displayed in the main cabin.

While exploring the Caribbean in 1970 they had met famed Caymanian diver and entrepreneur Bob Soto who offered them a job carrying tourists on sunset cruises. Soto was one Caymanian who could get anything he wanted, so Ralph and Olivia were lucky. My path and Soto's had not crossed, so I was no help there.

They were popular young Americans in Grand Cayman and enjoyed good reputations. I knew if anyone could help King find work for Sea Dragon, Ralph could.

The next day, I walked over to Seven Mile Beach. The Windchime was anchored several hundred yards offshore and I could see Ralph topside.

I waved my arms until he recognized my hail and jumped into his small, rubber, Zodiac. When he came ashore, I told him what I had in mind.

From what I knew, King and his wife had sailed around the Caribbean hauling tourists on day trips. He employed a crew of one or two young Americans and told us he normally hired temporary help to get from one port to another. None were experienced sailors.

Ralph and King hit it off almost immediately and I enjoyed a sense of accomplishment from arranging the meeting.

However, after a few minutes of small talk, Ralph said he had news. We looked at him. Ralph and Olivia looked at each other.

"We've decided to leave Grand Cayman," he said.

It was a surprising and somewhat distressing comment. I had not known Ralph and Olivia very long but it had been a promising friendship. Americans, especially young and adventurous ones, were in short supply in The Cayman Islands. The loss of any one of them was a blow—especially a couple of entrepreneurial free spirits like Ralph and Olivia, who owned a 36-foot trimaran.

"We just think it's time to move on," Olivia said. "We've decided to take our business to American Samoa. It's American and we won't have to go through all of the red tape we have here," Ralph said. "Besides, we've always planned to move on, and it's time…"

Ralph and King talked for a considerable time after that. I am sure King saw Ralph's departure as an opportunity, and Ralph indicated he would help.

But King faced rejection again and again. No matter what he did, no hotel was interested. Ralph, intent on sailing into the sunset, could offer no substantial help.

Two weeks later, Martha and I were having a rare afternoon outing alone at the Galleon Beach Club on Seven Mile Beach.

Offshore, floating on the calm sea several hundred yards away, the anchored Sea Dragon rocked slowly back and forth. Another spectacular sunset was materializing.

We noticed the Sea Dragon's Zodiac launch speed in and deposit King and Carline on the beach in front of us. They acknowledged our wave and headed toward our table.

"He looks a little grim," I whispered to Martha. "He's had no luck."

They joined us and King's handsome face showed the strain of repeated failure. We tried to cheer them up but there was not much to say.

Hundreds of native Caymanians made their living hauling tourists around the island's waters. Some wanted to fish, others wanted to reach the outer reefs for diving and others just enjoyed drifting in the sunshine. It was a fundamental, traditional industry in Cayman and the locals guarded it zealously, sometimes viciously.

King asked me to change seats with him and I obliged. I had been facing the open sea and he did not want to turn his back on his ship. He watched the distant shape with the intensity of a lifeguard.

We shared drinks and dinner and told each other stories about life in the islands. King's in-laws had come down to assist him, but Americans were powerless in The Cayman Islands. As absurd as it sounded, I was one of the most influential Americans and I could do absolutely nothing for him. In fact, he was probably better off without any overt attempts at help from me.

There was another American who had more clout with the government but we never warmed to each other with more than occasional, polite conversation and I did not believe enlisting his aid in this would help. I had nothing against him, but my suspicions about everyone on the island still haunted me.

Eric Bergstrom was the heir to the Bergstrom Paper fortune and had come to the islands in the 1960s with his wife Suzie. They opened the successful Tortugas Club for diving enthusiasts at East End and Eric built the Cayman Tourism Board from the ground up as a profession and avocation. Suzie created the little turtle with the pirate's cap that serves today as the official Cayman Islands' tourism logo. I was cool to both Eric and Suzy when I met them on social occasions because of my self-induced paranoia.

To maintain the government tourism position he enjoyed, Eric gave up his American citizenship.

King suddenly leaned forward in this chair.

"How long are you going to keep trying," I asked him. He did not answer.

"King, Dick asked you how long we're going to keep trying," Carline asked. "And I want to know, too."

"I think she's adrift," he said.

I turned and looked at the ship but she looked the same to me as she had for the past several hours.

"Are you sure?" I asked. "How about the guy in the Zodiac?"

"Rudy, but he doesn't know how to handle her and she's going to hit one of those big coral heads!" he yelled. "Look at those clouds forming out there."

Offshore, to the northwest, a huge thunderhead was indeed sneaking up on us.

Others on the beach were now watching us and looking at the ship quizzically. No one else thought of going with King.

"You've been drinking," Martha said, knowing what I was thinking. "You're crazy. You don't know anything about sailing even if you get there." There was no other boat is sight on the beach.

"Call somebody!" Martha said.

But even with more time, there was no one to call. By the time the police could get to the harbor and launch a motorboat, the Sea Dragon could have punctured her hull on one of those coral heads. The small dingy that had ferried King and Carline to shore had returned to the ship and there was no sign of life aboard. Rudy was below and probably unaware he was adrift.

I knew that King had been a competitive swimmer in high school and he had the long, lean musculature of the swimmer's body. I was also tall, but tended to be more tubby than lean.

For about ten minutes, I matched him stroke for stroke, but he began to pull away. The storm was closer and the waves began to build.

This added threat only gave King more energy and he was soon 40 feet ahead. I continued to pull as hard as I could but it was not long before I was drained.

After about five more minutes of this exhausting effort, I could see the Sea Dragon ahead. King had reached her boarding ladder and was climbing aboard.

About 50 feet from the safety of the ladder, I suddenly realized my predicament. I was having trouble breathing and swimming at the same time. To make matters worse, the slowly galloping Sea Dragon was moving faster. It would not be long before she outdistanced me completely, and I would be all alone doddering around in the waves hundreds of yards offshore in an approaching storm, a prime candidate for panic.

I thought of yelling for help but it was so embarrassing I resisted. Also, King would have had to abandon the recovery of his ship to rescue me and I'm not sure he would have, even if he heard my calls for help over the rising wind.

If the damn thing would just stop drifting I could catch it. I needed to turn on my back and rest. I thought of the unfortunate tug captain in the harbor during the last Biami. It is so easy to succumb to exhaustion.

The storm closed in around us. I felt alone in the sea, out of breath and energy. The fearsome currents dragged me along with the ship. The Galleon Beach Club was fading.

I wondered if Martha or anyone else ashore could see my predicament. Perhaps someone had called the police and a boat was miraculously on the way. I tried to look but there was nothing in sight but the Sea Dragon and me.

The drifting ship slowed a bit and I made headway. I struggled toward the ladder.

Something slapped the side of my face sharply and I thought a jellyfish had stung me. Then I realized it was a rope. Rudy, standing by the ladder, was yelling for me to grab it. I managed to grasp it and pulled myself toward the ship. I dragged myself on deck and asked in a gasp how I could help.

"Go forward and watch for coral heads," he said. "I've got to help King get her under sail."

I staggered to the bow and looked into the waters ahead.

There were coral heads everywhere! They stood eight to 10 feet tall on the sandy bottom like huge, concrete mushrooms. The ship was slowly rising and falling in the sea as swells began to build from the storm. When she fell between the swells, I could feel a soft "thump."

"She's hitting the bottom!" King yelled.

I envisioned the keel of the ship striking the sandy bottom. It was a miracle she had not already impaled herself on one of the rocks or coral heads.

Rudy, the part-time deck hand who ferried King and Carline to shore, had felt the anchor suddenly release the ship and raced around the deck in a panic. He tried to start the Diesel engine with no luck, then darted into the chart room and shrieked "Mayday! Mayday!" over the radio at the wrong frequency. No one within a hundred miles heard him.

King was able to get the engine started. It lacked the power to maneuver quickly against the rising wind. With Rudy's help, he began raising the main sail. We picked up momentum and tracked toward the open sea. Sea Dragon was vibrating like a frightened animal as she brawled with the wind. Ahead of us, coral heads appeared to block every route. Still we charged on and I gritted my teeth and cringed.

Repeatedly I yelled, "Coral ahead!" but King was steady at the helm. We swept right over them as I flinched in apprehension. I had no judgment of depth and the coral heads were passing below our wooden keel, six to eight feet below the waterline. To me, they looked ready to break the surface. No one noticed, or, if they did, didn't mind me making a screaming fool of myself.

Raindrops fell and the wind screeched over our decks as the thunderstorm struck full force. King and Rudy had the main sail up and King cut the engine and took the wheel. We were now a half-mile offshore and moving out to sea. Sea Dragon regained her composure. She was tacking with the storm, laughing at it, grabbing control and gaining momentum.

What had terrified me moments before now escalated into exhilaration. Sea Dragon sliced through the waves, rising and falling with a tremendous crash as she met each one. No longer did the storm concern me, even as lightning bolts crashed into the sea around us. We sailed for an hour, back and forth along Seven Mile Beach, three or four miles beyond the clutches of the outermost reef.

It was electrifying. Despite, or perhaps because of the potential disaster we had all experienced, we screamed into the wind like children on a roller coaster.

The storm passed and the sea calmed. There was no great damage to us or any other ships in the area. King brought Sea Dragon back to anchorage farther offshore than before. A spare anchor was brought on deck and lowered to the bottom. It held her soundly.

The three of us gathered by the wheel and examined the end of the torn anchor cable, a huge, thick nylon rope.

King fingered the neat end of the shorn rope.

"It looks cut," he said. "Somebody knew the current would bang her into the coral. They almost made it anyway with the help of the storm." We looked at the sea below as if searching for some clue in the black water.

Ashore again, I told Martha what had happened, leaving out the part where I almost drowned and embellishing my role as watchman for the deadly coral heads.

"Some of these natives are determined to keep him from going into business here, even if they have to destroy his ship," I said.

For years I wondered who had tried to sink the Sea Dragon. Whoever it was had come under water, since we saw no boats near the ship before her drift. It may not have been a Caymanian but another expatriate worried about the competition and sinister enough to scuttle such a

165

marvelous vessel. There were a number of ex-pats in the boat business in addition to Ralph and Olivia. The ex-pats were all expert scuba divers. Perhaps it had been partially sliced during the night, awaiting a sudden burst of wind to finish the job. Maybe it just broke.

King had managed a few day trips with tourists. Perhaps someone feared that if he stayed around he would become a fixture and obtain a legal relationship with a hotel. No one ever claimed responsibility and the police never came up with a suspect, at least publicly.

On the beach the revelers returned to their drinks and late meals after the brief storm. Everyone was oblivious to the drama that had played before them. To the unaware, it looked as if a couple of half-soused grown men swam out to a sailing vessel and took her for a joyride in the face of a thunderstorm.

It was enough for King and Carline. If The Cayman Islands wanted no part of them, it was mutual. King did not leave his ship again. Within a few days, they hoisted sail and headed for Jamaica. Neither King nor Carline said goodbye.

A few years later, Martha and I were driving by the crowded beach in Fort Lauderdale in heavy traffic when Martha shouted, "There's King and Carline!" I turned and looked. Sure enough, they were standing there on the beach.

"Should we stop?" I asked Martha.

We could not stop in time on the crowded road, and we kept driving. I now regret that. I believe we did not wish to intrude again in their lives. That was the last we ever saw or heard of them.

"Someone told me they were using that boat for smuggling," she said.

"They say that about everybody," I said.

A month later, we received a letter from Ralph and Olivia. They made the Panama Canal in five days and called it a "bureaucratic nightmare—unfriendly, inhospitable, and boorish." It cost $35 to transit and after a short rest they sailed for seven days to Perlas in the Galapagos. They stayed six weeks and left for the Marquesas, 20 days and 3,000 miles away.

They landed at Hiva Oa, the island where Gauguin lived and died.

"The Marquesas are much like Jamaica," they wrote, "high mountains, lush vegetation, few people, black beaches. The sea water is not clear and clean like Cayman."

Their letter was mailed from Tai Oa Bay, Nuku Hiva, Marquesas in French Polynesia, and it was the last I ever heard of them.

30

STORMS ALSO BREW IN THE SEA OF INK

Adventures in and around the sea can be as threatening as they are thrilling, but it was on the rock-hard, gray ironshore where my fundamental challenge waited. The minefield of Caymanian politics is subtle and combustible. At first I had been pleased to find expatriate American Bud Gordon working for me when I arrived. He pasted up copy and performed various production duties.

He had been a candidate for my position but was passed over. He was a large, amicable fellow with a quick smile and a talent for gathering worthwhile information and gossip. When he offered to write a folksy column about the natives and tourists, I was delighted. If Bud had concentrated on his journalism with the newspaper he could have become a real asset.

But he had other ambitions and could act hastily when distracted. He wanted to be a full-time, self-employed photographer. He now saw himself as a temporary employee marking time.

Bud had an easy writing style that poked fun at the island officials. He offered acerbic, biting comments about island life with a touch of humour. I thought it was valuable, innocent, and I encouraged him. On one occasion, he made some light-hearted, innocuous comments he called the "First Annual Cayman Islands Achievers Award." He praised the government for the cleanup of an old market area and then gave faint praise to the police for the formal installation service for the newly appointed Governor. Bud said there was the firing of "an almost-perfect" salute. A hint of sarcasm I found amusing.

He also mentioned an interesting visitor who had expertise in environmental affairs and had commented, "Our waters are wonderfully clean...but I wonder if development will let them stay that way?"

There were a few other harmless trifles.

The following week I received a letter from one of the most influential men in the country. Although I was never really close or politically allied with Benson O. Ebanks, I eventually grew to admire him. He was a native Caymanian who served as a legislator and as an appointed member of the executive council. Well spoken and intelligent, he had the serious presence of a no-nonsense individual.

When I received a hand-written letter from "Benson Ebanks of West Bay," following the publication of Bud's column, several of my Caymanian staff members were impressed.

"He's a big shot," Sandra said. Another pointed out that he was a political enemy of Dr. Roy's. At the time, I noted the hand-written letter's scribbling was all but illegible, even childlike. It surprised me, but I gave that imperfection no weight.

Ebanks suggested dropping Bud's column. "Since when has it been good policy to use the local paper to poke fun at people or even to suggest by inference that the people written about are important?"

He wrote further that he did not like the "foolishness" of a column called "Beach Patrol," written by reporter Marge Delello.

"We Caymanian people do not like to single out a few of the visitors to the island. We are happy to have all of them and I think the column should be left out..."

It was a benign letter following an innocuous column. I thought it was typical of what someone might do who was opposed to the newspaper, or to Dr. Roy, or to me.

Following the letter's publication I got a telephone call from Benson O. Ebanks. He said he wanted to talk to me. Curious, I invited him down.

The moment he walked in I knew that this was not the man who had written the letter. He wasn't angry. He just wanted to see the letter to see if he recognized the handwriting. He didn't, thanked me, and left after only a minute or so of conversation.

But his visit unnerved me. Here was a man that I knew was opposed to Dr. Roy, and thereby to me. He was polite but formal. I sensed a raw intelligence surrounding him and was sorry I wasn't able to draw out more of his feelings about the newspaper. Even if it were disturbing to me, it would have been insightful. The next week I apologized to him in my own column: "It seems that someone, for their own reasons, sent in the letter and signed someone else's name on it."

I never learned the identity of the writer. It was probably some individual mad that he or she never received any publicity and had used Ebanks' name to impress us.

One thing it accomplished was to add to my increasing apprehension. Did everyone have a secret agenda? Was anything to be taken at face value? Could I trust anyone?

The same week I printed the letter from the pseudo Benson Ebanks other forces were at work that would increase the government's distaste for me. When school resumed after the Christmas break in early 1972, our newspaper reported that no students showed up at the Cayman Brac junior high school. I thought that odd and suspicious.

Brac Headmaster Layman Scott told me the school was closed because teachers who left the last term had not been replaced. He referred us to the government for additional information.

The schools in The Cayman Islands are the same as schools in any country: A bellwether for the general health of the state and an open target for denunciation and rebuke for real or perceived inadequacies. And the Cayman government was as sensitive to criticism of its schools as any other political body. We were up to the challenge.

We persisted in demanding information and the following week were granted an interview. Scott's comments were a litany of complaints. "This school has always been plagued by staffing difficulties," he said. "For example, teachers often only stay for a short period. Often we have no replacement teachers for months at a time. Then, when we do get a replacement they teach a different subject from their predecessor and this causes a change in the curriculum and a lack of continuity of courses...Once I opened the school here and I was the only teacher present."

Scott unloaded his unhappiness with the small island school for page after page.

In the U.S., there would be no question that a parental protest to keep their children out of school would be newsworthy. There was a public outcry by the parents on the Brac. In Cayman, the reaction was a furious government.

"Mr. Layman Scott went out on a limb for his school by speaking openly to the press last week on the situation at Cayman Brac Junior School," I wrote in an editorial. "We would hope that no heavy reprimand is made against him, although I understand some steps may be taken against him for speaking out.

"There seems to be some rule in The Cayman Islands that forbids a public official from talking. On many occasions we tried to obtain information about certain police activities, roadwork, traffic, etc., and were told bluntly the government had an information office that provided that information.

"Forbidding department heads from speaking to the press seems a bit archaic in these times. His Excellency, the Governor, would earn our undying respect and gratitude if he could see fit to eradicate or modify this rule," I wrote.

"Since he is a former information officer, and a man who understands the need for communication, especially here, I believe His Excellency can appreciate our position." I had tossed the gauntlet.

In the following weeks, nothing happened to the outspoken schoolmaster, but the blanket of silence between the government and me grew thicker. To the bureaucrats, I was an irritating nuisance.

31

MARY, MARY, QUITE CONTRARY

Reinforcing the hostility between the newspaper and the government was the proposed new harbor. It was the government's passionate opinion that it should stay at its present location in the George Town harbor with major improvements to the facilities, including a new sea wall. It was Dr. Roy's opinion, however, that the new harbor should go in the natural, shallow harbor of North Sound. It offered more protection from sudden, savage seas such as the Biami that had brought tragedy to the island with the loss of the *Gulf Star's* captain.

At Dr. Roy's suggestion, I began a series of articles that called for more study and eventual vote by the legislature for or against the proposal rather than the present plan, which called for a unilateral decision by the Governor and his hand-picked executive council.

I took every advantage to force the harbor issue to a debate. One editorial noted that a famed British marine biologist named Wickstead had visited at the invitation of the government and had cast doubt on North Sound because of the pollution factor. "The pollution of South Sound was not discussed," I pointed out. I understood the constant needling of the government by me and my staff was an irritation, but I was trying to do a decent job of pointing out problems like any newspaper worth its sand. To the government, I was just an American stirring up trouble.

Mary Lawrence, born in Nicaragua of Caymanian parents, had immigrated to Cayman and married a Caymanian. She wrote a number of intelligent Letters to the Editor about the history of The Cayman Islands and its outrageous politics. She was a qualified teacher and had twice run unsuccessfully for the legislature. In the most recent election the redoubtable Jim Bodden, whose victory was now under challenge because of his dual American and Cayman citizenship, had defeated her.

171

Now that the production department was making progress, my most formidable task at the newspaper was to produce serious, knowledgeable, incisive writing. I desperately wanted reputable news reporting. More than anything I wanted a native Caymanian or a Caymanian citizen to write influential articles. So far, my editorial staff was all expatriate, unfamiliar with the culture, and inexperienced.

When Mary Lawrence suggested she might write a column, I was intrigued. I asked her for a writing sample and she complied. I was surprised. It was impressive. I hired her.

Mary called her column "On The March" and those within government ranks were immediately unnerved. A "march" in Cayman meant a headache for somebody, usually the government, which always overreacted. It meant Caymanians with a cause would have a rollicking march around George Town. But the gist of Mary's first "March" was pure apple pie—better education was necessary!

Mary's second column touched on the economic boom and I thought it showed common sense. She wanted progress to continue in the Caymans. I was thrilled with my new protégé.

Cayman had been a very quiet and somewhat depressed place in the first 50 years of this century, Mary wrote. During the Great Depression, Caymanians wandered leisurely around the country living off of fishing and light farming. Those who left Cayman earned very meager wages and did little to help those left at home.

In 1932 a devastating hurricane took a heavy toll on lives and homes in The Caymans and the tide from the storm saturated most of the land with salt water. Famine was averted only because of the British government and private companies in Belize and Jamaica.

When WWII began Caymanians began their great exodus, she said. Money was sent back home and the economy began to improve. By the 1950s the land was still contaminated with salt and was considered almost useless. Then, an expatriate savior named Greenall arrived and began buying land for speculation.

People begged him to buy their land for any price. He constructed the old Galleon Beach Hotel on Seven Mile Beach, the first one there. Visitors begin arriving. These visitors thought they had found paradise and returned year after year. Soon, however, a land boom began. Prices soared; land titles changed.

But foreigners were trading most of the land by this time and the cream of the profits was siphoned off the island.

More visitors were lured by the promise of financial reward. Most of the money left when they departed, although the government finally imposed a 5 percent tax stamp on land sales. In general, though, the ordinary Caymanians received little benefit.

"In 1963, with a view of putting the economy on a less fragile foundation, the government passed the Companies Law," Mary said. "This opened the door for a tax haven and companies around the world, weary of handing over their profits to keep the war machines of their own governments in the Western world going, began to move to our shores," she wrote.

"The resulting demand for facilities to house these companies, their employees and clients, have brought about the present building boom. It brings more and more real capital to our islands, and the first signs of real economic growth are in sight. These companies are coming to us in good faith, depending upon our stable government and liberal tax laws to maintain a haven for their operations for our mutual benefit."

She could also be biting. The following week she complained the new high school graduates would soon be "urged in a noble speech by a member of the executive council to join the civil service!"

But in the civil service they would find only the disappointment of low pay and disillusionment.

"There is an alarming discontent among civil service members," she said. "Except for those of the higher echelon who intend to stay where they are until they retire, there is a near unanimous vote of dissatisfaction with the operational policies of the service..."

The government was so annoyed it produced an immediate press release, claiming opportunities were "never better" than the present to join the civil service. "Admittedly, wages are invariably below those in the private sector but there are those whose sense of value includes a desire to serve their country."

In the same issue as the official rebuttal statement, Mary charged that the government hospital was in sad shape. Often the doctors had to telephone the pharmacy to see what limited drugs were available before prescribing, "And there is no hot, running water." She called the entire premises "shabby."

Even worse is lack of attention from the staff, Mary said. "Patients claim that calling out does not help...on one occasion a full, starchy dinner was plunked down in a chair by the bed of a stroke victim who had become paralyzed and could not even swallow the food had someone attempted to feed her. It was removed later with no attempt made to find out why she had not eaten it."

I loved it.

32

THE EARTH RESUMES ITS NORMAL TILT

As the months rolled by, the official clamor for my butt cooled following my scolding by Mr. Watler, His Excellency's stand-in. I discovered ways to avoid mistakes of protocol. My production problems were easing at last, thanks to my latest production manager, George. *The Caymanian Weekly* began to look like a real newspaper. It was still too small in size, but we were bringing the readability and appearance under control with the new computer equipment.

Mary Lawrence—who had not yet joined the staff when my banking story first appeared—continued to be a workaholic copy producer. Gone were our clip-art patches, poetry, childish drawings and filler copy. We were a long way from looking like a genuine newspaper—but we were making steady progress.

Mary looked like a woman who could be outspoken and direct, and she usually was. Although a Caymanian, her heritage was Nicaraguan and she had bright, dark eyes, black hair and light skin. Her countenance was pleasant and friendly. She was attractive and well spoken. Did I mention she was outspoken and direct?   I began to dream about a larger press and professional editorial help. I understood the economic potential for the company if I could get the staff and equipment we desperately needed.

In addition to her features on history and the constitution, the master copy-producer Mary also wrote her opinion column. Just as her political nemesis Jim Bodden, Mary's Cayman status also came under scrutiny by her political enemies. She said she had never sworn allegiance to any country but Cayman and, had she been elected, there could have been no legal challenge by the government because she held no dual citizenship like Jim Bodden.

I was so thrilled with her production that I let slide innuendoes that she was harboring a secret desire to re-enter the political arena now that the challenge to Bodden's seating had brought up the possibility of another election for Bodden Town's unsteady seat in the General Assembly.

The first meeting of the assembly following Bodden's questionable election began with foreboding. The question of his dual citizenship unleashed a constitutional controversy.

Possibly, one of my recent interviews with Bodden had frightened the government. In it, Bodden said his platform was for "full, internal self government." More than anything else, that scared the crap out of the tax haven community. The quickest way to destroy the tax haven would be to form an independent government and lose the protection of the British Crown.

Within moments of opening the legislative session, Governor Crook provided an answer to the official question. Before he could seat Bodden, the courts must decide whether or not Bodden was disqualified.

When angry shouts for discussion arose, Crook said it isn't proper to debate the question because it was now under judicial review. Bodden's supporters, fellow members Craddock Ebanks, Annie Bodden, Berkley Bush, Ira Walton, Anton Bodden and Alford Scott, stormed out of the assembly, followed by a crowd of onlookers and Bodden supporters.

For the first time, I wrote a front-page editorial to accompany the lead article on the legal challenge to Bodden's seat. In it, I urged patience, and said the answer will come from the courts, "not hotheads."

But I couldn't help twisting His Excellency's knickers by observing, "We do not fully agree that His Excellency should have waited until the legislature actually opened before letting everyone know what his official position would be."

Instead of reaction from the Governor, however, it was the six legislators who had bolted out of the meeting who responded.

They wrote me a lengthy letter, which reiterated their position that they thought the government had had plenty of time to decide the question prior to the assembly, and a simple telephone call to the attorney general could have settled it.

They saw my editorial as agreeing with the Governor's action and condemned it—when I was actually echoing the view they held! What a country! No matter what I wrote it was misinterpreted. De rigueur.

33

THE ROAD TO HELL IS PAVED
WITH GOOD PRETENSIONS

Mary Lawrence graduated from Cayman Islands High School and then taught at every school on Grand Cayman. She was married to a Bodden Town farmer, was extremely interested in government and politics and had been a candidate twice. However, I needed to face a nagging fear.

"Are you going to run for office again?" I finally asked her.

"I'm not sure," she said. I felt that slight lump of fright in my gut. "You know you can't work for the newspaper and be a candidate at the same time. That's not ethical for a professional reporter."

In the deepest reaches of my mind, I knew she was going to run, but I was so desperate for a writer who knew the internal politics of the country and was not afraid to write about it that I tossed judgment aside. "I need you to cover politics and government without any bias," I said.

She smiled sweetly, "Of course."

One of Jim Bodden's cohorts told a political rally that Mary had become The Caymanian's political "editor". I responded she would be reporting as a writer, not an editor. The locals never grasped the subtlety. The entire episode was moving to shaky ground.

Campaign meetings were the way politicians spread their messages in Cayman. They were like the campground gatherings in early America where politicians provided entertainment and free food in exchange for attentiveness.

Legislator A. J. Miller was an uneducated Caymanian whose political speeches rarely made sense. However, he was large, loud and dramatic. The crowd always responded to him. He owned a supper club on the south end of the island called the Eastern Queen and he had long been affiliated with Bodden.

176

Later that night, at another Jim Bodden's rally, A. J., turned his attention to Mary

"I have been opposed to Mary Lawrence since 1968 because I have been suspicious that she is a 'government agent'," A. J. said as he called the meeting to order.

"And when I saw the picture of her appointment as a political editor in *The Caymanian Weekly* this week, I told myself, 'Miller, you are a genius!'"

A. J. asked the crowd why would the government "go out on the street and pick just anyone as political editor?

"This is definite proof that, as I suspected, Mrs. Lawrence has been a government agent all along," he said. "She doesn't have the nerve to run again!"

The situation was ridiculous. I prayed A.J. would hurry up with his absurd conspiracy plot and change the subject. Here was a member of the legislature telling a political meeting that the government was now running *The Caymanian Weekly* and covertly appointing its own agents to my staff.

Unfortunately, A.J. was convinced of this preposterous scheme. I prayed that Mary would not rise to the bait.

I glanced at her. Her eyes, brimming with anger, were locked on Jim Bodden, who sat smiling in the audience. "What have I wrought?" I cursed myself. It would get worse.

In just two more days, in a column submitted to me for my approval, Mary announced her intention to seek election to the legislature by opposing Jim Bodden. The awful truth was that I was not even surprised.

"I have no intention at this time of resigning my job as Political Editor of *The Caymanian Weekly*," she wrote, "and it will be my job to report on the meetings of the campaign. Because of this, I will hold few meetings of my own but any voter can feel free to contact me with questions..."

I should have squashed Mary's column and asked for her resignation, as any legitimate editor would have, and she would have stormed out. We were now the talk of the islands. A huge crowd gathered outside of our offices when the paper went on sale. Advertising revenues soared. Mary's writings were invigorating the country and the newspaper. Everyone loved a political fight, the hotter the better. This one was beginning to steam.

With exhilaration, and the first pangs of actual success, thrusting rationality into the closet, I caved and let the announcement go to press. Mary immediately went for Jim Bodden's jugular: his support of full, internal, self-government that he had first proposed to me during an earlier interview.

Jim Bodden went to Jamaica and rejected his allegiance to the United States before the U.S. Council. He brought a copy of his letter to my office for me to read as soon as he got back. This was his last hurdle, and he had delivered it to me first.

With nothing left to derail Jim Bodden's run, Mary doubled her efforts. Now, I was allowing her to use her personal column for her efforts. I justified my reasoning by stating that her column was her own personal opinion, and not the newspaper's.

In her column, "On the March," she wrote that Jim Bodden had taken it upon himself to approach the Managing Director (Dr. Roy) and Editor (me) and asked them to remove her from her position because he (Bodden) does not like the way she reports on things. What Bodden had asked is that I assign Mary to cover areas other than politics. My reluctance to do this immediately was a professional abomination.

"If my employers (me) give in," Mary said, "they will leave us in the dark where they had us before and where they said they want to keep us—in the dark."

"Then, we will only be able to know what they want us to hear," she said. "That's how it started in Cuba."

Like political campaigns everywhere, the lively rhetoric was skin-deep. The more serious issue was a phrase in the new constitution making Mary's arguments more serious and easier for me to support. It was not widely understood by the public. The phrase is "discretion by the Governor." His Excellency has the right to take control if he feels the country is in danger. Period.

"To get away from (the Governor's discretion), this country would have to move to self-government," Mary said, "and then the discretion would be in the hands of a prime minister. The term discretion, as used in our constitution, is the only solid wall between us and self-government," she said.

"We have a stable government now. Foreign capital and investment are pouring into our country, creating more jobs, more ways to earn a living. But this can change overnight. Look at the Bahamas with their big hotels closed, weeds growing in their yards, people out of work.

"Look at Jamaica, all the problems she has: unemployment, illiteracy. Know what the leaders of these two countries did last week? They went to Cuba to form an alliance with Castro because they think he has been treated badly. Is this what we want in Cayman?

"The discretion is vested in the office, not the man," she said.

Unofficial government spokesperson and executive council member Benson Ebanks echoed the same sentiment at his own meeting a week later in West Bay.

178

"If the country is led into internal self-government or independence at this point, we are ruined. You will recall that Jim Bodden is a man who said a vote for him is a vote for full internal self-government immediately. This is a man who was also quoted in *The Caymanian Weekly* as saying, 'If you vote for me, remember, it is a vote to move this country as far as humanly possible from Great Britain'."

The pending election between the agitator for independence and the firebrand for status quo was dividing Cayman into two camps. Who knew where this would all lead? It could have been my personal zenith. Instead, it was an odious time for me as a professional journalist.

All my pretences of journalistic ethics were shelved in the heat of the campaign. I knew I should immediately muzzle Mary. Yet, I agreed with much of what she was saying. In addition, the newspaper was widely quoted throughout the tiny nation. It was intoxicating.

No one on my staff or within the newspaper made any comment about what I was doing. The directors said nothing. I guess they were enjoying it. The only suggestion came from an unsigned note left on my desk. Written in pencil, it just said, "Isaiah, 8. 7."

Curious, I looked up the passage: "For they have sown the wind, and they shall reap the whirlwind…"

I found it clever in a sarcastic way, and suspected Martha. She disavowed it. I asked Sandra if she had seen anyone around my desk.

"No sir," she said. "Except for that old witch from East End."

The witch is what the local employees called my "correspondent" from the East End of the island. Her name was Dorabella.

Days after the court cleared Jim Bodden to campaign, he contacted me with a subject long overdue:

"Dear Dick," he wrote in a personal note, "I am enclosing a copy of a letter which has been signed by several candidates in the forthcoming election. This is a letter stating our views as to how we feel concerning the writings in your papers by your political editor. We feel that this is not the high grade journalism and fairness for which your paper is usually known."

I read on, my sense of guilt increasing with every word.

"We would appreciate your accepting this as a representation of our feelings and not with a view to your publishing this letter. We intend it to be only a letter expressing our views to you the editor. Sincerely, Jim. "

"Dear Editor: The Political Writer with sly innuendoes and spectulations (sic) has insulted not only some of the candidates but also the honourable citizens who placed their names in nomination (for election).

"In the interest of fair journalism it is the responsibility of the editor, manager and directors to see that the Political Editor refrains from taking unfair advantage of fellow politicians in this diabolican (sic) manner."

It was signed by A. J. Miller, Ira Walton, J.M. Bodden, G. Haig Bodden, Cardinal DeCosta and six other candidates.

I showed the letter to Mary, informing her sternly that it was a private communication and not intended as a Letter to the Editor, or to be made public.

The new constitution adopted by The Cayman Islands at the time I arrived created an executive council of eight members, five of whom were elected by their fellow representatives from the 15-member general assembly, and three official members appointed from the assembly by the Governor.

In effect, this created a type of two-party executive council with the five elected members, the populist membership, and the three appointed members following the government line. His Excellency's three appointees serve as Chief Secretary, a Lieutenant Governor second in command (i.e., Mr. Watler); the Financial Secretary (the very efficient Mr. Vassal Johnson who helped write the original tax-haven laws) and the Attorney General.

The constitution also required the Governor to assign portfolios—management responsibilities for governmental departments—to the elected members, a system that would evolve into a system of ministers in the mid-1990s.

The Governor was required to consult with the executive council on matters of formation of policy but he could act unilaterally in matters relating to the police, defense, external affairs or internal security. There was also the caveat that if Her Majesty the Queen directed otherwise, the Governor could ignore everyone and simply do whatever London damn well wished him to do.

That, of course, was the panic button in the constitution. If the executive council ever got too wild or even if the Governor became insane, there was the safety valve of the Queen being able to set everyone straight in a hurry.

Mary was voicing my opinion in her writings. I certainly saw nothing but danger in the move for independence, which was the culprit lurking behind the grandiloquence.

My dilemma was a dichotomy. I knew I must dump Mary, who was out of control as a professional journalist. On the other hand, she was a motivator. Readership and sales for *The Caymanian Weekly* had never been better.

It should be emphasized that good reporters were a dime a dozen in nearby Florida, but they might as well be on the moon as far as the

180

Caymanian Protection Board was concerned.

It was not internal self-government, nor discretion, nor tax haven status that brought everything to a finale. It was I, and the appallingly sloppy way I exercised my responsibilities.Jim Bodden and Haig Bodden in Bodden Town called another political meeting. The hall was crowded by locals in anticipation of another wild session. The day before the rally, one of Mary's most controversial personal columns had appeared. She complained that Bodden was trying to get her fired.

As the meeting started, Haig Bodden held up a copy of the latest Caymanian. I wanted to head for the door, but all of the eyes turned toward Mary and me.

"This is an example of the biased reporting we are now getting in this country," he said. Jim Bodden took the podium and, looking directly at me, shook the newspaper. "Have I ever approached you and asked you to fire Mrs. Lawrence?" he yelled.

I answered very deliberately: "You never asked me to fire Mrs. Lawrence." After Mary's comment in her column, Jim Bodden believed I had betrayed his trust with his personal letter to me.

Mary shouted from the audience that she needed to respond because the exchange between Bodden and me had made her look like a liar. Bodden asked me to clear the air, but I shouted I had already answered what he asked and I did not want to get further involved in the argument. Silently, I wished I were 1,000 miles from Grand Cayman.

"You're already involved!" he yelled at me. "You also promised me before the election that if Mrs. Lawrence became a candidate she would be removed from political writing!

"It's a disgrace and poor journalism and I'm surprised at the type of journalism we have here. The people representing it should be ashamed to call themselves members of the press."

I turned crimson. It was embarrassment at being singled out in the huge crowd, but it was also shame. He was right.

Craddock Ebanks, incumbent candidate and Bodden supporter who was unopposed as representative from the North Side, joined to blast the Caymanian, charging that nowhere in the world would anything like this happen except in Russia.

Craddock Ebanks made me particularly uncomfortable. He was a man who had made no secret of his passionate hatred of me. He had denounced me from the floor of the parliament after an editorial I had written against the establishment of a censorship board. It involved movies on Sunday and I had asked, "If you can buy a drink on Sunday why can't you see a movie?"

The Ministers Association of Cayman objected to my rationalization and I wrote another editorial defending myself: "If we (*The Caymanian*

Weekly) were a church, our congregation would be composed of Christians, Jews, Muslims, Agnostics, Atheists, Drunks, Teetotalers, Negroes, Caucasians, Idiots, Geniuses and every other creature on God's green earth.

"It is the job of any newspaper worth its salt to defend individual freedom and the right of a man or woman to make a choice of their own will, dictated by their convictions."

* * *

Craddock Ebanks, devoutly religious, voiced the opinion of many who could not abide my rationale. Protocol does not allow denouncement of an individual by name in the legislature, but I understood perfectly when he stood in that august body and railed against "foreigners who come to our shores and try to tell us how to operate our government."

One day after an accidental drowning in the harbor, he met me on the street and stopped directly in front of me, blocking my path. The man who had drowned was an associate editor for Billy Bodden's newspaper. His name was Vernon Campbell and he had died of an air embolism while scuba diving.

A newcomer to the island and to diving, something frightened him while he was on the bottom of George Town harbor. He had raced 60 feet to the surface without exhaling as he flailed upward. The sudden increasing pressure of his rapid ascent ripped his lungs and he bled to death. He was a decent chap, and I attended his funeral.

Standing face to face on the sidewalk where he had blocked my path, Craddock Ebanks glared at me. "Well, I'm sorry to see you," he snarled. "I heard an editor had drowned in the harbor and I was praying it was you!" Stunned and startled by the hostility, I could not reply.

* * *

Mary's husband, James Lawrence, stepped toward the platform to defend his wife. He announced he would read the private note that Bodden had written to me.

"Wait!" I protested, "That's a personal letter!" But Lawrence began reading it before I could get to the platform.

Mary stood defiantly at the close of the reading and announced she was going to have a political meeting at this same spot tomorrow night to pick up where Jim Bodden left off.

"He who robs me of my good name enriches not himself, but leaves me the poorer for it," she shouted.

Bodden shouted back, "I have not robbed anyone of his good name.

What I have said was printed in *The Caymanian Weekly*."

I do not think anyone in the room understood the significance of Mary's husband reading that letter, except three people: Mary, Jim Bodden and me.

I took the unusual stance of writing a "Letter from the Editor" for that week's newspaper; a statement from me that the letter read to the public at the meeting by Mary's husband was without my permission:

"At a political meeting in Bodden Town," I wrote, "Mrs. Mary Lawrence, a candidate for the Legislative Assembly and political columnist for The Caymanian, made the comment that Mr. James Bodden, an opponent, took it upon himself to approach the Managing Director and the Editor and ask them to remove her from her job because Bodden does not like the way she reports on things...

"Last night, during discussion at a political meeting attended by Mr. James Bodden, I, as editor, was asked by Mr. Bodden: 'Did I, James Bodden, come to you and ask you to fire Mrs. Lawrence from your paper?' To which I replied, 'No, you did not come to me and ask me to fire Mrs. Lawrence.'

"What I said was true. I was never asked to fire Mrs. Lawrence. However, if there are those who construe this remark to mean that Mrs. Lawrence was not telling the truth in her comments about being fired, I will add the following:

"Mr. Bodden approached the Managing Director and myself and suggested Mrs. Lawrence, since she was a candidate herself, should remove herself, or be removed from political writing until the campaign was over. It was not suggested that she be fired, but that she should handle other assignments.

"Mrs. Lawrence has told me she feels that to remove her from her political writing post would be the same as firing her."

Mary and I never enjoyed closure on the issue. She and I both understood that her time with *The Caymanian Weekly* had come to an abrupt end. She did not come to the office again and I did not contact her. She was both a powerful politician and a passionate writer. I believe she chose the wrong one of these gifts to pursue. To say I could have handled the entire incident better would be the understatement of my life.

Two of the top three candidates filled the two vacant Bodden Town posts, Haig Bodden and Jim Bodden. Mary came in third with two others behind her. She lost by 40 votes. After Jim Bodden took his legislative seat, he lost interest in full, internal, self-government.

A few days after Mary walked out, Billy Bodden paid me a surprise visit in the newspaper office. It was our first face-to-face meeting. Both of us were curious.

Billy was almost as tall as I, six-three in my socks, but much thinner. His straight black hair, fringed by gray at the temples, was parted and combed straight back from his forehead. A Caucasian, his face was deeply lined and darkened by years in the sun. Billy looked haggard, weary, like someone who drank too much and too often. His eyes were large, grey, very intense and bloodshot. They seemed curious, not kind.

After introducing himself, he said, "I just dropped by to make sure you're taking good care of my business. And I see you're learning about local politics."

Immediately, I tensed. My cheeks turned scarlet. His retention of ownership still rankled me. Billy's own Compass was in operation now, but I rarely paid attention to it.

"You know, Dick," he said, enjoying my obvious discomfort, "One of your girls told one of my girls that you had called me a son-of-a-bitch."

I looked at him, not sure what to say. He was obviously baiting me. "Did you call me a son-of-a-bitch, Dick?"

I knew intuitively that Billy, as I had learned about all Caymanians, wanted to test the waters.

Actually, I admired him for coming face to face. But, I was determined not to back away. I still felt very intimidated at being a foreigner, but not at being me.

"Did you, Dick?" he asked again.

There was nothing threatening or intimidating in his manner, although he was not smiling.

"Billy," I said, "I'm sure I have called you a lot of names since I have been here."

"I can't imagine a gentleman like you calling me a son-of-a-bitch," he said.

"Well, I can't remember all of the names I've called you," I said. "And I'm sure they weren't very nice."

It mollified him and we both relaxed. He smiled as he turned to leave.

"Take care of the place for me, now," he said over his shoulder as he walked out the door.

I felt like yelling back, "You can have the son-of-a-bitch back right now if you want it."

34

WINDS OF CHANGE BLOW ACROSS THE HARBOR

My arrival in Cayman originally had coincided with that of Dr. J.H. Wickstead of the British Marine Biological Association. Wickstead was to assess the country's many environmental concerns. The government saw the environment as the largest single unexploited resource available to Caymanians and was looking for a way to develop it in a manner benefiting all.

When he completed his report he said that dredging was killing North Sound and the island needed a sewage treatment system. As for North Sound's use as a harbor, he said, "You do a deep-water harbor in North Sound and that will be the end of it. And you will probably spend more than the harbor costs keeping it clear. Don't touch North Sound. That's my considered opinion!"

The issue continued to be a newsworthy theme for months. Captain A. A. Reid, friend and ally of Dr. Roy's, was one of the strongest supporters of a North Sound Harbor. It would only require three miles of channel to dredge, he said. We would then have a beautiful land-locked harbor.

The harbor was a decision that would be made solely by His Excellency and his executive council.

Reid initiated the opposition to the Governor with a series of letters to the editor, the normal political tactic when events became serious. Reid admitted he knew nothing about the ecology report, said he thought it was ridiculous and that at least 90 percent of Caymanians supported the idea of a new port in North Sound, an area of 49 square miles. No more than three square miles would be used for the port, with two miles of channel.

The North Sound Development Co., of which Reid, Dr. Roy and my friend Sir Anthony Jenkinson were directors, proposed a joint venture with the government for the construction of a joint airport/seaport.

Sir Anthony was an English baronet and had married an American.

185

He had always taken an interest in Martha and me and we had visited the Jenkinsons socially. He also owned Morgan's Harbor resort in Kingston, Jamaica, a hotel complex on the bay almost exactly where old Port Royal had been plunged into the sea by an earthquake. His friendship was another reason I had tried in the beginning to get the government to consider the North Sound proposal.

Reid followed his letter with a second proposing that Cayman needed to open its doors to others who wished to settle here. "America opened its doors to Caymanians, and Cayman should do the same!" he said.

That was a popular theme with me. As an American, I resented being treated like a pariah when there were more Caymanians living in America than there were in Cayman. As for the Brits, after America had bailed their asses out of two world wars, I resented the attitude that as Yanks we were all second-class yeomen.

"If there are other nice people, cultured, educated and creative, who want to make The Cayman Islands their home, we should be happy and welcome them," Reid said. It was another dichotomous predicament. My better judgment was in battle with my sympathy for Reid's amity for Americans.

Reid's comments prompted a letter to me from Benson Ebanks, who again spoke for the government's position. This time, I made certain it was actually from him. Ebanks' letter began to turn the tide of what would become a sea-change in my thinking.

"He seems to think Cayman is developing too slowly," Ebanks wrote. "If the government's concern was only for the present generation, then the decision would be simple - let development proceed at an uncontrolled pace and everyone worth his salt should make a financial killing before it is over. But what of the next generation?"

Ebanks also posed the question of who would care for the "nice people, cultured, educated and creative," that would come with increased population. "The maids, baby sitters, construction workers?"

Ebanks said he thought the Caymanian people would welcome the newcomers, "but the hard truth is that with the best will in the world our limited population, and thus our limited labor force, will not accommodate this.

"In spite of what Captain Reid says, the wise course is to control development to the extent that it can be serviced and supported by our local population and a tolerable amount of immigration."

Reid again responded, but his letter revealed a little more of the history behind the feud. The angry captain said he had not mentioned Ebanks previously, since he did not hold him responsible. (Reid, as did I, regarded Ebanks as the government's true spokesman).

The problem began with the previous chief of state, Reid said. "I more or less regarded Mr. Long (former Administrator prior to Governor Crook) as a very forceful Administrator who wanted his way and got it...Everyone knows that Mr. John Cumber (Administrator prior to Mr. Long) with his great personality and ability, got Cayman started on the road to progress and prosperity. He liked everyone: Americans, Canadians and Caymanians and got along with all.

"Then along came Mr. A.C.E. Long—Caymanians labeled him 'All Cumbers' Efforts Lost'—and he started applying the brakes so fast and hard that he almost broke the necks of those in the rear seat."

As for where the laborers Ebanks mentioned will come from? Cayman can do as Bermuda has done, he said: "Get Portuguese and get them from the Azores! They are good waiters, good carpenters, good builders and the best farmers. They're nice people who would integrate well."

I was fond of Captain Reid. Not only was he an ally and partner of Sir Anthony's and Dr. Roy's, but he held populist views that appealed to me in this little country of contradictions. My son Steve's best friend in Cayman was Captain Reid's grandson Andrew. Dr. Roy and his chums had a huge economic interest in further development and it was their right to pursue it. On the other hand, vision weighed heavily on the side of a government which detested me.

The older generation of men like Dr. Roy, Captain Reid and their ilk had once pointed the way for Cayman to prosper. They had created a Crown colony and paved the road to create one of the finest tax havens in the world. But the world was changing around them.

Governor Crook said of the economic dilemma, of which the proposed new harbor was a big part, "...Virtually everything which has led to the recent expansion—the development of the offshore financial industry and tourism—essentially requires that there shall be no direct taxation, out of which the funds for this kind of development (roads, sewage, harbors) would normally come..."

What I didn't like and have never liked was concealment when government conducts the public's business. The government felt this was a sinister view for an editor to have in Cayman, and that attitude was responsible for much of my woe. But I did pursue it as honorably as life there permitted. Although I believed the government's position on the new harbor was the correct course, the secrecy surrounding it was inappropriate.

Shortly after the exchange of letters between Benson Ebanks and Captain Reid, I wrote a front-page editorial demanding the government unveil its intent for a harbor and explain why it was acting covertly.

I got a press release in response that informed me the government could not reveal where the harbor would be—but then told me exactly where it would be: "The government cannot give out full information

187

until the project is further along. An announcement will be made at the appropriate time." It added that the "most probable location of the new harbor would be the improvement of the present harbor. Hopefully, work will begin next year."

About 10 days later, I received the official notification that the present sea wall at George Town harbor would be extended at a cost of approximately $1 million. Dr. Roy and his cohorts were furious and I was told to initiate an editorial campaign against the proposal by the government. I declined.

"I'm sorry Dr. Roy," I said. "It's not in the best interests of the country." He hung up the telephone without comment. For a moment, I couldn't believe what I had said.

I had boated on North Sound. It was and is a magical place. It was the future home of Stingray City. You can drift around all day in the warm sun. Anywhere you slip overboard there's an enchanting world of colorful, underwater life waiting in the turtle grass to be discovered. We paddled around, drank beer, gathered sunlight, and plopped into the clear, shallow water occasionally to gather conchs for a perfect twilight picnic of fried fritters on a solitary beach. A harbor would have spoiled such experiences forever.

Had I been more astute, I could have avoided the entire contentious era by pointing out that the government's financial support for the harbor was a loan from the Caribbean Development Bank, whose experts had already informed the government that George Town was the only option for which it would hand over the funds. Then again, I'm not sure anyone but the bankers understood that.

I wrote an editorial imploring the government to require a customs statement from those who visited (and shopped) in the U.S. and other Caribbean islands. We estimated a simple declaration statement might add as much as $100,000 a year to tax coffers. Hey, I wanted to preserve the tax-free status of the islands!

We called for a Cayman Islands Conservation Law. "Almost daily," I charged, "passengers leave for the U.S. and England with huge plastic bags containing coral formations—including rare black coral. There are THOSE who want the entire island chain turned into a national park that protects all wildlife and natural formations," I editorialized. "This may not be such a bad idea," I wrote, "although provisions must be made for legal fishing."

"THOSE,' included me.

Jean-Michael Cousteau came for an environmental conference at the time, and was interviewed by reporter Ursula Gill. "I haven't dived here but I'm pretty certain I know what is happening," he told her. "You have all these hotels going up here for visitors attracted by the sea. And it is not spoiled yet. But if there are no strict regulations, it will be gone in a few years."

Cousteau lamented spear fishing, which surprised us. "It takes 10 years for a grouper to grow to 50 pounds," he said. "If that is killed it will take another six to 10 years to replace it. When the large fish are killed, spear hunters kill smaller and smaller ones."

Encouraged by such words from the progeny of Jacque Cousteau, I called for the creation of a non-resident fishing license. Fines would support a conservation fund to employ a game warden who would enforce Cayman's conservation laws, which we urged the legislators to provide.

Several years after my pleas, the country began creating a system of marine parks surrounding all three islands. In 1978 and again in 1986, legislation was passed creating some of the Caribbean's most effective laws protecting the coastal and territorial marine environment. In 1993, the most severe penalties in the Caribbean were passed against marine pollution. A fine of more than $600,000 was possible against vessels convicted of polluting territorial waters.

The Caymans today have strict marine conservation laws enforced by marine parks and marine police officers. Any harming or collecting of any marine life in park zones, including coral, is illegal. In addition, the taking of any conch, lobster or fish in season is prohibited while using scuba gear, and spear fishing is strictly prohibited. Even the importation of a spear gun into the Caymans is now illegal.

I can't claim responsibility for all of these covenants, but I do claim credit for planting seeds.

As my confidence grew, I was sure the best was still to come. However, there were still one or two gates to hurdle and distress was never far away.

One of our saddest moments came after Martha and I returned from a buying trip in Miami. Nolan met us at the airport with the news that our beloved Smokey was dead. "I gave him a burial at sea in front of your house," Nolan said. "We're all sorry."

Following his nefarious entry the day Martha arrived, Smokey had spent most of his time lying in the sunshine in front of our home, a friend to all and a threat to no one.

It appeared that he had been deliberately beaten to death. I was furious and considered it a personal attack on my family. I offered a $200 reward for information about who may have killed Smokey. All I wanted was a name. There were no takers. We really loved that animal and it was a painful loss, and a portent of things to come.

35

THE BEST THINGS COME IN SMALL PACKAGES

The most interesting "correspondent" I had was the extraordinary woman who covered the east end of the main island for me. Dorabella was a most unusual-looking woman. Extremely tall, six feet or more, very thin, the darkest, most leathery skin I have ever seen and penetrating, startlingly blue eyes. When Dorabella watched you with those piercing eyes looking out of the depths of that unfathomable black face, she created the sensation of disorientation—she was an apparition from the Haitian highlands of two hundred years ago. It was impossible to turn away when Dorabella looked at you—into you—and you knew she was reading the thoughts behind your words as you spoke.

Dorabella was the woman whom Sandra Parchment had called the "old witch from East End," the day someone left the psalm on my desk. East End was the appropriate name for the far eastern end of Grand Cayman.

She neither smiled nor frowned when I met her the first time. She extended her long, bony hand, clasped my hand firmly, and welcomed me to the islands. She might have been 60 years old, or 90.

"You will be happy here for several years, Mr. Dick," she said. It wasn't a question or a comment, but sounded more like a directive.

"Thank you, Miss Dorabella," I said respectfully. "I hope I'm going to be happy here for the rest of my life."

She looked at me intensely, but said nothing.

The local staff in the room watched the old black doyenne intently. No one approached us.

"I must go," she said. "Here's my story for this week."

She handed me a single sheet of lined notebook paper with her hand-written notes. It was about a birthday party, a few trips to Miami by residents of her neighborhood—always a special occasion for the rural Caymanians—and a sentence about my arrival. "East End welcomes

Mr. Dick Gentry to *The Caymanian Weekly* from Texas."

Everyone already knew about my arrival but I decided I would allow it to remain in her column anyway. She was paid a meager 10 cents per column inch for her work and I didn't want to cut her wages, even by a few pennies. The correspondents averaged only two or three dollars per week.

"I think she likes you," Sandra giggled when Dorabella walked out of the office. "And she don' like nobody."

"Well, I hope she likes me," I said in return, "because she couldn't be doing this just for the money."

"She's an obeah woman," another said in a hushed tone, looking behind her toward the doorway to make certain the giant black lady had really disappeared.

"A what?" I said.

"She's a witch," the girl said, her eyes widening.

"Come on," I said.

"It's true, Mr. Gentry," she said. "She was in jail once for practicing voodoo out there on the east end."

"That's ridiculous," I said

But I knew she wasn't kidding.

"Don't nobody ever get cross with Dorabella," Sandra laughed. "She'll fix you good."

"Get your butt back to work," I said. "You're gonna scare me back to Texas."

She relaxed, grinned broadly, and strolled back into the rear of the editorial offices to discuss her conversation with me with the other local staff members.

The practice of voodoo was still feared in the Caribbean by much of the native population. Just having the accoutrements for the practice was against the law in The Cayman Islands. A spell by an obeah woman could be psychologically paralyzing—if you bought the twaddle that voodoo actually produces results.

Dorabella had allegedly been arrested in the past, but I was never able to learn much about the incident, which had occurred many years ago. There were scattered bits and pieces of information about some ritual, but I could never confirm it, and I certainly did not believe it.

When I got to know Dorabella better I tried once to broach the subject. Fortunately, she was not angered with me about the question and almost smiled as she replied.

"Ah, Mr. Dick," she said, "I don't know anything about that bad stuff, nothing at all."

I wanted to know more about obeah but I didn't want to press my luck with Dorabella. I was never scared of her alleged witchcraft powers, but I didn't want to lose her as a "celebrity" correspondent.

Every time she brought her column in for publication she insisted on bringing it to my desk. If I wasn't there, she would leave it there for me.

One day a few weeks after my third Christmas, my correspondent from the smallest island walked into my office.

"I'm Diane Evans, your correspondent from Little Cayman," she announced. "I've been trying to get by to meet you. I was over here for supplies for the club, and, here I am!"

Diane was a divorced Texan who had come to the islands on vacation and fallen in love with the place, especially Little Cayman. Her bubbly personality and appeal had landed her the job of manager of The Southern Cross Club, a loose association of owners from around Cayman and the U.S. who had constructed a rustic, one-story hotel on Little Cayman. There was a main dining area and kitchen, and about a half dozen cabins on the grounds.

She wrote the weekly column for the paper because she enjoyed it.

"I also want to know when you are coming over to see us?" she said. "There are a lot of people on the Brac and Little Cayman who want to meet you."

I knew very little about the other two islands. The newspaper had correspondents on each who filed weekly columns about social events, marriages, and other mundane occurrences.

I hadn't thought about visiting the other islands, but I had to admit it sounded like a great idea. The thought there were Caymanians anxious to meet me had its appeal. It would be nice to get away to a place where I might not have to watch my back every time I stepped out in public.

I would take my family and even write a few articles about it, making it a working vacation as well as a getaway from the pressures and perils of "big city life" in George Town.

36

THE TALE OF THE TAPE

As the months passed, I learned that George and Erleen were growing closer to Dr. Roy. They had been to his house for dinner several times. I thought it was terrific.

As for myself, I had unintentionally ignored Dr. Roy and was glad that he was receiving attention from them.

Mr. Arthur and I had become close friends and it was easier for me to work with him than any of the other directors. In addition, hardly a day passed when Mr. Arthur didn't visit *The Caymanian Weekly*.

I knew Dr. Roy had grumbled to Mr. Arthur that I was not spending enough time with him, and he missed the weekly reports that he used to get first hand from me. I insisted to George that he keep Dr. Roy abreast of events at the newspaper. He complied.

I can't remember when I first noticed the frost in the voice of Dr. Roy. But it was unmistakable. At first, I was positive that he was resentful that I was working so closely with Mr. Arthur and Norberg instead of him.

In the past years of *The Caymanian Weekly*, Dr. Roy had been closely associated with the newspaper. He met weekly with Billy Bodden and his signature was always one of the two required on company checks.

There were a number of reasons this changed. First, it was a matter of convenience. When Martha took over the bookkeeping, it was easier for her to grab Mr. Arthur and have him sign a few checks. In the earlier months, when my signature was not yet authorized as one required on the account, Dr. Roy would sign several checks in advance. When Martha was pressed, it was easy for her to go to Norberg's bakery or to his home for a second signature.

Bringing Martha aboard had been a godsend. When most of the staff had abandoned me for work with Billy at the Compass, the company's loyal bookkeeper went with them. I needed immediate help from someone who could be a quick learner. I looked around in desperation, and there was Martha. She moved into the operation with a vengeance. She is an organizer, a hard worker and a doer. She took over the finances and started looking at the money—who got it, who spent it, who we owed, and, more critically, who owed us.

One factor in Cayman that did not enhance good business practice was the matter of collecting accounts receivable. Basically, it wasn't done. Except for the banking community, businesses didn't want to offend their customers. It was not considered polite. No one was in a hurry in The Cayman Islands, and that included the paying of bills. It didn't take Martha long to understand why the newspaper had such a cash crunch.

"Dick," she said soon after assuming control of the accounts, "Take a guess how much money we are owed?"

"I don't know," I said, "I left all of that up to the bookkeeper. I never had time to get involved. I'd guess anywhere between $500 and $1,000?"

"Try $25,000!" she said.

In the early 1970s, this was an enormous amount and most of it was at least six months overdue. Some of it had been owed for years. There was no wonder we used our overdraft at the bank to pay our own bills.

Martha took on the challenge with a vengeance. She wrote letters, threatened lawsuits, telephoned again and again, and even camped out in offices, refusing to leave until the bill was settled. Cayman had never seen anything quite like her assault. Instead of being insulted, the majority of our debtors quickly settled up. A few even tried to hire Martha away from me. I was proud as hell of her. She was hell on wheels if anyone was lax in paying their bill.

Another reason for our lethargic, self-destructive line of communication with our managing director was the overdraft. Although it is a common practice in English banking systems, it made me uncomfortable to operate on an overdraft. Still, I often did not have enough money to cover the necessities. This was especially true on payday. Rather than have to go sit down with Dr. Roy and explain over and over that we were indeed making progress—"in spite of this little overdraft request here"—it was easier to work with Mr. Arthur and Norberg.

Also, Dr. Roy was aging rapidly and I was uncomfortable talking to him about my expansion plans. I realized that I was neglecting him and promised myself that I would pay him a personal visit and attempt to bring him out of what I thought was a temporary malaise.

By this time, Erleen had brought upon herself the enmity of the entire company. It was no secret that she thought her husband was working too hard. Erleen had her own spin on everything that happened at *The Caymanian Weekly*, and it was: if not for George, the place would collapse.

I tolerated her attitude for a number of reasons. First, George was indispensable to me and he remained one of the hardest working individuals I had ever seen. I was also a very tolerant person by nature and saw her as being protective and supportive of her new husband, traits that I admired.

Martha, Risë, Sandra and the other women on staff, however, were becoming more and more annoyed with her constant complaints that she was "exhausted," and with her favorite remark, "Somebody's not doing their job," which she employed instead of confronting someone directly about some unidentified, non-specific responsibility.

Erleen, of course, had not been exposed to the raw challenge of business in Cayman. She expected the company to operate with American efficiency and she never quite figured out she was in another country.

I could see George was not immune to her manipulation, although he never spoke openly in my presence about his feelings.

One morning, I arrived to find Erleen on the job without George.

"Where's George?" I asked.

"He's home," she said.

"Is he sick?"

"No, he's just so tired that I made him stay home and rest," she answered.

I was both confused and concerned. George had never missed a day, and the behavior was unlike him. I decided to ride out to their apartment and find out if there was something I might do for him. I had the feeling that something was amiss. I was determined not to let another problem build into something that would end abruptly with loss of another valued employee and friend.

George and Erleen had rented a cottage on a bluff overlooking the sea near Bodden Town.

When I arrived there was no one at home. I strolled over to the bluff and saw George far below me. He was sitting quietly at the edge of a small tidal pond throwing scraps of bread at the fish.

I yelled at him and walked down.

"What's the matter?"

"Nothing, I just thought I would take a little time off," he said. "I'll come back with you."

"No," I protested. "For Christ's sake, stay here and rest. I didn't come to get you; I was just worried about you."

But he wouldn't hear of it and insisted I take him back to town. I tried to draw him out on the way back to town, but he was quiet and non-communicative. I was worried. George was hiding something from me, something I now believe he was ashamed of. But not Erleen.

When Erleen saw us, she scolded George, but he brushed her off.

Throughout the day, I would catch glimpses of her glaring at me. She was scowling but would always turn away when I looked at her. I had the distinct feeling she hated me.

It was at this crucial time that the board decided to reward me for my performance at *The Caymanian Weekly*. In a special meeting, I was voted a seat on the board of directors and issued stock in the company. That night, I celebrated with Martha at home. It looked like things in Cayman were going to work out for us after all. Risë and Nolan arrived to find out what action the board had taken. They were excited too.

"Right now, let's just keep this to ourselves," I said. "I'm not ready for the staff to know yet." They nodded, realizing it wasn't the staff I was concerned about. The thought brought a cloud to the festive atmosphere.

George didn't ask me anything the next morning about the board meeting, but I volunteered to tell him that I had been made a director. He offered his congratulations. Erleen, listening intently from her post at a nearby table, said nothing. At that instant, Mr. Arthur arrived in the print shop. He was in his usual bubbly mood.

"Hey there George," he said, "did you hear about what we did for our good friend Dick?"

I was suddenly on edge, hoping Mr. Arthur would simply end with that remark when George nodded.

"We gave him 5 percent of the shares of the company," Mr. Arthur said, "and someday we'll do something for you!" With that, he patted George on the back.

George grinned broadly, and said, "That's terrific!"

I cringed when Mr. Arthur reported such delicate news at this point. George now understood that I had deliberately withheld the stock information from him.

I also knew George well enough to recognize the subtle sarcasm in his manner. Mr. Arthur didn't. He believed George was genuinely happy that I was now a part owner.

I could only imagine what Erleen would tell him when they got home that evening. I was beginning to understand that Erleen was now overly ambitious on George's behalf.

37

THE BIG CHILL FREEZES ALL

Several weeks passed without incident following Mr. Arthur's announcement that I was now an owner. I had called Dr. Roy a couple of times, but he had not returned my calls. I became anxious. After talking the situation over with Mr. Arthur, I decided the time had come for direct action. I would pay Dr. Roy an unannounced visit at his home and find out what was bothering him. Perhaps he was still annoyed with me that I had not editorially supported his North Sound project. There had been a lot of money and development at stake.

In addition, some major changes at the newspaper were on my mind in terms of equipment and personnel. I also wondered what was going on in George's mind. The old days, where we were open and frank with one another, had disappeared. There was now reticence between us. I didn't like it, and had decided to marshal my forces in case another tough decision was brewing.

I knew Dr. Roy was particularly fond of George and Erleen and I doubted he would understand why I was suddenly losing faith in the couple. I wasn't ready to fire George. In fact, that idea would have been absurd only a few days earlier, but the weather was not the only thing that can change quickly in Cayman and I needed reassurance that I was still in full command. Getting rid of them, if it came to that, would pose a particular problem and I wanted to know if Dr. Roy remained on my side.

He received me at his front door and appeared both surprised and nervous to see me.

"I just wanted to talk," I said.

He looked at me and motioned me inside. He was reluctant to speak.

When we were seated at a couch inside his living room, I jumped right into the problem.

"I'm wondering what the matter is." I said. "You haven't said anything to me for weeks and I want to know what's wrong?"

He looked at me silently and I tried to fathom the thoughts behind those dark, fierce eyes. His long, sharply pointed nose and bushy brows gave him the countenance of a giant angry eagle when he frowned.

"I'm here today because I know something's changed and I need to find out if we're still friends," I blurted out.

I had never thought of Dr. Roy as a close friend, but my survival instincts were now in control.

He sat back and scowled at me.

"Friends!" he shouted. "You want to call yourself a friend of mine after what you said about me?"

He was shaking with sudden anger. I was dumbfounded and could only sputter, "What are you talking about?"

"You know what you said!" he answered. "You can imagine what my wife thinks!"

By this time, I was as alarmed as I was confused.   I thought he had suddenly lost his senses and believed I was someone else.

"Dr. Roy," I said sternly, "This is me, your friend Dick."

"You're no friend of mine," he shouted. "Not after what you said. And I'll tell you something else: I want you to get out of my building!"

He was shaking so violently I thought he might collapse if this continued.

Still startled, I rose and started for the door. This was all some kind of strange misunderstanding. It had to be. Not only was he furious with me personally, he had just ordered the newspaper to move the company out of his building. This was something I had wanted to do for months, but I had yet to find a suitable site and I certainly never expected to be tossed out by the managing director.

I hardly remember driving back to the office. George and Erleen were nowhere to be seen. I told Martha briefly what had happened and she urged me to see Norberg and Mr. Arthur immediately.

Something was terribly, horribly out of order.

I drove to Mr. Arthur's little shop and told him about the baffling meeting I had just had with Dr. Roy. He listened, nodding after each sentence, and said, "I'd better drive over and talk to him."

I rushed back to the office to wait. George and Erleen were still nowhere to be found.

By 5 o'clock, Mr. Arthur had not come by. At 6, I closed the office and drove to his shop. His car was in the driveway. I walked to his porch and met his wife at the door. She said he had just gotten in and had lain down on the bed. I was concerned, but prepared to leave.

He heard me on the porch and came to the door.

"Dick, lad, give me a minute. Go into the print shop and wait. I'll be right out."

Outside the open window of his little shop, the broad Caribbean stretched westward. The sun was sinking and the brilliant sunset was only moments away. It was another beautiful, strange day in Cayman.

He came in and sat down in his rocker. I waited.

"I talked to Roy," he said quietly. "It seems he thinks you said he had something going on with your mother-in-law..."

"What?" I yelled.

"Wait a minute, now, lad," he said. "He said you told people that he, well, that he didn't love his wife and was crazy about your mother-in-law, Miss Agnes..."

I was dumbfounded.

"Arthur, I don't know what in the hell you are talking about."

I could see he was searching for the right words. He wasn't sure himself what had happened. He was sure of one thing: whatever had happened, in Dr. Roy's mind it meant big trouble.

"Erleen told them 'something'," he said, avoiding my face.

"Erleen?" I said, "What the hell does she know?"

"She told Dr. Roy and his wife 'something' about 'something' you said to Agnes," he said, struggling.

"This is insane, Arthur," I pleaded. "When did this happen?"

He said it had happened when George and Erleen recently had dinner with Dr. Roy and his wife.

"I wish I knew what she said," I said, sinking down on a bench in the shop.

"There was something about a tape recording," Mr. Arthur said.

Then, in a flash, it was clear. Everything jumped into sharp focus. Erleen had told Dr. Roy about the gag message I had made for Agnes, the one where I had imitated Dr. Roy's deep, rolling voice.

"Wait a minute," I said, "this is very easy to explain. I know what she was talking about. It was a joke. It wasn't even a joke on Dr. Roy. It was a joke on Agnes's husband Tom."

I explained the tape to Mr. Arthur. He nodded, said he understood, and urged me not to worry.

"I'll straighten this all out with Dr. Roy," he said.

But I was concerned. I wasn't certain Mr. Arthur had completely understood. He was merely reinforcing his support for me.

"Now, I don't know what I'm going to do with George." I said.

I was curious about Mr. Arthur's reaction and more than a little worried. Mr. Arthur appreciated George's work as much as anyone, and had never said a bad word about him. I wondered if I was really going to be able to count on his support. He didn't keep me in suspense.

As he walked out of the print shop toward his house, he looked back at me once and growled:

"That bastard!"

As long as I was in Cayman, that kindly old man was the one person who never deviated from giving me 100 percent support in anything I did.

I shared my disbelief in what had happened with Martha, Risë and Nolan. They were distressed, but not necessarily surprised with what Erleen had done.

I decided to confront George and Erleen as soon as possible and I was waiting for them the next morning. Erleen failed to show, but George was there as usual.

I took him aside and told him what had happened. He looked at me for a moment, and then said, "Isn't it true, Dick?"

It was not the reply I wanted. I had wanted him to chastise Erleen and reassure me that I had his support. The last thing in the world I wanted to do at that moment was to fire George.

"True?" I said. "George, it was a joke! You know that. We never even mailed the damn tape!"

"Well," he said, "all I know is that she just told the truth."

"Nothing could be further from the truth, George," I said, "and both you and Erleen know that.

"You've grown resentful against me and God knows why. I brought you down here and then sent for your girlfriend. I've done everything I can to make you two happy here."

He looked at me silently, unsmiling, subdued.

"Well, you can tell your wife not to come back. She's fired and I don't want her in here again. You two think you're going to get me out of here. Well, there ain't a way in hell! Especially after this stab in the back."

With that, I wheeled and stomped out of the pressroom.

I didn't know what he would do. I couldn't bring myself to fire him on the spot. I was not certain of the board's reaction. I knew I had Mr. Arthur's support, and he owned the majority of the company, but I wasn't sure about Norberg.

There was also the company to worry about. Without George, I would be back in a familiar fix again. It would not have been a complete disaster, since I had taught myself to run the presses, but everything would suffer. I could make them roll, but I was no professional printer. Our growing commercial business would certainly deteriorate.

The financial condition of the company would come under close scrutiny again. If I fired George and our revenues from the commercial printing operation took a dive, I would have a tough time keeping our bank account out of the red. I knew, too, that Dr. Roy would immediately begin impeding me because I had fired Erleen.

To me, she had become a cobra. I hoped never to see her again. But I was certain Dr. Roy saw her as his loyal confidant. She had played her role with considerable skill. I suspected she had been cultivating him for weeks. In retrospect, I should have suspected it. My own naïve, trusting nature had deceived me once again.

Dr. Roy, by nature, did not have a great sense of humor. At his advanced age, I knew that he would never understand the nature of the prank with the tape.

In short, I understood I would never be forgiven. Still, I had to hope that somehow I would be able to maintain something of a relationship.

After all, I was grateful to him for offering me an opportunity to live and work in Cayman. But above all else, I hated for him to believe such a terrible lie. That was what was so difficult—that he would believe that I had turned against him. The realization that he believed I had betrayed him caused physical pain.

It wasn't long before I received a solid assessment of the damage. I received word through Derek Wight, Dr. Roy's nephew who managed one of Dr. Roy's grocery businesses, that Dr. Roy wanted to talk about company finances. He was "concerned" and wanted to know my plans for the future of the company.

I was anxious to meet with him. It would give me the opportunity of opening a dialogue with him, which might lead to rapprochement.

The staff of the Caymanian became excited when I told them Dr. Roy was coming to the office. He had not visited the paper since I had been there, and his rare visit would be a special occasion. We decided to make it a genuine event. Everyone pitched in. We cleaned and polished and bought fresh flowers and donuts. On the day of his visit, everyone dressed in their church-going best.

At 11 a.m., when his arrival was due, the staff crowded toward the front office. They were eager to greet the managing director and show him there was solidarity within the company. By this time, several days after Erleen told the old man about the tape, word of "an incident" had leaked throughout the company—and therefore around the entire country.

Intrigue reigned again.

When the time came I stood at the front window looking for his car. I wanted to walk out and explain that the employees were waiting inside to greet him. It was the general coming to pay his troops a visit.

From my office widow, I could see the grocery market that Derek managed. I saw Derek walk out of the store and head in my direction.

201

Dr. Roy was planning to bring him along, I thought. That was okay with me. I liked Derek and appreciated having him at the meeting. Perhaps he could help Dr. Roy understand what had happened.

When he walked in, however, he immediately trampled our hopes.

"Dr. Roy isn't coming," he said with some difficulty. "He asked me to sit in for him."

My disappointment clearly showing, I told the staff to go back to their jobs, and that Dr. Roy was not able to come. They were crushed.

During the meeting with Derek, I attempted to broach the subject of the problem between Dr. Roy and myself. I couldn't tell if he was sympathetic or not. He just said, "Dr. Roy is an old man now and can be difficult."

I tried to explain to Derek that I was encouraged about our finances and it appeared that we would end the year with a modest profit, something I had not managed previously.

He nodded and said he would report the good news to Dr. Roy.

"By the way," he said as he rose to leave, "Dr. Roy did tell me to inform you that he would like for the company to move out of his building as soon as possible."

"It's not fair," I told Martha later. "Goddamn it, it just isn't fair for it to happen this way. Not after all of our hard work here. It's like from the very beginning there was always something standing in our way. Every time we were able to crawl a foot, something kicks us back a yard."

I made the decision then to do something about George. He had continued to work as hard as ever but our friendship had evaporated.

We were both polite, but few words were wasted between us. I didn't want to continue working this way and I was beginning to recognize that I didn't have to. My mild-mannered ways, accommodating personality and sometimes outlandish sense of humor had brought me nothing but grief. I was beginning to learn how to properly manage a company, even though it was very late in the game.

I placed another advertisement in the Miami Herald for a printer. My first acceptable response came from Bob Hodges, a printer from the Florida west coast area who claimed he could manage a printing company. I flew to Miami, met Bob, and had a lengthy discussion with him about the situation I had in Grand Cayman.

"That doesn't bother me, Dick," he said. "I can manage the shop and I won't have any problem managing George if you want to keep him around."

That was enough to convince me to hire him on the spot and I returned to George Town armed with the knowledge I wouldn't be held hostage much longer. On my return flight, I suddenly decided it would be best to get rid of George before Bob arrived. Why turn the problem of George over to Bob? I had to think about the business. In spite of everything, I hated my decision.

There was nothing gratifying about firing George. I didn't know what to expect from him. I had seen him almost come to blows with one of my writers and I knew how angry he could get and how impulsive he was.

Although he was short in stature, he was built like a fireplug. As for myself, I was large, but as powerful as a bowl of pudding. My conditioning program consisted of lifting glasses of rum punch. It wasn't a confrontation I relished.

I approached him as he was cleaning a press.

"George, this ain't working," I said. "I'm going to let you go."

"Now wait a minute," he said, "you're just upset about all of this."

"No, George," I said. "It's over. I want you to get out of here."

He looked crushed, deflated. There was no anger in him. It appeared to be disappointment, but I didn't know. I no longer trusted him and I now knew that he was devious.

"I would really like to stay," he said, almost begging. "And your new man is taking over anyway. Don't you think it should be his decision? I'll be a help to my new boss."

Taken aback by his reaction, I hesitated. I had expected a fight; I had gotten a plea. And, he was right. I had hired a new manager. And George had been a tremendous worker.

"Okay, George," I said, giving in one more time, "here's what I'm going to do. I'll put it in writing for you. You screw up again and you won't be here five minutes."

I had him follow me to my desk where I typed out a short memorandum advising him that Bob Hodges would be the new press foreman and George would be demoted to pressman. He signed his name.

"But one thing," I told him bluntly. "Erleen is history."

He said nothing but nodded that he understood. I hoped that I had made the best of a bad situation.

38

THE MAN WHO WOULD BE PAPERCLIP KING

There was only one office supply store in George Town, and it wasn't us. We were able to sell a few stationery supplies to our printing customers. It caused me to consider expanding our office supply business.

The rift with Dr. Roy and the forced relocation we would soon be making made me hesitant to increase the printing supply business within *The Caymanian Weekly*.

I approached Mr. Arthur with the idea of a separate business from the newspaper with a new ownership. He listened as I explained my idea for creating a retail office supply store. His son Truman, who still worked in the Cayman attorney general's office, was also interested and lent his legal support by incorporating the venture and signing on as a director and shareholder.

Truman suggested we might be able to capitalize the company on the strength of an overdraft. Even without Dr. Roy, my new partners had wealth.

Mr. Arthur, Norberg, Truman and I approached Barclays Bank and easily obtained a $25,000 overdraft to initiate the business. We located a site to lease not far from our newspaper building and immediately began plans for our grand opening.

Martha and I had become friends with one of Alison's Caymanian teachers at the private, American-styled Triple C elementary school, and her husband, Jay Hargest, an American. He was looking for something to do, and I approached him on the possibility of managing the store for us. He had been in the retail business in the islands working for his father-in-law in one of the island's largest hardware stores so he had qualifying experience.

Jay signed on and as a reward I suggested offering him stock as an incentive. The other directors agreed.

I took $8,000 cash from our new bank account, flew to Miami, and shopped for wholesale office supply dealers. I looked in the Yellow Pages, found a distributor and called for an appointment.

To the salesman's astonishment, I told him I was starting an office supply store in Grand Cayman and needed supplies to sell and I had no idea of how to stock the store. Would he select $8,000 worth of general supplies for me using his discretion?

"You're serious?" he asked.

"I've got the cash in my pocket."

"Then I've got everything you need."

Fortunately, I had blindly stumbled onto an honest salesman. He outfitted our small shop with everything necessary, from paper clips and rubber bands to portable typewriters and shipped it to George Town in time for our opening.

The business was a success from the opening bell. Several years later, the Miami wholesaler notified every one of its Caribbean customers that it was becoming too expensive and too difficult to supply them. They would have to find a new wholesaler, or fold their tent.

There was one exception, the little office supply store in George Town, Cayman Islands.

"Because of our special relationship," our company was told, "we will continue to fill your orders indefinitely."

The islands occasionally suffer a fool even if he's not a son of the soil.

39

SOME DAY, YOUR PRINCE WILL COME

When official word was received that His Royal Highness Prince Charles would be aboard the cruiser HMS Minerva when it called at George Town, the island erupted into mass delirium.

For hundreds of years, the loyal Caymanian subjects of Her Majesty, His Majesty or Whomever Majesty wore the crown had prayed for a royal visit. It had never happened. Once, when I editorially criticized Her Majesty Queen Elizabeth for not visiting or ever acknowledging The Cayman Islands, I was shocked by the government's reaction.

Information Officer Olive Miller actually gave me a pat on the back. "It's about time something was said," she remarked.

Day after day Caymanians would gather at the dock to watch the horizon for the prince's ship. Everyone knew exactly when it was scheduled to arrive but it was fun to go and wait with the excited onlookers. After all, time was relative in Cayman. Maybe the prince would show up early.

But he arrived on schedule. The huge, gray navy vessel came over the horizon and dropped anchor a quarter-mile offshore. The crowd waited for an hour until a small launch with a British flag could be seen approaching shore.

The crowd quieted respectfully as it drew closer and closer. Inside the launch we could see at least a dozen naval officers in informal, khaki uniforms. There was no official party waiting to formally greet the boat, since this was only a semi-official visit by His Royal Highness. He was merely a lieutenant aboard the warship, or so the official announcements said.

He was easy to spot. I noticed his mop of hair appeared reddish in the bright Caribbean sunlight. My first impression was that the familiar face was much healthier looking and handsome than the photographs of him I had seen.

As he stepped ashore the crowd began applauding and cheering. Charles smiled, turned, and waved at us, acknowledging the welcome. He quickly disappeared into an automobile driven by one of the officers of the police department for a tour of the island.

During his visit, the local police closely guarded the prince. Rumors were that he had taken several local ladies to dinner aboard his ship, and had spent time sailing with them off Seven Mile Beach in a little Sunfish sailboat.

The social event of the year, perhaps the decade, was staged in honor of the HMS Minerva's officers. That meant, of course, that it was really for His Royal Highness. There were only a limited number of invitations available. As publisher of *The Caymanian Weekly*, they could hardly ignore me.

And they didn't. Martha and I were delivered a hand-lettered invitation to His Excellency the Governor's home to meet HRH.

I arranged for Nolan to attend and take photographs. Risë had to stay at home, disappointed. I didn't make any special effort to have her invited. She had improved on her annoying habit of becoming rowdy and flirtatious in a hurry at the cocktail parties and I was still nothing if not a Southern, male bluenose. I knew she would have headed straight for "Chuck" after a few drinks.

Risë was in her early 20s and tended to be embarrassingly vocal after a few drinks. At her very first Cayman cocktail party, she shocked the circle of stuffy colonials present by describing a cocktail party as a place where, "Cocks chase tail." Nolan couldn't have cared less but I was particularly irked because I held a fatherly culpability for Risë's behavior.

The leading form of entertainment in Cayman, for lack of anything else to do, was the cocktail party. At a party, you get a cocktail and start talking. After four or five minutes—no matter how interesting the conversation or how attractive the participants, it's required by etiquette to politely exit your group and join another. As you arrive, someone will detach and move to another group. The process is repeated over and over—atoms bounced away to form a new molecule. When one atom strikes your group, it knocks someone loose to bang into another and creates something brand new.

Eventually, you end up talking to everybody. After enough cocktail parties, you are an integral part of local society. Everyone gives cocktail parties. They are both business and social events. And they are wonderful without exception because they force people to communicate. Sometimes, you end up talking to your friends or even your spouse.

The downside, of course, is that it creates a lot of drunks.

Martha practiced her curtsy and I was curious about what to say. I was told I should call him, "Your Highness," or "Prince Charles." I was relieved and Martha disappointed when we were told since we weren't British subjects, no bowing or curtsying was required. And I was not at all prepared for what happened.

The crowd on hand was small, and select. There were perhaps 40 or 50 people, a mixture of the British banking elite, high government officials and a few token Caymanians who owned businesses. Dr. Roy, I noticed, was not present. I was certain he must have been invited. Perhaps he was ill, or, perhaps, he didn't want to be in the same room with me.

The guests arrived in couples and they systematized themselves into practiced groups of four. We stood drinking our cocktails, talking polite nonsense and waiting expectantly and nervously, hoping the next party to arrive would be the HMS Minerva's captain with HRH in tow.

Finally, the front door opened and the captain entered, followed closely by the prince. They were fashionably late and incredibly dashing, as only British Navy officers in full white dress uniform can be. His Excellency the Governor walked over and officially welcomed the captain, who then introduced His Excellency the Governor to His Royal Highness. A white-coated butler approached and offered the cadre drinks. They accepted and then turned to work the main room of rigid guests.

I thought of pinching myself to see if this was really happening. My group of four was first in line as His Excellency ushered the captain and His Royal Highness into the main room to begin the introductions.

I remember thinking to myself, "What the hell am I doing here?"

I wasn't thinking about here at the Governor's House, I was thinking about little Dicky Gentry in the middle of the Caribbean, on a warm, moonlit night, surrounded by the elite of the small island nation, clutching a rum and Coke and watching a tall, gleaming, smiling, golden future monarch march directly toward me looking me squarely in the eyeballs.

Then, the Governor was there in front of us, introducing the prince to Martha and the other two with us.

"Just shake his hand," she had been told, "but only if he offers it first."

He smiled at Martha and extended his hand. She reached out, missed it on the first try, and then awkwardly grabbed it. The other two were introduced.

The Governor then turned to me. "This is Mr. Dick Gentry of *The Caymanian Weekly*," he said.

I stuck out my hand.

"Oh yes," he said, "accepting and shaking my hand firmly. You're the fellow that's giving the local boys such a hard time. It's silly, you know. Damned silly. I can't understand why you're doing this."

I was stunned. Here I was face to face with the future King of England and he was chastising me for the newspaper tactics I was using as a competitor against Billy.

I was totally unprepared to review the issue in this place at this time, but quickly mumbled something about the competitive nature of our business. Even then, I felt imbecilic discussing competition with someone who had never had to compete for anything off the playing fields.

"You know, you could do the country a great service," he said seriously. "The people could have two newspapers, on two different days, if you would give the local boy a chance."

I was so flabbergasted I couldn't even react. I cursed myself for downing three rum and Cokes to steady my nerves before his arrival.

"It's highly unimaginative, ridiculous and a disservice to the community," he added. "I would think you could do better by us."

"But, he's my competitor," I blurted. "You have no way of understanding that, I'm sure. I'm not going to stand by and let that son-of-a-bitch chase me back to Texas!"

Those within earshot gasped in horror. I wondered myself if I had overstepped the line, but I was angry and hurt. I wondered if this was the reason I was invited.

He looked at me in surprise. I don't know how much contact he had had with Americans before and I didn't mean it as an insult, but I suspect it was the first time anyone had told him flatly that as a member of the royal family he had no business meddling. The guests who overheard our conversation glared at me. The comments also ended our conversation abruptly.

"Well, it's just damned, bloody silly, and quite a shame," he said, and turned to another fawning group. But first, Nolan stepped in and asked for a photograph, to which the prince obliged. Nolan captured the moment forever on film. Unfortunately, he was still experimenting with techniques and decided this was the shot where he would try to bounce the flash off of the ceiling to get a softer effect.

Since the ceiling was about 20 feet high, the strobe light barely reflected off of it. The photographs are dark and cloudy, but still recognizable.

In the ensuing years, people would stare at the photograph closely, and then recognize him: "Is that...Prince Charles?"

When he was out of range, I said to Martha, "He's been briefed about Billy and me, probably by the Governor. He told me to quit picking on the local boy. I can't believe this. I'm so goddamned sick of this. Did you hear any of that crap he was giving me?"

"He was looking at my boobs," Martha giggled. "Did you see that?"

40

REINFORCEMENTS ARRIVE
FOR THE BATTLE OF GEORGE

My new foreman Bob Hodges arrived with his wife and her young son. His manner was a refreshing change from George. Where the latter was gruff and increasingly sullen, Bob was friendly, warm and hospitable to everyone.

He knew his job and had no trouble fitting in. I never knew why any of my expatriate staff chose to give up life in the comfort of the United States and come to the Caribbean. The enduring seductiveness of the tropical island fantasy stood alone in most cases.

Most only daydream about it. To actually move to the middle of the Caribbean with the hope of a job and just enough money for a ticket is madness to most rational people. More than one visitor confided to me it is a great place to vacation but they didn't want to live here.

Then, there are the rest of us.

I knew only that Bob had remarried and was looking for a fresh start. He said, as I recall, that there had been some problem with his previous employer in Florida and he had quit. That was a common circumstance. Many people were trying to leave some unhappy situation or job problem behind. Like many of us, Bob did his share of drinking. But if that had been a barrier to a job in Cayman there would have been very few people employed.

George kept an increasingly low profile. There was little doubt he resented Bob and even less doubt that he blamed me personally for his situation. But he was on his best behavior. Erleen was now completely out of the picture.

Rarely did George and I have a meaningful conversation. I had tried my best to prepare Bob for George. Still, I knew there would be a confrontation at some point.

It didn't take long.

Bob came to me with an exasperated look on his face his second week and told me George had just cursed at a representative from one of the banks who had come by to pick up an order, which wasn't ready.

It was not the first time George had been rude to customers, but previously he had me over a barrel. Now I had Bob.

I walked over to the press shop with Bob to confront George.

He appeared to be waiting for us. A slight smirk was on his lips.

"So what happened?" I asked.

"Oh, the bastard was over here bitching about us not having his job ready," George said.

"Well, did you have to curse him out in front of everyone?"

"Well, the son-of-a-bitch was rude to us," George said, "He said we couldn't do anything right."

"Well, goddammit, we can't," I said.

"Maybe if we had someone here running the place who knew more than dog shit we could," he said, looking me right in the face.

Bob looked on in amazement. I also noticed Walwyn had come to the front of the shop and was watching. His grin told me he was enjoying the confrontation. Walwyn had been with me longer than any other pressman. We had never grown closer than boss and employee because of his participation in the early strikes at the company. He had not walked out when Billy started the Compass, not because of loyalty, but more likely because he was not a Caymanian and might have had problems switching his work permit. Billy had probably not asked him to join. At least not yet.

"George," I said, more exasperated than angry, "get your ass out of here and don't ever come back."

He feigned a broad grin, loosened the belt on his shop apron and tossed it aside, wheeled, and, swinging his arms, strode cockily out the front door without a word.

"Well, it's up to you now," I said quietly to Bob.

"Don't worry about a thing, Dick," he said. "Believe me we're much better off without that guy."

I walked back to my desk and sat down. Walwyn followed me.

"Mr. Gentry," he said.

I turned toward him.

"I'm gonna have to have more money now, sir," he said.

I wasn't surprised. Every time I got into a jam, everyone wanted more money. But not this time. It may have been foolish of me but I was as flat against the wall as I was going to get.

"Walwyn, you're fired," I said without emotion.

I expected him to recant, but he just nodded and walked back into the shop to gather his personal belongings. I watched him leave with a note of sadness. Walwyn had been with me almost from the beginning. I had never known him well, but he was another familiar face that would be gone. I did not yet understand that Walwyn was covertly linked with George.

It was a night of celebration and despair. Martha, Risë, Nolan and I went to the Galleon Beach Hotel for dinner and drinks.

Mostly, it was drinks.

At the bar, I noticed Reid Dennis from Billy's Compass. The former Marine lieutenant who had lost a leg in Vietnam had been with Billy before my arrival. Reid had chosen the warm sun and clear water of The Cayman Islands to recover from the loss of a limb. He found a warm reception in the islands, and became a permanent resident.

When the *Gulf Star* and *Sharon Michelle* had sunk in the harbor during the Biami, The Compass had not yet started publication, and Reid had offered me photos of the rescue attempt for my extra edition. I accepted, but we had never been more than speaking acquaintances because of his loyalty to Billy. He was drinking with a companion, another visiting former-Marine.

"Hey Gentry," he said when he noticed our group. "Come up and have a drink to the Corps."

It was an offer I couldn't refuse. I was reminded it was November 10th, the Marine Corps annual birthday celebration. We downed several depth charges—a shot glass of 190-proof rum in the bottom of a huge draft beer—and the night quickly faded from reality.

I told Reid about firing George, but he already knew. George and Walwyn had applied several weeks before to go to work for Billy.

41

THE GATHERING STORM

Dr. Roy made no secret that he was finished with me. George applied to the immigration department to have his work permit transferred to Billy's company.

I went to Truman for advice. He had recently resigned as an assistant attorney general to open a practice with former law school friend Casey Gill, whom I also knew well.

I had hired Casey's girlfriend as a writer. A native of Germany, unassuming, exceptionally bright, Ursula had met Casey in England. They were later married in George Town. Both Truman and Casey knew about my problem with George and Erleen. So, both had a personal interest in helping me.

They told me to write a protest letter to the protection board and I did, claiming that I had brought George to Cayman and had fired him for insubordination. The government had no right to allow him to stay, I argued.

Dr. Roy, however, implored the department to let George remain. He threw his considerable weight into the effort and personally vouched for George, writing a strong letter of support. He also made a few key, personal telephone calls to top government officials explaining that he was no longer my mentor in The Cayman Islands.

There was no way that I could oppose Dr. Roy's wishes. He remained one of the most powerful men on the island.

Nor could Norberg help me when Dr. Roy weighed into the battle. Norberg had been appointed to the new Caymanian Protection Board, a powerful committee that ruled on new companies—making certain they had their appropriate 60 percent local ownership—and work permits. I had viewed his appointment with great satisfaction, thinking he would be able to assist me with guiding new personnel from the United States through the ever-increasing protectionist bureaucracy.

This was not too much to expect. However, in the case of George, Norberg was unable, or unwilling, to successfully challenge George's permit. I think he saw the issue as a personal problem between George and me, not between George and *The Caymanian Weekly*.

George got his work permit and so did Walwyn, and both went to work for Bodden. As quickly as he entered my life, George departed. I never saw him, or Erleen, again.

It wasn't the catastrophe that it would have been a year or so earlier. I was now used to the woes associated with local labor problems, and, whenever possible, tried to stay ahead of the game by continuing to cast for future employees, both in production and editorial.

My support group was also growing. I had begun to make some real friends in the island, many of them from England who had come to the island for business reasons. David Kendall-Carpenter was one such Brit. He was the manager for the local Cable and Wireless Telephone Company. Every year *The Caymanian Weekly* published the telephone directory for Cable and Wireless.

It was a lucrative contract. We printed the catalogue for free for the company, in return for the "yellow pages" advertising. There was a stiff battle for the contract with Billy Bodden's company my third year in Grand Cayman, and I desperately wanted to hang on to it. The multi-year agreement was worth about $80,000 to my company.

We won the contract, and I have always credited my success to friendship with Kendall-Carpenter and the mutual respect we held for each other.

I had enjoyed a friendship, too, with Ed Oliver and his wife since our arrival. Ed was a former art teacher with the Famous Artists School who had run away to Cayman. He invited my family over for our first Cayman Christmas celebration. Ed was instrumental in helping to initiate an arts festival that continues to this day.

I remember the first Cayman Arts Festival primarily because of the dubious behavior of Martha and Risë. A crowd awaited His Excellency the Governor at a large buffet dinner at the La Fontaine hotel to kick off the celebration.

We waited and waited, growing hungrier and hungrier. Still, no Governor.

Finally, to my horror, Martha and Risë told Nolan and me, and the others at our table, to follow them.

"Martha, you can't eat before the Governor gets here!" I cried.

"Oh no?" she replied, "just watch me!"

She and Risë walked to the front of the buffet line, picked up their plates, and began filling their plates.

Nolan and I watched dejectedly, hanging on the ledge of

215

embarrassment.

Then, one by one, others in the crowd of more than 200 started straggling toward the buffet line.

By the time His Excellency arrived, many of us were already starting our desserts.

It was an item of discussion for some time, but eventually the local aristocracy lost interest. Martha and Risë were well known in George Town for their behavior. Or, perhaps it was their demeanor. Both were tall, extremely intelligent, and attractive; and both possessed a kind of regal bearing attributable to their backgrounds. Martha had been a ballet dancer for a dozen years in her youth, and Risë had been Tupelo's head majorette and band drum major throughout junior and senior high schools.

When they walked into any social situation, they entered as if they owned the joint.

Nolan and Risë also developed their own circle of friends. They entered, and won, the local bridge championship, which delighted me, since the majority of contestants were Brits, contemptuous of American skills.

My relationship with the government also started to improve. I was finding that more and more I agreed with much of its thinking.

I received a letter from a woman in Washington, D.C., who had bought beach property for her children. She was responding to an article and photograph we had published about the theft of sand from the beach by builders. It was near the Spanish Bay Reef, on the north shore of Grand Cayman.

It was a shocking letter, which claimed that she had purchased the land in question, and that she had bought it with the help of Jim Bodden.

Bodden, she charged, had sold her a piece of beautiful beach with palm trees which now was the "open pit" shown on our recent front page.

"...A man from West Bay approached him (Bodden) about buying sand from it," she wrote, "and was told, 'It now belongs to a lady in Washington. I can't give you permission but I can't stop you from taking it'."

When she discovered what was happening, she had gone to Police Commissioner Doty several times and was told he was powerless to do anything about it.

She built a fence, but that didn't stop the theft of sand.

"I have lost all faith in British justice," she wrote. "After two years of trying to save my children's investment I have received no help from anyone that I have approached in the government."

216

I decided that I would forego placing the letter in the newspaper for an act that would be less offensive to those involved and might actually get results.

I wrote a short letter to His Excellency, and sent a copy of my note and the letter to the woman in Washington and to Commissioner Doty.

To my surprise, a week letter I got a hand-written reply. Inside, was an even greater surprise.

It began, "Dear Dick," and briefly thanked me for the information. It was signed, "Roy Crook."

The chink in the old amour was small, but definitely there.

42

YOUR EDITOR IS MISSING

There was an infection continuing to spread within the board of directors because of Dr. Roy's unhappiness with me, but I blithely believed my persistence in recounting it a bad joke would eventually prevail. I concentrated my efforts on maintaining and improving the newspaper.

After poring over the applicants for a managing editor who would come to the Caymans for the meager money offered, I made my decision based on their experience and correspondence.

It was too expensive to bring someone down for an interview, and I had no time to go to the U.S. I had one long telephone interview with my final selection, and he sounded marvelous. I was pressured to move because reporter Ursula Gill was pregnant and needed time off.

The man I hired, Grant, had owned a newspaper in Illinois. He was a widower, and looking for a challenge. In short, he wanted another chance to run a small newspaper. "I thrive on challenge," he wrote.

On paper, he looked perfect. I was as excited and expectant as a child on Christmas Eve when his plane was due. I even rented him an apartment within walking distance of the newspaper. The apartment was another of my ideas to retain workers. Since housing was such a problem, I rented a three-bedroom apartment near downtown and planned to deduct a modest rent fee from the wages of my new employees.

I had hired another printer. This one was a young man from Miami named Tom Buffenbarger, who had walked into my office shortly after George and Walwyn left and I had offered him a job with Bob's approval. He proved competent at running the smaller presses and I gave him one of the rooms in the apartment.

The night Grant was due from Illinois I was scheduled to attend an important cocktail party, so I asked Risë and Nolan if they would go to the airport, meet and greet Grant and bring him to the event. I would meet him and begin to introduce him to Cayman society at the same time.

At the party, I couldn't contain my excitement about Grant's arrival. Since he was a recent widower, there was no clinging woman left behind in his life to torment him or draw him back. There were many young Caymanian women who loved Americans and were willing to do everything in their power to discourage depression. I had urged long-gone Roy Kratt to open his eyes to this, but he simply never tried.

I was certain that Grant wouldn't be so shy and I would encourage him at every opportunity. I wondered if my new editor was on the ground yet.

At that moment, Nolan and Risë were watching as the LACSA jetliner unloaded its passengers at Cayman International Airport.

"Do you see anyone who might be him?" Nolan asked.

"Yea, I'll bet that's him," Risë said, pointing to a balding, graying, rail-thin man in a dark suit who was being assisted down the steps of the jet by two attendants.

"Poor Dick," Risë thought as she watched the man reel toward the gate. They decided to try to sober him up before they brought him to meet me and the general public of Cayman. He never made it to the party.

Grant never enjoyed a completely sober day during his short stay in Cayman. He wasn't a bad writer but he was a bad drinker. Usually by 10 a.m., he was well into his cups.

After two days, Risë greeted me with a doleful greeting: "Good morning, your editor is missing."

He was close to the sad end of a long, busy career of hard drinking. Like many members of my own family, he had been a boozer for so many years that even the first drink would recognizably alter his personality. I knew from experience there was no way he was going to quit just because I threatened him.

He was finished—as a writer and as a productive person. He was so scrawny his eyes were sunken into his skull. The dark bags under the eyes enhanced the suggestion of a walking cadaver. I was furious with him. Not only did I believe he misled me about his condition, but he reminded me of many drunks who had been involved in my life—a family full of them going back for generations.

I confronted Grant. He could stay and work, but I would give him an antabuse tablet every morning when he came to work. The agreement was that I would give him the pill. I would watch him put it in his mouth and I would watch him swallow it. I would make him open his mouth when he was finished so I could tell it was gone. I knew a lot of drunks.

He agreed and promised that with my help and encouragement, and God's blessing, he would begin a new life. He thanked me profusely and promised he would change. I had heard this all before.

Everyone in the plant knew what I was doing. The office wasn't a place where anything remained a secret. The printer, Tom, approached me about Grant. Tom was no angel, but he was sharing the apartment with Grant, and he confirmed the obvious.

"You had better get rid of that guy," he said, "He's nuts!"

The next day, Grant refused to take the first pill.

"Why not?" I demanded. "A deal is a deal."

"You can't do this to me," he said angrily, "It's against the law to treat me like this. I've got my rights!"

"I'm the law here! Take the damn pill!"

I could see the desperation mounting in his face. He was as sober as I had seen him, and I realized the need for a drink was more urgent with every passing minute. He was shaking, and having a difficult time standing.

I was growing angrier, too.

He swallowed the pill and I relaxed. Maybe he would make it.

Within 15 minutes, Grant was at my office door, gray and shaking. He looked like death. He was holding his stomach. He walked into my office and fell into a chair, his chest heaving violently.

"You ignorant son-of-a-bitch," I yelled, "You're drinking! Don't you puke in my office."

"I'm not ever going to do it again," he promised. "Help me," he pleaded. I got up and started shoving him toward the restroom. I knew he was in pain but I wanted to strangle him.

I told Grant the next day that he was fired. He angrily denounced me and said he was going to sue me.

"You won't get away with this," he threatened. Of course this wasn't America and he had no civil rights other than those I allowed him.

"You're going home, Grant. You're a drunk," I said. "It didn't work. I'm sorry."

He demanded I give him airfare back to his home.

I called LACSA and made him a reservation.

He said nothing as he climbed aboard the jet and didn't turn to wave before he disappeared inside. He would need assistance when he landed in Miami. I wondered who would help him down the steps.

I fretted over Grant. Unfortunately for him, his behavior unleashed a rage against drunks I had suppressed. I was no angel when it came to drinking, but I had never in my life awakened after a bout and wanted the hair of the dog.

To me, drunks are those who continued day after day, never drawing a sober breath for weeks at a time. I could deal with functional alcoholics, for a time, but Grant was a drunk who had lost the ability to function.

Almost every male member of my family, excluding my brother and me, had problems with the bottle that threatened their lives. My mother's father would often come in from work riding backward in the saddle because he was so drunk. My uncles Leon and Clyde each ruined their lives because of alcohol.

Clyde lived through W.W.II and joined the merchant marine. When ashore, he drank a case of beer a day. Without fail. He was never falling-down drunk, just a little tight all of his waking hours, all his life.

When we lived in Hawaii, his merchant vessel arrived once and he visited us for a day. I drove him back late that night on our motor scooter. We stopped at a liquor store on the way and he stuck several fifths in his jacket to smuggle aboard, since he couldn't hide enough beer.

He visited again when we were in Port Arthur, Texas, and once again I made a last stop with him at a liquor store for emergency rations.

"I've got some hidden on board, but there's always room for more," he said.

Leon was the bender champion of all of my relatives. He rarely missed a day of drinking. Even though I knew he drove my mother and aunt crazy with his drinking, I didn't fully understand it until I returned from the Marines.

I thought it would be harmless to take Leon out drinking one night. We bought a case of beer and drove around the back roads all night drinking and talking.

By 5 a.m., I was tired and wanted to go to bed. Reluctantly, Leon agreed to head for the barn.

Our house was only a few hundred yards away from the family homestead, where Leon lived with his sister Dot.

My aunt Dot was furious with us, and I quickly ducked out to head for home and bed.

As I stretched out, I could hear them arguing across the yard.

The argument lasted about a week. Leon refused to quit boozing and his rampaging continued until he and everyone else in the family were exhausted.

When he was able to quit these binges, he would collapse in his bed, pull the curtains, and stay in bed for a week while his sister fumed and nursed him back to health.

My own parents were furious with me, and I never attempted a drinking bout with him again.

Leon, one of the sweetest, gentlest and kindest men I've ever known when he was sober, was an uncontrollable rascal under the influence. He was finally forced by his family to quit, but was successful only with the help of daily antabuse and the powerful drug Thorazine, which he took for the last 25 years of his life.

I wondered how Grant would be received back in his home by his children. Had they hoped for a new life for him down in the warm, healing, Caribbean sunshine? Had they prayed for a miracle cure under the magic spell of the islands? I'm sure they had. Children always do. It just doesn't work that way.

My own mother and father, alcoholics for most of their lives, could pull some dillies, which didn't help my disposition in interacting with a drunk. In one shameful episode, I coaxed my mother to Grand Cayman to get her out of Tupelo where she had lived alone after my father died a decade previously.

I had forgotten how angry I became when she drank—and she started drinking heavily in Grand Cayman no matter how much I protested. It took only one drink for her to begin slurring her speech, but I could always detect it immediately. I had promised her she could attend a cocktail party with us one evening, and she was tremendously excited by the prospect.

When I went by after work to pick her up, I found her pretty well soused. I was so incensed I told her she couldn't attend.

"I've got enough problems down here without taking my embarrassing mother to a cocktail party," I shouted at her.

"I'll behave," she pleaded.

"You don't know how to behave!" I snapped back, almost in a frenzy by this time.

"Dick," Martha said, "Everyone will be drinking. It's no big deal."

"She's not going," I said flatly.

We left her all dressed up in our home on the front porch—alone, sad, tipsy and dejected. The kids weren't even there. They were at the babysitter's.

It wasn't until many years later that I learned through counseling why I became so out of control with my mother's alcoholism. But by then, it was too late for reconciliation.

A lot of time passed before I understood how deeply I had hurt her that night.

Martha had learned to input type for the computer at the Caymanian and pulled her wedding ring off while she worked. Afraid she might lose it, she placed the little silver band with the tiny diamonds in her jewelry box. It wasn't there one day when Martha looked for it, and we thought she had lost it. My mother had passed it down to me to give Martha.

Almost 15 years after we left The Cayman Islands, I was looking for an old insurance policy in the dresser drawer in my mother's bedroom in Tupelo. A flicker from the back corner of the drawer caught my eye.

I reached in and pulled out the missing silver ring.

Mother was in the kitchen when I found her.

"Mama, where in the world did this come from? I've been blaming Martha for losing it."

She looked at me and sat down in a chair by the kitchen table.

"I took it back that night," she said.

"What night? What are you talking about?"

"The night you wouldn't let me go to the cocktail party," she said.

I couldn't think what to say.

"You stole the ring?" I asked, incredulous.

"I hated you that night," she said.

"It wasn't a good night," I said, unable to tell her how sorry I was.

"Can we have it back, now?" I asked, dropping it in my pocket.

"No, you can't," she said. There was no anger, just resignation.

"OK, I'll put it back," I said.

The two of us were never able to resolve the ownership.

After we buried Mama, my brother Roy and I and our wives sat in his living room one evening in Starkville, Mississippi and tried to divide our mother's small bounty of family jewelry and memorabilia.

When we came to the little diamond ring, Roy picked it up and handed it to Martha.

"This doesn't count in our 'negotiations,'" he smiled. "I think this belongs to you and you should have it back."

Grant unwittingly ran into that psychological buzz saw when he came to work for me.

I was sorry for him, but also a little sorry for myself. I had invested time, effort and money in attracting him to the island, and the whole escapade ended up being another zero on my success chart. It was time for a break, and I recalled Diane's open invitation to visit the smaller islands. "They like you over there," she had said.

43

A GIFT OF MAGIC AT THE FOOT
OF THE SOUTHERN CROSS

A few days later Martha and I and the two kids boarded the older, twin-engine Cayman Airways DC-3 that made regular weekly runs to Little Cayman and the Brac. At the controls was George Thompson, Cayman's first son-of-the-soil to make captain on the airline. He was a big, pleasant fellow that I had met at several cocktail parties. Eventually, he would captain one of the jets when Cayman Airways began Miami flights.

Below us, East End began to slip away. The hulks of the wrecks on the reef passed below us and the soft blue hue of the ocean grew darker as we moved higher over the deepening waters.

Olice Yates, our Caymanian stewardess, asked me if I wanted a drink.

She brought me a rum and Coke and I looked around the cabin. There were about 10 people aboard.

"This is about average," she said. "Most of them will get off on Little Cayman. They are the tourists. This is normal. Those who fly to the Brac are usually local folks."

Like most newcomers, I knew little about the smaller isles. My reading told me that the first recorded note about them was made in 1655. Columbus spotted the Lesser Isles in 1503, but, having no offshore funds to invest, sailed on by. Until 1700, there were reports of activity on Little Cayman, but for the next 100 years it appears to have been deserted.

After almost an hour, the shades of blue in the ocean began to change back from deep blue to a lighter turquoise. We were approaching land. Little Cayman began to float by our port side. It looked like the rural East End of Grand Cayman, except there were not as many houses. We dropped lower and flew across a huge sound.

"What's that?" I ask the stewardess, pointing to a small cay.

"It's Owen Island," she said. On the shore near it I could see the scattered cabins of Southern Cross Club. We flew on. We were going to Cayman Brac first. It is about five miles farther from the east end of Little Cayman. The airstrip is on the western tip of the Brac.

There was a soft landing on the asphalt strip. The bluff from which the island gets its name cannot be seen from the straight-in approach unless you're in the cockpit.

We rolled up to the small terminal, even smaller than the one on the main island. The captain let us all get out and stretch our legs. The first thing that hit us was the silence. Not a sound. The entire island looked deserted beyond the airfield. It was hard to believe about 1,200 people lived here.

Within minutes, we reboarded and were soon aloft. Captain George skimmed over the waves since it was a short flight. He banked steeply and we could see the airfield below. It looked just like a huge pasture. The plane landed smoothly in the field and pulled up to an open shed about the size of a small garage.

The "fire truck" was parked inside it. It was a single tank of chemicals about six feet tall that rolled on two metal, spoked wheels about five feet in diameter. I knew it was the fire department because it was painted red.

Diane was waiting for us.

"Well, you made it," she said.

Diane, in addition to being manager of the club, was official taxi driver in her pickup truck, and also kept the official air traffic log. The club, I learned, owned the airport.

We piled aboard the pickup and roared off down a sandy road. There is no asphalt on Little Cayman. The scenery was greener than Grand Cayman, and Martha observed it was probably because of the lack of dust from the traffic.

"There are about 100 members," Diane said as we rode along. "It was started about 10 years ago by a Dr. Logan Roberts. Everyone is welcome during the day, and you can spend the night if there is room," she said. "After a trip or two, they want you to buy a membership."

Offshore, I could see Owen Cay in the distance. "We can walk out there and have a picnic one day if you want," Diane said, "The kids will love it and you can walk all the way. It's not deep."

It was approaching sunset.

"I'll take you down to your cottage and you can change," Diane said. "Then, it will be time for dinner and your party."

My party? I asked.

"Yea," she said, "The whole island is throwing a party for you tonight in the dinner hall."

"Is anyone bringing a rope?" I asked.

"No," she laughed. "Just relax and enjoy yourself."

I was worried about leaving Alison and Stephen alone in their cottage, even if it was close by. It would be dark soon.

"Oh, they're invited too," she said. "They're going to love it!"

I looked out over the small bay to Owen Cay. Beyond, the sky was red, gold and purple as sunset approached. Behind me, the torches were lit and lights began to dance in the dusk around the club. The day was slowly shedding its tropical heat. In the distance, a few cumulous clouds began their nightly transformation into huge, mottled mushrooms. Near shore, waves churned listlessly.

My rum punch, perhaps my third, fourth, or fifth was delicious. While Martha and the children dressed for the party, I walked alone down to the shore.

That moment on the sandy beach in the twilight with no one else around, no one trying to insult or offend me, no one furious over one of my articles, was my happiest moment since I had arrived in Grand Cayman.

Sitting alone on the sand as the stars began to glimmer, I savored the quiet dignity of the universe spread before me. To the east the Brac rose from the sea. It sparkled in the rays of the setting sun like some huge sea monster's fin breaking the waves.

If I had been sitting here 470 years ago, any sail that crossed between that Brac and me would have belonged to Christopher Columbus. This is where he first passed by.

To the south, the constellation Crux stoked its lonely fires. Not visible in most northern latitudes, Crux was hidden from early Greek and Roman astronomers who surely would have attached some ridiculous myth to it. But when explorers finally sailed to this southern part of the world, Crux, shaped like a tiny Latin cross, proved a faithful buoy anchored in the skies with the upper and lower stars aiming like an arrow at the South Pole.

Gazing at the beautiful little constellation, I knew it belonged exclusively to me this night. I knew a secret the ancient explorers did not. There were not four stars securing the points of this bright little diamond, but more. Astronomers discovered Acrux, the brightest point at the bottom of the cross, is really two stars orbiting each other.

Slowly, the Southern Cross shifts farther to the south as millennia pass. It's a result of what astronomers call precession, a drift caused by the circular wobble in the earth's axis.

What a fitting talisman this cross is for most of us commoners, I mused. It hides from the intellectual majority, drifts in a limitless universe, no myths, no legends. Goin' south with a bobble. Certainly not among the brightest points of light, yet it plays its role just fine, thank you.

"Now there's a clan for the rest of us," I said aloud to the waves, "I christen myself First Knight of the Southern Cross!" I was very pleased with myself.

"It's very hard to see your sorry ass," I called out to my newly adopted talisman. "Why don't you get up there where people can see you?"

Crux usually hangs so low on the horizon in The Cayman Islands it is almost impossible to spot unless you are looking for her. And low on the horizon usually means cloaked by low clouds or haze. But on a starry night in the middle of the dark southern sea, many a lost navigator believed it magical.

I was happy and my party waited. I rose from the sand, spiritually buoyed, and one of the stars winked.

"It's all the luck of the draw, Gentry," it yelled down at me. "Deal with it!"

"By God, they ain't got me yet!" I bellowed back as I wobbled toward the dining hall, feeling suddenly I was master of the entire universe. "I have not yet begun to fight!"

Diane had invited everyone on Little Cayman to my party and almost all of them came. There were hurried introductions, blurred a bit by my latest in a long line of rum punches. But Diane told me not to worry about formality since I would meet them again tomorrow when everyone would be sober and much more businesslike.

The club's chef served up roast pork and chicken, corn-on-the-cob, syrupy sweet potatoes, black beans, plantain and mountains of rice and black beans. Her name, like hundreds of others in the country, was Mrs. Eden, a likely descendent of William Eden, who arrived in Grand Cayman in 1765.

Old man Eden died in Nicaragua, but his two sons remained to begin a family that is probably the largest in the country today, maybe larger than the Bodden clan. Before he left, Eden, using slave labor, built a huge stone house in 1780 at Pedro's Point on the southern end of Grand Cayman. He called it Saint James Castle, but to locals today it's Pedro's Castle, a tourist landmark. A friend of mine, Tom Hubbard, owned it. As you will see, Tom was a character right out of a James Jones novel.

The supply of frosty beer, Jamaican rum and Irish whiskey following Mrs. Eden's dinner was infinite.

Loud, reverberating music was provided by a portable record player interspersed with live action from a small band—reggae to the core.

It was odd that our children were with us enjoying the evening. They stayed close by the dance floor and clapped and yelled with the crowd. We were completely comfortable with them so close. No worry about baby-sitters or illness or whatever. No running off every half hour to check on them.

It was soon beyond midnight and the party was staying the course, but Martha and I had had our fill. It was darker than normal, and I could see no stars overhead as we made our way to the cabins, no reassuring little diamond-shaped cross anchoring the shapeless heavens.

Small waves were now crashing against the sandy shore. A breeze had quickened, and kept the mosquitoes grounded. Unlike Grand Cayman, the lesser isles still experienced a problem with the pests since there was little expenditure by the government for extending the eradication program. And as there were only about a dozen permanent residents, I understood that. Several of the residents told me later it wasn't the mosquitoes that were the problem, but sand fleas. They trapped people inside the way mosquitoes used to do in Grand Cayman. Fortunately, we met no sand fleas during the visit.

Even as we drifted off to sleep with our heads swimming dizzily we could hear the beat of the music thumping away to the Jamaican beat and the sound of excited, happy, rum-and-Coke enhanced revelers. I was looking forward to morning and a picnic to little Owen Island. There, offshore from the club, fish are caught, cleaned, and cooked over an open fire on the beach.

Morning brought disappointment—rain. During the early hours a Nor'wester had blown through the islands and its remnants spoiled our first day.

We walked over to the Club for breakfast. The place was a mess. Cups, plates, food and trash littered the floor. But Diane, perky as usual, was up and about, and greeted us with a warm smile.

"There's not much entertainment here, so when we have a party, everyone comes and they don't leave until the food and booze run out," she said. Looking around, she added, "This place is a mess, isn't it…don't worry, we'll get it fixed up. In the meantime, how about breakfast?"

We were led to a large picnic table in the kitchen. At the stove, the indefatigable Mrs. Eden was busy with ham, bacon, potatoes and eggs. While we waited, Diane poured us steaming cups of black coffee and gave the still-sleepy kids icy orange juice.

As we dug into the bounty—there were also huge, fluffy, buttered biscuits with brown milk gravy—Diane told us about the country's smallest island.

"There's a sandy road that almost circles the island," she said. "There are some houses but most are owned by non-residents and they're empty now. Our club manages them for some of the people. They are an interesting assortment of people," she said. "Burgess Meredith, the actor, has a home here, in fact. But," she added, "None are as interesting as the people who live here permanently."

Diane had the club pack us a lunch and Martha, the kids and I set out in the club's dilapidated old Dodge pickup with Diane in the cab driving.

As we drove along, I couldn't help but notice the heavy foliage and isolation. Like most of the Caymans, mangrove swamp was omnipresent, along with breadfruit, sea grape and banana plants. The woods were thick with azalea, hibiscus, oleander, jasmine, honeysuckle and several species of wild orchids. Plants thrived year-round.

"What about customs here," I asked her. "This looks like an ideal site for smugglers and dope peddlers?"

"Sammy McCoy is the customs man, part-time," she said. "You met him last night at the dance. He also works for the club."

"Was he the one playing in the band?" I asked.

"No, that was Andy. He's one of our managers," she said.

"Does everyone on the island work at the club?"

"Just about everybody," she said.

"And there are permanent policemen over on the Brac. They keep a close watch on us over here and can get over here in minutes if something's not right."

"Unless we're in the middle of a Nor'wester," I suggested.

"Yea," she said. "But there is talk of a permanent government official stationed here."

"Is that good?" I asked.

"Maybe," she said.

Before I got her to expand on that remark, we arrived at the eastern end of the island and pulled up to a long house that looked new. There was a sign hanging in the yard: "Paradise Inn, the Keeners."

A man walked out to greet us. He looked familiar.

Aubrey Keener, formerly of Tyler, Texas, had moved to Little Cayman about a year previously with his wife, and they built the home for themselves and friends. There were four apartments with the house, which they rented to tourists.

The extraordinary thing about the Keener's home was not the house itself, but the furnishings. Almost everything in the place had been hand-made by them on Little Cayman.

He showed me an old wooden, hand-carved plaque about two feet wide a little more than a foot deep. It was an African man working in a village with an oar or some other type of instrument.

"I've been offered $500 for it and no one even knows what it is," Keener said. "It just drifted in from the ocean one day."

I wondered about his decision to leave Texas and build in this

229

beautiful-but-isolated spot.

"Any regrets?" I asked as we returned to the truck.

"By God, no!' he said. "I'm gonna be buried right behind that stump there," he pointed to the remnants. "I salvaged it from the northern shore. It was probably dumped there by the '32 Hurricane."

We waved as we drove away and he waved back and shouted, "We enjoyed your party last night!"

That's where I saw them, I thought.

"What's next?" I asked our driver.

"I'm going to take you to the Good Ship Lollypop while I do some shopping," she said.

Soon, she had stopped behind the beach's sandy ridge. Over the top, I could see the mast of a large ship. Naturally, I had to see it up close.

"That's it," she said. "Go on over by yourself for a visit while we drive into town. It's just down the road. I'll wait for you there."

As I crossed the ridge, I could see a large barge pulled up to the beach with its huge front ramp resting on the sand. It was a sea-going barge, manufactured to transport tanks and trucks. It had a pilothouse and cabin for its crew when it was at sea. It appeared oddly out of place on the deserted beach.

I walked to the barge and noticed its name was "Cleo," not "Lollypop." That was just a local term.

The ship appeared deserted but well anchored to the beach. I walked into the open bay and shouted.

There was nothing but silence and no one in sight on the beach, so I climbed to the pilothouse. There were some charts and assorted food goods, but not much else. Behind the wheel there was a cot for sleeping. It was unmade and rumpled.

Leaving the empty barge, I started walking toward the town.

After a few minutes, I came to an old cemetery and paused for a closer look at some of the headstones: Hyman Bodden Sr., 1830-1899; Eunice C. Scott, 1893-1899; John Scott, 1828-1899...So many of those buried had died in 1899 I wondered what terrible catastrophe had occurred that fearful year.

I walked on, admiring the solitude - until I heard my name shouted:

"Dick, come here!"

Surprised, I walked toward a modern house in a break in the heavy brush. There were several locals on the porch. They had all attended my party and wanted to welcome me again to Little Cayman. It was early, but they were enjoying a rum punch and I accepted one. It was pink, icy, sweet with pineapple and rum, and delicious.

Among them was an older man, about 60, who told me he had been born on Little Cayman.

I asked him about the changes on the island.

"When I was born, there were 140 people here and the island was worth something," he said. "There were big coconut plantations all over the island, and schooners. We had about 20 schooners. Now, the equipment is gone, the people are gone, and we can't catch no more turtles…"

I thanked my new friends and walked on toward "town," not knowing what to expect. After only a few steps I was in downtown Blossom Village. At the center of downtown was a telephone booth. There were one or two other structures close by; one of them a small grocery store.

Two men were intently engaged around the telephone booth.

"We have two telephones," one of the men told me without looking up.

If there were two, I wondered where the other telephone was. There was no phone at the most obvious place, the Southern Cross Club.

"When one of them gets full, we switch it to an empty one," one of the workers volunteered without my prompting.

So, he meant there were two telephones, not two locations. When one filled up with coins, they replace it. I didn't ask them why they didn't just empty it.

Alison and Stephen ran up, followed by Martha.

"This is the kind of "city" I'd love to call home," she said. "I wonder if all the residents came downtown at the same time if they'd have a traffic jam."

"I'm not sure how many cars you have to have to call it a jam," I said. "I doubt there's a half dozen on the whole island."

A small gasoline engine chugged nearby. It was on a portable generator charging the battery for the telephone.

"Sometimes it works; sometimes it doesn't," one of the workers shrugged.

"We hope Cayman Airlines will give us a short-wave radio soon," said Diane, who had walked over to join us. "The only way we know the plane is coming in is when we hear the engines," she said.

I saw the "Lollypop," I said, "but there was no one around. It was just sitting there. Strange…"

"Oh, not for Little Cayman," she said. "Come on, I'll take you to meet the owner."

As we drove off, both workmen stood up and waved. One of them shouted something.

"What did he say? I couldn't hear," I told Diane.

"He said they enjoyed your party," she said.

We were driving in the general direction of the airport. That feeling was reinforced when we pulled up in front of a large aircraft hangar.

But it wasn't close to any runway, nor was any aircraft close by.

"I want you guys to meet Mr. Friend," Diane said. "He's one of our most interesting residents, and one of our most valuable."

With that, we walked up to the hangar, opened a door near the huge sliding doors and entered.

Extraordinary, astonishing objects littered the tables, the floor and hung from the ceiling. Every recess of the gigantic building was crammed with mechanical relics. There was everything, except for an airplane—and there might have been one or two of those if you had time to poke through all of the materials.

It was as if the world's richest tinkerer had gathered all of his treasured bits and pieces and brought them to a far corner where he could spend his time with them in private, blissful isolation. That wasn't far off the mark.

John Friend could have been 60, or 70, I couldn't tell. Looking like a blend of Bogart and Randolph Scott, he appeared while we were exploring and was delighted to see Diane and to meet us. I was a little embarrassed at being discovered inside his private building, but he didn't care. I asked him the purpose of the contents.

"I'm an executive whose corporation was sold to another corporation," he said. "Consequently I had some spare time, so I'm here for a vacation."

I managed to drag out of him that he was "an electrical engineer, a mechanical engineer, with a splattering of naval architecture mixed in…" And, he was from Milwaukee.

"I own the barge, Cleo, and lease her to people, and the government, to lighter freight from island steamers," he said. "But, I don't think she's long for Little Cayman. There's not enough work for her here."

I wanted to know much more about this peculiar character, but Diane informed us it was time to head back to the club for dinner. I was surprised that the day had gone so fast. We drove past Cleo on the way back.

"He brought all of this material down here from the states for his hangar," Diane said. "He just enjoys playing around with his ship and all of his equipment. He's installed electric lines all across the island. A lot of the homes have electric lights now. He's some kind of genius, I think."

I asked what she knew about his company and his background.

"All I know is that he's one of the richest men in Cayman and maybe the United States," she said. "I don't know exactly what he sold but I've been told his company made diesel engines for ships. It was a huge company. The biggest diesel engine maker. Still is."

"Was he at my party?" I asked.

"I think I danced with him," she said.

"If I had known who he was I'd have made sure I danced with him," Martha piped in. "Maybe I could have married him."

"Make up your mind," I said, "You said the same about Mitch Miller."

"He turned out to be too short in person," she said. "But he was cute."

Dinner that evening was quieter and it was early to bed for all of us. I still hoped to get to the tiny Owen Island for some fresh, grilled-on-the-beach sea bass.

The May day dawned clear and bright, but the Northwester had brought unseasonably cool temperatures and it was too chilly to swim or walk to the tiny island.

So, we again climbed aboard the old truck. We were going around the western end of the island. I wanted to see the vacation home of actor Burgess Meredith.

Our first stop, however, was on the Salt Rocks, an area where the deep sea comes right up to the rocky shoreline. Diane told me this was the area where ships used to load phosphate from the old mine, now abandoned about 100 years.

"Where is it?" I asked Diane.

"I've been told it's back in the bush. No one goes there any more."

"I'd like to go," I said.

Before she had time to answer, we had turned around the western tip and there was a cleared space with a neat white house all alone on the bluff overlooking the sea. The place looked brand new.

Again, the resident looked familiar. Otto Reiner was a former vice president of Sterling Drug Company, which makes Bayer Aspirin. He was a huge man, with thick gray hair, good-looking in a craggy sort of way, and very friendly.

A former tackle with the University of Tampa back in the 1930s, Otto had been the star of a series of television commercials produced by his company. He was "The Tough Guy With A Cold" who took Bayer aspirin for comfort. I remembered it.

Otto and his wife Barbara had turned their backs on the U.S., preferring to live in the isolation of Little Cayman. Like the Keeners, they had built everything inside the house, even the furniture, by themselves.

Otto owned quite a bit of property around his house. He had cleared several acres north of his home down to the shore, where the sea was rough because of the rocks. "Great bone fishing down there," he said, inviting me to come back during the season.

Otto showed me a small boat that had washed ashore at his doorstep and he had bought it at a public auction. It was called Pilon, about 10 feet long and Cuban made.

"You can see where it was hastily altered for two sets of oars," Otto said, somewhat sadly. "Strange for such a small boat. Someone had planned a long trip."   \

To Cayman, I thought, or Jamaica...and freedom.

"I guess they didn't make it," Otto said.

As we looked at the boat, another resident joined us. He was Torrey Tatum, who lived on the Brac and had some business to conduct with Otto.

Torrey said great mahogany forests once covered Little Cayman.

The Great Storm knocked most of them down, he said, but there are still hundreds growing in the interior of the island.

"They are huge," he said. "Only one has ever been logged and brought out. It was used to 'timber up' a cabin cruiser for the Bacardi (rum) family of Cuba in the 1930s. One tree did the whole job."

Burgess Meredith's home was a disappointment. I thought it would be a mansion in the wilderness. But it was only a small, green house with a large screened-in porch.

Martha and Diane walked off along the shore with the kids, beachcombing. I was content sitting in the back of the truck looking out over the Caribbean and enjoying the quiet. Except for the little sandy road, the place probably hadn't changed in millennia except for what The Great Storm had readjusted.

"All along the shore down there are millions and millions of tiny iron filings," Martha said.

"They must have come from a shipwreck," Diane said, "but I've never heard of one this far up here."

We passed Bloody Bay where the English wiped out a band of Spanish privateers in the old pirate days. I would have loved more time to explore the area, looking for more relics.

The next morning brought the unhappy realization that I would go back to George Town late that afternoon.

44

THOSE PIRATES OF THE CARIBBEAN

Little Cayman and its isolation gave us time to reflect.

Martha and I had accepted the daily grind at the newspaper but we were concerned about our two youngsters. We had no time to discuss the future of Alison and Stephen before we left the United States and were afraid they would shrivel into turnip-truck cargo without their peers and Captain Kangaroo. We were wrong. They blossomed.

We learned television is a curse. Never did our children or we miss the tube. We read every night and so did our children. We talked. We enjoyed our meals together. We played in the sun. They thrived. Stephen, a hyperactive child, flourished in Cayman; his behavior modified and his schoolwork improved.

We ate fresh vegetables and fish. We had fresh, low-cal, low-fat turtle meat to eat with rice and beans and fried plantains.

On the downside, Martha and I consumed enormous quantities of alcohol. There was hardly a night that passed when we didn't sit outside, slurp rum punch and watch the kids play in the yard as the sun set over the ocean in front of our house. We had one music tape. It was by Gordon Lightfoot and we played it night after night. His rendition of "Island Goodbye" became our theme song.

During those long, alcohol-sodden evenings, it was easy to look beyond the front yard and imagine what the view would have presented 50, 100 or even 500 years ago. We wanted to know more about our new home. We read plenty of lore and legend, but there wasn't much accurate information available. In my attempts to teach our little family about our home, I discovered a worn copy of what is probably the first history book about The Cayman Islands in the local library. It was written by an Englishman who had headed the government around the turn of the century. The author was less than impressed with the country.

In his study, Notes on the History of The Cayman Islands, George Hirst chides the Caymanians for not writing down their own history: "Parish churches in England scrupulously cared for family and property records," he says. "In The Cayman Islands, this research fodder was skimpy or completely unavailable.

"A few families here and there kept records," he writes, "but many valuable diaries have been lost in the hurricanes and other storms for which the Carribean (sic) Sea is so renowned."

One thing remained unchanged from the time Hirst wrote his book until my arrival 75 years later: The attitude of the typical British colonial civil servant.

Hirst, who published his history in 1909, was at the time the Administrator. Whereas my infamous banking article allegedly insulted the British, his portrayal of the Caymanians was condescending, chauvinistic and anti-American.

"This history, I hope, is published on the verge of a new era which I have no shadow of a doubt will ere long prove that Caymanians still carry in their veins the blood of the stolid, persevering Briton, who from nothing has built up the greatest Empire this world has ever known, and who means to keep it.

"Let Caymanians now enter with their hearts and bodies into this laudable object, let them vie with one another in building up this Dependency and thus help in building up this Great Empire. Let it be that when this history has to be written afresh, or revised at least, the name of one Caymanian will be introduced as a patriot of whom the British Empire throughout the world will have occasion to honor and hold up to the rest of the world with pride. If Corsica could give to France an epoch maker, cannot the Caymans do the same for the British Empire?

"The Tendency of the present day however is to denounce the British nation and scorn the patrimony one ought to be thankful for. The young men of Cayman are too fond of renouncing Britain and embracing citizenship of one of the numerous modern republics the American Continent is so notorious for.

"Whether any of them are of any more credit to the republic of their selection than they were to the British Nation has not so far been proved. We hope, should another edition of this history ever be published, that this stain on the loyalty and patriotism of the Caymanian will have been wiped out and redeemed by the uprising of a native of Cayman either as a great soldier, sailor, patriot, or in some other capacity useful to his nation at large."

I'm not sure why the Cayman's first historian had his knickers in such a twist about the local failure to produce a Napoleon, or why fleeing to America was such a stain on loyalty and patriotism. For his sake, it is best that he is long dead, since the Caymans failed to produce such a hero and the British Empire has failed to maintain its glorious momentum.

Before I winged over the blue Caribbean in 1971 on my first flight to the capital city, George Town, I was, like most Americans, oblivious to the fact that the British, and almost everyone else, did not worship America with the fervor that I thought they did.

45

YO HO HO, AND A BOTTLE OF BLOOD

There is a fine line between pirate and privateer, depending on your nationality.

If an Englishman had a stout sailing ship in the 16th century, a crew of rowdies, cannons, little conscience, and a need for hard cash and barrels of grog, he could sign as a privateer to attack Spanish merchant ships. The successful crew could claim a portion of captured loot as payment.

Today, it might be compared to allowing rednecks in Georgia, Mississippi, Alabama, South Carolina and Panhandle Florida to team up with their hunting clubs, militia units and bowling buddies to roar 90 miles from Key West to Havana in their 1,000 horsepower Cigarette powerboats and pillage the country with the full support and encouragement of the American flag.

I suspect privateering in the early Caribbean was a popular avocation as well as a profession. Privateering must seem alien to contemporary Americans, but in reality it was seriously suggested in 1962 when the Russians were constructing offensive missile sites in Communist Cuba.

In an essay in LIFE, Senior Editor John Dille suggested several avenues the U.S. government might take to stop the Soviets from transporting supplies to Cuba. Along with full and partial blockades, he said, "Another option would be to outfit old-fashioned 'privateers' to go after the Russian shipments in the fashion of John Paul Jones. This is a real long shot, but it has the merit of lessening the chances of international combat."

Following the terrorist attack on the Twin Towers in 2001, columnist Nikolas K. Gvosdev, a senior fellow for strategic studies at The Nixon Center, a bipartisan Washington, D.C. think tank, wrote that the U.S. government should "revisit the power granted to it by Article I, Section 8, of the U.S. Constitution to 'grant letters of marque and reprisal, and make rules concerning captures on land and water.'

"In other words, it is time to consider reviving privateering for 21st century conditions," Gvosdev wrote.

Another term was "buccaneer," which originated from the burning of green branches to smoke meat. In French, boucanier means "smokers of meat." Outlaws used to rustle cows in Haiti and sell their smoked meats to passing ships.

All the carnage and cooking mattered little to The Cayman Islands until 1655 when the first mention since Columbus was recorded by Henry Whistler, the sailing master of Admiral Penn's British Flagship, The Swiftsure.

On June 26, Whistler scribbled in the ship's log: "...in the afternoon we brought it to bear North, and within hauling a more Northerly course did intend to touch at the Kie of Manus to get some turtle for our sick people..."

How "The Cayman Islands" grew from "Kie of Manus" is a lengthy construction with few hard historical bricks for support. Suffice to say, it did, but no one can say irrefutably why or even what it means. There's another school that believes the name Cayman evolved from the caimans (crocodiles) that were once prolific there.

The significance of Whistler's comment is that The Cayman Islands were an important turtle fishery and that is presumably the only reason it was first inhabited.

In England during this era the British Parliamentarians had the good sense to topple the monarchy with a ferocious civil war.

Oliver Cromwell, a populist and possibly one of my ancestors, took over the government. A major leg of Cromwell's foreign policy was to snatch the whole West Indies and its reputed mountains of gold and silver. As it turned out there were mostly mountains of guano and precious little gold. But there was land.

Santo Domingo, founded by Columbus's brother Bartholomew in 1496, was the oldest continuously inhabited European community in the Western Hemisphere. It was a possession of the hated Spanish, as well as the center of the new Western civilization. It even had its own university, founded in 1538. Whoever possessed Santo Domingo, Cromwell reckoned, owned the West.

To grab Santo Domingo, he dispatched a mighty armada commanded by two admirals—Sir Robert Venables and Admiral Penn—who stormed ashore following a naval bombardment. But they were sternly rebuffed.

In those times, expeditions against the Spanish were financed in part by wealthy civilians who were repaid from the spoils. Today, it would be like Home Depot and Wal-Mart financing Operation Desert Storm for a share of the oil revenue. Soldiers, even lowly privates, could expect a handsome cut.

Embarrassed by their failure at Santo Domingo, Admirals Penn and Venables were dejectedly sailing home. They looked at their map for a face-saving opportunity. They knew their shareholders were going to be pissed.

There were a number of possibilities. There were the useless Caymans, turtle-rich and still unclaimed by any of the major powers; Cartegenia in Central America, and Hispaniola. What to do?

Cartegenia, with treasures to loot, was more heavily defended by the Spanish than Santo Domingo. Hispaniola—modern day Haiti and the Dominican Republic—was a French possession.

And there was Jamaica.

Jamaica had some agriculture. There was mining potential in the mountains, and, best of all, it was a great strategic location. Jamaica was in the middle of the Caribbean. It would make a magnificent midway naval base from which to plunder.

Best of all, it was lightly defended.

On May 10, 1655, the discomfited British fleet dropped anchor in Kingston harbor, fired a cannon and demanded surrender. The 200 Spanish soldiers defending the country's 1,500 settlers and their 3,000 black slaves felt discretion was the better part of valor and tossed in the towel.

When it learned of the loss, the Spanish government was furious but unable to mount any counterattack before the Treaty of Madrid in 1670 ended hostilities between the two nations.

The enraged Spanish citizens, seething over the cowardly capitulation by their soldiers, prayed for the destruction of the English base in Kingston harbor, Port Royal. Their prayers would be answered by the horrific earthquake and resulting tidal wave which swallowed Port Royal in 1692, drowning more than 2,000. Even today underwater archaeologists explore the ruins of the sunken city, marveling morbidly at the destruction.

Admiral Penn, in appreciation for his military service, was granted a huge tract of land in the American Colonies. His ambitious son, William, had a natural flair for real estate promotion and developed a huge housing project which he dubbed Pennsylvania. Sales were splendid.

With the British in control of Jamaica for the next 300 years, the stage was set for the slow development of The Cayman Islands. Many British invaders were ordered to remain in Jamaica to defend the newly captured country. The occupation force included a dozen small ships and a garrison of 6,000 men. History again teases us with too few facts,

240

but it is very likely that the invasion force of 1655 contained within it the first residents of The Cayman Islands.

If this is true, they were the founding fathers from hell. Sir Robert Venables described the men left behind as, "the dregs of the British Isles and Barbados...the most profane, debauched persons we ever saw..."

Among them was almost certainly the son of a farmer, a young Welshman about 20 years of age named Henry Morgan. No one knows what drove Henry to the West Indies, but he would become the most intriguing privateer of the epoch. His bloodthirsty rampages against the Spanish are renowned. There's little doubt he frequented the Caymans, possibly even operated from there for a while, although a lot of conjecture has to be applied.

Morgan's life shows how truth can be more imaginative than fiction. It provided fodder for dozens of novels and movie exploits. His daring escapades earned him the title of Chief Buccaneer of Tortugas, a rocky island and legitimate pirate stronghold roughly the same size as Grand Cayman a few miles northwest of Haiti.

Because Columbus had called The Cayman Islands "Las Tortugas" when he spotted them, I suspect contemporary Caymanians have confused the two different places, especially when they wanted to strengthen the image of Cayman as a lair of pirates.

On January 23, 1674, Morgan the pirate became Sir Henry Morgan, and was appointed lieutenant Governor of Jamaica. He served briefly as Governor. That also made him Governor of the swamp that would become The Cayman Islands.

Morgan's two uncles were prominent English soldiers. One was a major general under George Monck, a powerful Cromwell crony who proved to be two-faced. Monck turned against the Parliamentarians who had overthrown the Crown and wasted King Charles I, then helped place his son, the exiled Charles II, on the throne.

An appreciative King Charles II made Monck the Duke of Albemarle, and the two Morgans (and their spirited nephew Henry) had a friend in very high places.

There's no doubt Henry Morgan was an intrepid, dauntless, dynamic individual, but it never hurt to be chummy with the king. Unfortunately, history claims Morgan indulged too much in the extravagances of the good life and died of "debauchery" on August 25, 1688 at the age of 53.

Morgan's grave is lost somewhere on the floor of Kingston Harbor. When the earthquake destroyed Port Royal, it dragged the seaside grave where he was buried into the depths.

46

BEATING THE BUSHES FOR EVIDENCE,
UNDERSTANDING

Diane was busy my final day on Little Cayman, but Andy, of party band fame, volunteered to drive me around to visit a few of the oldest residents and indulge me in a quick trip to try to locate an old mine.

We were near the old salt docks where they once loaded the phosphate.

"Can we get there from here?" I asked Andy.

"Maybe," he said, and I was overjoyed that we were at least going to make the attempt. Andy pulled over to the remnants of an old road leading back into the brush.

"This is where the rails came out," he said.

They hauled the phosphate out to the sea on rail carts, beginning in 1883. A few pieces of the track have shown up as bar rails at the Southern Cross Club and in private homes.

Excavations began in George Town using Jamaican labor. The following year a group of investors from Baltimore formed the "Carib Guano Company" and discovered the rich deposits on Little Cayman. They worked the mine seven years and there was employment for everyone who wanted work.

Andy and I followed the old road through the brush. It looked too easy. It was. The trail played out after a mile or so. There was no sign of a track but we found a mound of "something."

"Phosphate," Andy said. "This is where they used to dump it."

"I'll find it when I have some time and the next time you're here we'll come back," he said.

I nodded dejectedly. I was falling in love with the little isle and everything tangible that I could grab on to strengthened my connection with it. There was also something about finding a century-old mine and walking in the tracks of those men who labored there so long ago.

It was obvious that few people, if any, had been here for the better part of a century. I also had a secret agenda that I had not spoken about. I wanted to find a "soccer field" back in the brush.

No official record of inhabitation of the islands by the earlier Indians has ever been documented. The peaceful Arawak were fishermen, not hunters. Huge mounds of conch shells mark their historical sites and they raised their crops in a large, reinforced mound called a conuco. They also played a game similar to soccer. There were references to stone fields created for this sport. Would there be any evidence of these after hundreds of years?

We were getting into the truck at the main road when Andy suddenly said, "Wait a minute. I want to check something out."

And there it was, another trail. Even after a century, this trail was possible to follow. There was no doubt we were on the right track. Where else could it go? Soon, Andy began to point to large hollows in the stony ground along the trail.

"That's where they scooped it out," he said. Here, sweating workers dug out the phosphate-laden soil from the rocks and carried it in baskets to the dumping ground. From there it was loaded into the small rail carts for the trip to the dock at Salt Rocks, a quarter mile or so away.

There were wild flowers growing everywhere. Multicolored birds—parrots, doves, bull finches, flycatchers and woodpeckers—chirped angrily at our intrusion. Andy pointed out dozens of wild orchids, lovely hangers-on which attach themselves in abundance to larger trees.

If you didn't know what we looking for, you would have missed it. I would have without Andy. There was a large mound of earth by the trail. The soil had a reddish tint to it and was covered with grass.

"That's the main dump," Andy said. He spotted a piece of rusted rail sticking out of the brush. It's the only relic we found.

"It looks like the men have just walked away," Andy said.

They walked away when deposits of phosphate were found in Florida about 1892. The Carib Guano Company went broke and was abandoned to its creditors.

No, it wasn't much of a mine but I couldn't have been more thrilled if we had found The Lost Dutchman. A century ago, it would have been a busy place. Now, it was just a few holes in the brush guarded by angry, multicolored birds and pastel orchids.

I took several short side trips into the brush looking for long lost Indian signs. I found several stacks of long-abandoned conch shells, but who's to say how old they were. There were a few mounds of earth, but here again, they could have been natural. As for the soccer field, there was no trace. Of course 400 hundred years of time and tide could have easily covered them up. I wanted to look longer, but time was running out.

Back at the club, I told Martha of my mine discovery.

"So, what's this guano?" she asked. "Some kind of jewel?"

Sarcasm was Martha's favorite form of humor when she was not happy with me. It was only months later that she told me she thought my Little Cayman correspondent was paying too much attention to the editor.

"Well, guano is a kind of crap used in fertilizers," I said.

"You spent all morning of your last day wandering around in the jungle looking for shit?" she said.

"It was booby guano," I said.

"Little Cayman is one of the largest breeding colonies in the Caribbean for the red-footed booby bird," I said, repeating what I had learned.

"So you found a red-footed, booby birdshit mine," she said.

"An 'abandoned, long-lost,' red-footed, booby bird crap mine," I corrected her.

"Your mother will be proud," she said.

Actually, I was as happy as Columbus must have been when he first spotted this place hundreds of years ago.

"I met someone else you might find interesting," I said.

"Who?" she asked.

"I talked to a man who was aboard the Balboa when she sank. Not only was he aboard her, he was the bosun!"

Up until that time, the Balboa was the most famous shipwreck in The Cayman Islands. Even more famous than the highly-suspect Wreck of the 10 Sails.

The Balboa sank right off George Town harbor and even today the most inexperienced snorkeler can splash into the harbor and gaze down at the bones of the steel hulk 60 to 70 feet below.

We had done it half a dozen times. We dropped into the harbor from the ironshore near the Lobster Pot restaurant and paddled a few hundred yards straight and there she lay. She was also the popular target for divers. A few hardy souls, like legendary local diver Tom Hubble who owned the ancient Pedro's Castle, could free dive all the way down to touch her. Hubble was a reclusive man I had heard a lot about, but had not been able to meet. He had a reputation for not being very friendly.

Andy had taken me by the bosun's house on the way back in from the mine. It was down another trail on the north side of the island. We drove to a small, frame house and the man's wife came out to greet us, smiling.

"Where's Captain Woody?" Andy asked.

"He's working in his garden," she said, pointing to yet another trail.

"Just past the half-way tree," she added.

As we trudged along, the trail became rougher and rougher. Once more I began looking for Indian signs.

I wondered how an 80-year-old man managed this walk to tend his garden every day. And the truth was we had hardly started.

"Where is the half-way tree she was talking about?" I asked Andy.

"Its half way there," he said, matter-of-factly.

Andy stopped ahead of me and surveyed the brush. Then, he walked off into it while I stayed put. I looked around in case this was the halfway tree but there were no particularly impressive trees. Then, Andy was back.

"I found him," he said. "Follow me."

Captain Woody was standing in a small clearing. In his hand was an ancient hoe. He wore an old, tattered straw hat and faded, dirty overalls over an equally old, faded blue cotton shirt. His hair under the hat was silver and his face tanned and lined by thousands of days outside, both ashore and at sea. We shook hands and I introduced myself, half expecting him to tell me he had enjoyed my party.

"Sit down," he said, more of a command than an invitation and I looked around for something to sit on. But he plopped down on the dirt and there was nothing to do but the same.

"Will you tell me a little about the Balboa? And the Great Storm?"

He studied the question. And as he did, he reached in his pocket for a sack of tobacco. He shook some of it on a piece of paper he had torn from a brown paper sack, rolled it up, licked it, and then fired it up with a silver Zippo.

"We'd been to Port Arthur," he said. "You know where that is?"

"Captain, that's where I lived before I came down here," I said.

He smiled and offered me a smoke. I sensed I had established a base for camaraderie.

I was trying to quit, but I didn't want to offend him. I clumsily tore off a patch of paper sack and held it out. He dumped tobacco from a small cloth sack in his pocket onto the paper and I rolled it into a stumpy cigarette and stuck it in my mouth. He flicked the Zippo and I took a deep drag.

"I grew this myself," he said proudly. "It's real tobacco, just like the Indians used to grow here."

Not certain he was aware of it, I told him the Arawaks cultivated tobacco.

"I've seen wild tobacco plants way back in the brush," he said.

"From Indians?" I asked.

"Nobody knows where it came from," he said.

"Young man like you shouldn't be smoking," he told me. "Tobacco will surely kill you."

"I'll quit soon," I said. "Tell me about the Balboa."

"We left Port Arthur and went to Pensacola for lumber. We headed out for Jamaica with lumber and Texas products."

I looked at Andy's face. He was listening as intently as I was. He told me later he had never heard the story before.

"I was bosun. She had 180 feet of straight deck and we ploughed right into the storm."

Things were violent, he said, but the small steamer continued to make headway and they thought they might be able to pound through the storm to safety in Jamaica.

"Then her engines started giving out," he said. "The ship was too heavy for her engines in that kind of weather." He paused, and looked out distantly to the empty sea, lost for a moment in the memory of that raging ocean of many years ago.

"We decided the best thing we could do was to run for Grand Cayman, so we turned her and made it to George Town harbor. I let out two anchors, each one weighing 8,888 pounds—one of them 60 fathoms and the other 75 fathoms.

"That was all we could do. We all made it to shore except for one man: The Donkeyman—a big, black Jamaican who, like a fool, decided to try to ride it out."

I asked what a donkey man was.

"There's a little engine on deck called the donkey engine, a winch," he said. "This man—Edwards I think his name was—ran that little engine when we loaded and unloaded things."

"So he was killed?" I asked.

"When we went ashore the wind was out of the southeast," he said. "It changed to the northwest that night and it was so strong the Balboa started bouncing in the waves. Even with the bottom 60 feet below she rose and fell so much she struck the coral with her hull and busted open. She was doomed." Another biami casualty, I thought silently.

"And Donkeyman?" I asked.

"When the sea broke over her it washed Donkeyman off the deck, but it also pushed a lot of the lumber we were carrying overboard. Donkeyman fell on the flotsam and it washed ashore. All he got was some bumps and bruises. He went back home to Jamaica and I never saw him again."

After a half hour visit we bid our good-byes and started back down the trail. I hated to abandon this peaceful spot. It was like walking away from a living history book. When I looked back he was down on his knees in the dirt again, pushing earth back and forth around his sweet potato plants, a brown-paper-bag cigarette dangling from his lips.

246

As Andy and I walked back to the truck I asked him what he thought it would have been like here on Little Cayman during The Great Storm.

On Little Cayman, or on Cayman Brac, you don't have to explain which storm you are talking about. Everyone knows the hurricane of 1932 was The Great One.

"We wouldn't want to be here," Andy said simply.

I told him I had talked to Joseph Grizzell, who had been born on Little Cayman and he had told me he understood the entire island was under water except for one little spot.

"Do you know where that little spot is?" I asked Andy.

"I guess you want to go there?" he said. He was smiling.

"I sure would like to if there's time, Andy," I said. "Can we?"

"I'm not sure where it is," he said. "It's not like there's a hill or something on Little Cayman."

More than 100 had perished on Cayman Brac, the second largest of the Cayman archipelago, five miles away. The coast on the southern side of the island backs up against the brac.

Most of the people on Cayman Brac in 1932 built their homes on the narrow coast that backs up against that bluff. It is easy to picture what happened when that mother-of-all-hurricanes roared out of the blackness. Those who died were trapped against the bluff and drowned in the huge tidal flow.

There are accessible caves all along the side of the bluff and they proved a safe haven for those lucky enough to recognize and understand what peril was approaching.

"I wonder how many people lived here that night." I asked Andy. "There's no bluff to climb on Little Cayman."

"I want you to meet someone else," Andy said, pulling up to a new house at the edge of tiny Blossom Village.

Mrs. Ella Scott had heard us drive up and stepped out on to her small porch. I was immediately taken by her friendly, bright, intelligent eyes. She had that rare gift of grace and beauty in her deeply lined face that made her stunning, even though she was well into her 80s.

"Miss Ella," Andy said to her, "this fellow wants to know about The Storm."

She grinned and invited us into her small, neat living room.

"We knew it was coming," she said, "but we didn't know it would be so bad."

Her father owned a barometer and the family watched it fall, fall, fall, all afternoon long.

"It was November 9th, 1932," she said. "The first sea struck our home at 5 p.m. It didn't do any damage and the wind really wasn't so bad. We weren't that frightened, yet."

It grew darker. The second big wave brought an almond tree limb with it.

"It knocked a hole in our house," she said. "Water was coming in like someone was throwing it out of a bucket. We began to be afraid.

"Our family and friends gathered 'round and we started singing, 'Jesus, Save Your Pilot Me; Over Life's Tempestuous Sea'..."

The storm subsided the next day. Reefs offshore from the tiny island broke much of the force and saved the residents. She told us the hurricane was the second one that had devastated the coconut trees, and added to the flight of young men and women away from the island.

Who knows whether it was the 1912 hurricane, or The Great Storm that started the depopulation of Little Cayman.

With the young men and women leaving, the population dropped to a handful and the government decided to close the island and move everyone to the Brac.

Captain Woody told me earlier that day that everyone had been ordered to move to the Brac. "The government has never done anything for this island," he said. A few families stayed on, barely making it.

The birds chirped, the sand fleas rejoiced, the sun rose and set, a few crops grew and time passed. It was hard to imagine the life those hardy souls lived.

One day Captain Woody looked up and saw a sailing ship coming in. "It was the Neptune," he said, a yacht belonging to Dr. Logan Robertson. It was in the early 1960s and Captain Woody ended up building the Southern Cross Club for the entrepreneurial Dr. Robertson.

More time passed and Dr. Robertson looked up Captain Woody again.

"Captain Woody, we need an airport here," Dr. Robertson said.

"I've never seen one," Captain Woody said.

"Well, I still think you can build one," Dr. Robertson said. And Woody did.

Unbelievably, no one died on Little Cayman during The Great Storm, according to Miss Ella. With her astonishing memory she began naming off everyone who had been on the island that terrible night. She knew all of them.

"I've heard that there was only one spot above water that night," I said.

She nodded and pointed across the street toward a small church. "Everyone gathered right there," she said.

It was the only place where the water didn't cover the land.

After thanking her, I asked Andy if he would wait a second while I walked over to the church.

It didn't seem any higher than the surrounding real estate. But on a frightful night in November of 1932, it had been a haven for 71 souls, all of them named and remembered by Miss Ella. It was a special place. Possibly, a miraculous place where Little Cayman's pilots were saved from the tempestuous sea.

Now, it was time to return to reality.

I walked down from The Southern Cross Club to the beach, where I had looked up into the heavens and found my starry mentor. And there was another reason I wanted to remember the spot.

Had I been standing here in 1669, I would have seen a Spanish privateer named Manuel Rivero Pardal sail outside the reef with a fleet of five ships. He was allegedly looking for a fight with Henry Morgan, who had been sacking Spanish vessels. He spotted the Jamaican vessel Hopewell, whose captain Samuel Hutchison was entertaining several other captains, including one Captain Airy, referred to by Hutchinson as "Governor of The Cayman Islands." After abandoning the Hopewell when they saw the Spanish ships, the captains fled into the trees, along with the "residents" of some 20 fishing huts that housed turtle hunters.

Captain Pardal took several hundred soldiers ashore and scoured the woods looking for the group, but could not find them in the swamps. I'll use conjecture since the episode is hand-me-down history, but it goes, as Pardal was leaving, the group came out of the woods and began shouting insults. Pardal was taking the Hopewell as a prize along with all the turtling vessels as he could find.

Once back in Jamaica, he pinned a message to a tree bragging of his Cayman exploits and challenged Henry Morgan to a hand-to-hand fight. Morgan had already left the area to invade Panama, and the two never met. The turtling huts on Little Cayman, recorded in the sketchy reports of the battle, are used as proof of the first settlement in The Cayman Islands.

*   *   *

As the DC-3 roared into the headwind and lifted into the air on the way back to reality, I looked a final time at the small terminal dropping away beneath us bearing the name: "Edward Bodden Airfield."

Little Cayman history will remember Edward Bodden as the legendary son of the soil who built the club and—without ever having seen one in his life—the airport.

I remember him warmly as Captain Woody, a wise, kindly, old gentleman who gave me a home-grown tobacco cigarette rolled from a torn brown paper bag on a lazy afternoon during a fascinating history lesson in the middle of a sweet-potato patch on a small pebble in the middle of the deep, blue sea.

And, even if it was only petrified bird shit, I found the lost mine.

47

IF THAT'S THE SUN GOING DOWN,
THE DAY MIGHT BE OVER

In my last month with the newspaper—although I was unaware of that impending development—I prepared a series of editorials in which I planned to lay out my proposals for the guaranteed prosperity for Cayman. In this lofty series, I wanted to plead, if necessary, with the government to initiate steps to protect the fragile environment.

When the assembly approved an appropriation of $100,000 for a Natural Resources Study in 1974, my editorial hoped the survey would be the impetus to end "the usual procrastination of our Assemblymen as regards our natural resources.

"The survey will say we are destroying our coral, our beaches, our conch, our lobster, etc. We know this now, do we not? Yet, what has been done? Nothing! In this past assembly, a motion was put forward calling for more restrictions on the taking of beach sand. It was not passed!

"Hopefully, putting the official seal by experts on our problems will instigate the action necessary to prevent further spoiling of the isles."

Vassel Johnson, the financial secretary of the government and one of the kindest government officials I met in Cayman, set the stage for my final opus. In his address to the legislative assembly, he spoke of the evil of inflation that was beginning its reign in the country.

I called inflation a "dragon" in my editorials and indeed it was. Costs had spiraled as much as 50 percent in the past two years. Hardest hit were the poorer Caymanians. Some food staples had taken jumps of as much as 200 percent in two years.

"The majority of our citizens, without the knowledge to understand what is happening, can only complain and look to government to 'do something' to help," I editorialized.

"Government must find itself in a difficult position. The budget proposed for next year is inflationary...yet with our rapid expansion and the need for more services, how can government justify a cut in its budget? Over a million dollars will go into salary increases and will probably be followed by 'catch up' raises in the private sector.

"The dilemma is that the raises will most certainly be lost to inflation. Add the fact that our economy is narrow and fragile at best, and we ask, 'How do we cool the spending without slowing our remarkable progress?'"

Part Two of the series explained the inflation factors that were punishing the population: higher prices in the countries which exported to Cayman; the 20 percent duty on import prices which increased as insurance and transportation rates soared, and the demand for the ever-decreasing supplies themselves—not only food supplies but building and construction materials—as Cayman produced nothing internally.

My editorials were in concert with what some officials in the government were reporting to me privately. They were as concerned as I.

The Caymanian Weekly was now regularly reporting the inner politics of the government. We were fortunate, as a news medium, to have various members of the legislative assembly providing "minority reports," which we printed in great detail. We finally were enjoying some respect.

It was dry writing to most of our readers, but I wanted to squeeze every piece of information I could out of the bureaucracy. After three years, I was more comfortable than ever. My articles had the ring of truth and the government began to respond like an old creaky railroad engine discovering a little oil made the wheels turn easier.

Our situation was complex. I thought, and so put it down on paper, that the inflationary rate and resulting erosion of the purchasing power of the Cayman dollar could cost the country its competitive position in attracting tourist and investment dollars.

What were the alternatives and solutions? I thought we should report them and explain how they were being used in other Caribbean countries:

Price and wage controls: Guidelines established by government covering prices, wages, dividends and interest rates, governed by a special board.

Moral suasion: Again, guidelines recommended by government but without force except for an official urge for cooperation. The government would sit down with business to establish the guidelines that would be the best for the country.

Fiscal policy: Gaining control of the budget, and balancing it.

Monetary policy: Manipulation of the country's money supply and general climate of credit for the purpose of achieving desirable results in the national economy.

Government policy: The government would take a cooperative and coordinated approach to achieving its official objective while cooperating with the private sector.

I promised in my concluding editorial, "The ramifications of the various alternatives will be discussed in greater detail in the near future."

The Caymanian Weekly was at last playing an important role for the country's posterity. At least that was my belief. I saw a danger that Cayman was losing its rustic charm and becoming another high-priced, over-developed tourist destination for the world's wealthy elite. I privately believed there were some in the government with the same fear.

I had battled the prejudice against me and was finding my voice at last. At the least, I was being tolerated. Some were even beginning to listen without their habitual resentment. No longer did they demand my resignation.

I was never able to get into the ramifications of alternatives as editorially promised. The final newspaper that abruptly ended the series came just weeks before the Christmas holidays.

We would not publish for two weeks during the Christmas break, and, although I did not yet know it, the very first edition of the New Year would contain the front-page notice that The Cayman Weekly was under new management.

But before then, the annual board meeting was scheduled with much pent-up business on the agenda. I knew it would be crucial, and I was eager to confront it.

I SHOULD HAVE FOUND A HORSE
BEFORE DRIVING THE CART

It is ironic that reporter Little Dicky Gentry failed to read a "nut graph" before the bon voyage from Texas. This is the paragraph reporters use for perspective. For example:

"MEMPHIS (Aug. 16, 1977)—Elvis Presley died today at Graceland from a congenital heart defect. He was only 42.

"(The nut graph) The legendary King of Rock and Roll was born on January 8, 1935 in Tupelo, Mississippi in a tiny frame house built by his father on Old Saltillo Road in East Tupelo, Mississippi. With 33 motion pictures, countless gold records and legendary performances in Las Vegas, Presley was a music-industry icon who will be long remembered by his millions of fans."

My nut graph—call it "exposition" if you like—should have read like that before I ever set foot on the ironshore:

This is not Key West. The Caribbean nations do not get along with each other, and never have. The region has a complex, violent past that reaches beyond Columbus's first footprints in the Bahamas. The plundering nations of Spain, Portugal, England, France, and to a lesser degree, the Dutch, fought each other for the wealth that slavery, sugar, silver and tobacco could provide.

As of 1900, there were no truly independent countries in the Caribbean. Cuba and Puerto Rico were virtual U.S. colonies ceded to the U.S. by the Spanish-American war. Haiti and the Dominican Republic were each occupied by Marines. When the Marines left Haiti in 1934, the first independent nation in the Caribbean settled into a period of rapid decline. The America-approved dictator Rafael Trujillo governed the Dominican Republic until he was assassinated in 1961. In 1937, Trujillo had ordered the murder of every Haitian living in his country. He killed about 35,000. Even after he died the country remained in chaos.

The Marines went back in 1965 to restore order. Ironically, the Dominican Republic has always had difficulty in governing itself. In the 19th century, it wanted to sell itself to America for $1.5 million. President Grant wanted to buy it, but Congress wouldn't allow it.

The Danish sold the Virgin Islands to the U.S. in 1915. Looking back at the nut graph from 2009, I have to say that the United States should have had it all, the entire Caribbean! If they had acted boldly, so much suffering would have been avoided, and think of all the beachfront property that would be available.

We missed several chances to own Cuba. We took it away from Spain, but we gave it back to "the people." There had been an earlier attempt in 1854. The "Ostend Manifesto" wanted the U.S. to seize Cuba from Spain and pay no more than $120 million for it. If Spain refused, we would just take it. Northern newspapers editorialized that the South was behind the purchase because it wanted to extend slavery, and the prospect died.

Jamaica, Trinidad, Barbados, Guiana, Anguilla and The Caymans were part of the British Empire. Aruba, Bonaire, Curacao and Suriname belonged to Holland. The French owned Guadeloupe, Martinique and French Guyana.

In 1935, strikes, riots and civil unrest began in earnest. The sugar workers of St. Kitts and British Guiana struck. A coal strike followed in St. Lucia and St. Vincent. In 1937, the oilfield workers in Trinidad went on strike. Jamaican dockworkers refused to work without a pay raise. It wasn't really about money; it was about life, and the difference between the lives of the colonials and the natives. The British rushed troops to Jamaica and when it was over, 29 were dead and 115 wounded.

In the decade before I stepped ashore in Cayman, many countries declared their independence, assumed some sort of self-governance, or were independent.

One of them is Anguilla, a Crown Colony. It probably set me up for my biggest headache with the Cayman government. The British misunderstood what happened in Anguilla much as they misunderstood the Cayman Island's "march" that brought a British warship cruising back and fourth on the horizon.

Anguilla is a lot like Grand Cayman in many respects.

They are both about the same size, both magnificent and both have chickens roaming free all over the place, even today. Like the Caymans, it is a semi-self-governing Crown Colony. Anguilla is named after the eel, and Cayman is possibly named for crocodiles. In the 21st century, they are both expensive places to live. Anguilla is hard to reach by air; Cayman isn't.

In the late 1960s, the united islands of Saint Kitts, Nevis and Anguilla, were given the right to become self-governing with protection by the Crown. They accepted, but Anguilla wanted to separate from the other two. What happened next depends on which recorded history you care to believe. Then, there's my version: It was another case of lack of proper intelligence and overreaction by the Crown. The police chief from St. Kitts came over to protest what the Anguillans were up to, which was to remain a Crown Colony. Someone fired a pistol. No one was hurt.

The British government, believing a full-scale revolution was under way by the Anguillans, dispatched 315 Red Devil Brigade paratroopers, supported by helicopters, to squelch the "revolution". The Anguillans actually wanted alignment with the Crown. What they did not want was to be aligned with Saint Kitts and Nevis!

So when the troops landed on March 19, 1969, screaming, dancing, hyperactive Anguillans met them. Thank God the Red Devils held their fire. When the celebrants explained the situation to the brigade commander, everyone relaxed and gathered around for a cold beer.

Some historians refer to the incident as "The Bay of Piglets."

All around the Caribbean the common folk were acting out. In October 1966, Jamaica had declared a state of emergency because of rioting in West Kingston. The police got it under control. It happened again in 1968 when university students rioted. In 1969, rioting broke out in Curacao and Dutch troops had to take control.

This was probably happening around the time I was leaving Artesia, N.M. bound for Beaumont, Texas, pulling that huge trailer with our possessions.

In the spring of 1970, riots broke out in Trinidad organized by Black Power leaders. A section of the Army mutinied. The loyalists in the Army and the police put down the mutiny.

The only thing the Americans cared about was a tiny, violent country in Southeast Asia. The only thing I cared about was the pending destruction of my own bowels by ulcerative colitis.

So, with the Caribbean in a foul mood when I arrived, it would have been prudent to wait before I mentioned in one of my initial articles that put the English government into such a rage, "…the Caymanians were tired of taking so much crap from the English."

Oh, if only I had understood that no one anywhere wants any crap from a newcomer, especially any outsider who starts telling them what's wrong with their country. For example, the South wanted the North to stay out of its business before the Civil War. The citizens of Mississippi resented the federal government ordering Ole Miss to enroll my friend James Meredith. Slavery and segregation are terrible things, but they are red herrings in man's natural aversion to foreign hegemony.

Now that I had finally educated myself and was ready to experience amity in my new country, I saw a light at the end of the tunnel. And then I heard the whistle.

49

CHRISTMAS IS A GREAT TIME FOR A PUNCH

At the board meeting, I was not full of Christmas spirit, but ready for war. For months I had been spoiling for a man-to-man confrontation, not with Dr. Roy but Billy Bodden. As a shareholder, he had every right to be present.

I planned to accuse Billy about the original pilfering of company profits with the Carib Ad Agency ploy that I had uncovered my first week in Cayman. And there was the taking of my priceless subscriber lists. I wanted him to explain his role in setting me up for the ill-fated employee walkout, and, more than anything else, I wanted to gloat in front of them all that it had failed, that we were stronger than ever! I now understood the Caymans, and my place here. The future never looked brighter.

I would outline my plans for the future of the company. I maintained a small hope that Dr. Roy might be persuaded into letting us stay in his building. I had made no move toward moving. But, even if he refused, there were other spaces available.

Mr. Arthur and I had talked about trying to buy Dr. Roy's share of the company if the occasion arose. I hoped that if my expansion plans didn't meet with the managing director's approval, the old man would wash his hands of *The Caymanian Weekly* and me forever and be willing to sell out.

Mr. Arthur's consistent comment whenever I mentioned that prospect was a simple, "He'll never sell."

We all arrived at Dr. Roy's office about the same time. I was talking to our accountant Richard Graham-Taylor—the first person I met on the shore when I arrived several years ago—when Dr. Roy drove up. He nodded at us and then abruptly dismissed Richard with a curt, "We won't need you for this." Richard looked at me in surprise, but I could only shrug. I had no explanation.

I was disappointed. For the first time, we had squeezed out a tiny profit and were turning around the once-deteriorating company. It was not much money to men who once took thousands in annual dividends, but the bottom line was out of the red for the first time under my stewardship and I wanted our accountant there to hammer that point.

We gathered around Dr. Roy's mammoth desk in his office as he called the meeting to order. I couldn't help thinking back to my letter in the middle of that very desk three years ago—an eternity now. At the time, he was convinced I would come with the blessing of God. Now, I was the Devil.

There was also so much confusion, so much misunderstanding, and so much sadness at that table. The worst moment came when the inevitability of what lay ahead arrived. There would be no reconciliation. It did not take long.

Billy and I avoided eye contact but when Dr. Roy told us to begin, Billy immediately asked for the floor and Dr. Roy told him to speak his mind. I was surprised, and annoyed, that Dr. Roy had allowed Billy to open the meeting. But my surprise was about to turn to shock.

As soon as his first words spelled out, I could tell Billy was drinking.

"I have a proposal for you fine gentlemen," he said. "There's not room for both the Compass and *The Caymanian Weekly* in my country." He looked directly at me, and I struggled to hold my temper. I knew I would get my chance even if I had to force it on the group.

"So," he said, "I propose a buyout!"

"What kind of a buyout?" Dr. Roy asked, although I was keenly aware that he knew exactly what Billy would propose.

"I will sell you The Compass for $10 a share or I'll buy out *The Caymanian Weekly* for the same price."

Dr. Roy cleared his throat, but said nothing. His eyes gleamed and there was a slight smirk of satisfaction on his lips as he looked around the table at each of us.

We were so stunned by the surprising turn of events we didn't know how to respond. I had expected Billy's motion to be to fire me and I was ready with my rebuttal. I was eager. But a sell-out?

I sat mutely and waited for someone to say something.

"Has anyone got a comment?" Dr. Roy boomed, shattering the silence.

"All right, then," he said immediately, "I recommend we accept the financial report and adjourn."

I straightened up and opened my mouth to object that I hadn't even given the financial report yet, but before I had a chance Billy rose to his feet and walked unsteadily out of the meeting.

259

Even with Billy gone no one could do more than shake his head. Mr. Arthur and Norberg were speechless. Truman Bodden, our legal advisor who had attended at his father's and my insistence in case I was brought under legal attack, looked at me with a blank expression. The managing director was the only one who was ready for action.

Dr. Roy looked directly at me for the first time in months. I had come to gloat but he had stolen the opportunity and was relishing it. The meeting lasted only ten minutes.

Billy's bombshell had disrupted everyone's strategy but the managing director's. We walked outside and found Graham-Taylor still standing on the sidewalk outside Dr. Roy's office, where he had been summarily dismissed.

"I thought I had better hang around in case anyone had a question," he said. I told him about the bomb Billy had just dropped and his mouth opened in surprise. His shocked eyes were huge behind his thick, black-plastic-rimmed glasses.

Truman joined us and we three began walking slowly toward Truman's office.

"What the hell can we do, Truman?" I asked. "It's pretty obvious Dr. Roy knew what Billy was up to."

"They're cousins, you know," Truman said, as if that meant nothing more than if he had said, "They're Caymanians," or, "They're human beings."

I stopped and looked at him incredulously.

He nodded slightly. "Distant, but cousins," he said.

I shouldn't have been surprised. This was, after all, Cayman.

"We could call him on it," Truman said.

"What do you mean, call him? You mean try to buy the Compass?"

It was a thought that had never crossed my mind. I couldn't imagine buying the Compass, even without all of our problems among the board members. I was certain that if given enough time I would squash the Compass into oblivion.

"I mean sell *The Caymanian Weekly*," he said, looking up at me.

I was astonished.

"Billy doesn't have the money to buy the Caymanian even if we wanted to sell it," I argued.

"Maybe he does," Truman said. "We could call his hand on it. If he can't do it we'll sue him. Billy owns real estate. I don't know how much but he just might have it. He has some family land...and there's Dr. Roy to consider...He wants you gone."

We walked on toward the office contemplating this latest twist.

The idea of winning a lawsuit against Billy if he couldn't get the money was engaging. How ironic if I could make him pay for the new printing equipment I desperately needed. Maybe we would even get enough to purchase our own building, free of Dr. Roy's control.

On the other hand, as far fetched as it sounded, the thought of Billy Bodden gaining control of *The Caymanian Weekly* after all of the grief he had caused over the past three years was appalling, not to mention potentially disastrous to me personally.

It would certainly be a defeat. I had gone to the board meeting prepared to fight, and ready to outline my plan not only for survival but also for growth and ultimate victory. The thought of giving in to Billy had not once occurred to me.

Now, everything was topsy-turvy.

There was a subdued atmosphere in the office of the Caymanian. Few details were known by the staff but they understood that momentous decisions were being made that would affect all of us.

As I sat in my dejected reverie, a shadow fell over my desk and I looked up to see Dorabella, holding her weekly story for me to read. She never missed a week. I hadn't heard her come in or seen her approach.

"Hello Miss Dorabella," I said, unsure what I should say to her.

"You goin'?" she asked solemnly.

I looked up at her. The eyes watched me intently but with no display of anything but concern.

"I'm not planning to," I stammered, caught off guard by my most faithful correspondent. She might have been asking if I was going to dinner, or to the beach, but I knew instinctively that she was asking me if I was leaving Cayman.

"Oh, I'll be around for a while, Miss Dorabella," I said.

"You and your little wife and children be fine," she said. "Here," she said, looking around the office, "It won't be so good."

"Why thank you, Miss Dorabella," I said, interpreting her remarks as a compliment, "I appreciate that, but I don't think I'm going anywhere."

"You will do what you knows is right," she said.

"Miss Dorabella," I asked tentatively, deciding to take full advantage of the intimate moment to satisfy my curiosity about her clandestine reputation, "I've heard about obeah since I've been here and I've wondered if there is any truth to it. I sure would love to write a story about it."

It was a reckless stab in the dark and I didn't know what to expect. In spite of everything, I was still the inquisitive reporter looking for that big story. She looked at me intently and I instantly regretted opening my stupid mouth.

"Without mentioning any names," I added quickly. The last thing I wanted to do was offend her. But she didn't appear angry. Her piercing, dark blue eyes narrowed and she leaned toward me.

"Mr. Dick, do you think I's a witch?"

"Well, no," I said, "but if you were, I could certainly use a little help right now, and not only with an article."

I smiled, trying to indicate I was joking, even though there was truth in my comments. I would love to have help, any help, witchcraft included.

"Mr. Dick, there ain't no witches."

"So, you're saying there's no obeah, no witchcraft?" I asked, encouraged and intrigued by the old woman's willingness to talk to me.

"Mr. Dick, there's nothin' scary except'n the minds of fools," she said.

"Miss Dorabella, you're quite the philosopher," I said.

"You gonna do good with your little family," she said. "Poor Mr. Billy..."That seemed an odd statement, but she turned and walked away as I watched, surprised and perplexed by the unexpected sophistication of her comments. Oddly, no one approached me to ask what she had said, as usually happened. No one even glanced up from what they were doing. I wondered if they saw her come in, or leave. Except for her column on the middle of my desk, I might have imagined the entire episode.

I didn't see Dorabella again but I never forgot her simple logic. I know she was a witch, but to me she was a good witch, and she never missed a deadline.

50

OH COME ALL YE FAITHFUL, LET'S GET DRUNK

Christmas that year was dismal. The specter of losing out to Billy hung over everyone at the newspaper. On Christmas afternoon, I was sitting alone in front of Nolan's house in Bodden Town with a bottle of rum and a bottle of Coke, watching the weak, gray waves crumble on the reef. They were subdued. It was a rare gray day in Cayman. The ocean was flat and lifeless, its surface opaque, forbidding. But I understood the sea now. There were no terrors left. The shadows contained no hidden phantoms—just sea eggs.

Dr. Roy had ordered us again to vacate his building and had shown no sign of either relenting or forgiving me for his perceived injury. I understood finally that he was actually serious.

Our equipment was ready for the scrapheap. Our cash situation was dismal. I had no permanent home for my family. Billy was right about one thing: There was no longer room for both of us on the island.

But even if he could raise the money, I wanted more than making Billy pay for *The Caymanian Weekly*. I wanted justice. I wanted to torpedo the Compass and send it plunging to the bottom of Hog Sty Bay where its bones would rot alongside those of Captain Woody's long-lost Balboa.

Sitting there in my chair, brooding on the beach, I could see no way of blocking Billy's momentum. I was whipped. It then struck me to think as an American businessman might, not as an honorable Caymanian. And why not? As it was constantly pointed out to me, I was an American.

Out of the blue, the infuriating veil shrouding my brain parted and there appeared in its place an astonishing strategy. It was a simple voice from a part of me I had not listened to for a long time. The epiphany was so mean-spirited I initially dismissed it as too out of character. But if it worked it would be more than satisfying; it would be astonishing!

The more I thought about my idea, the more appealing it became. The question was, "What would my partners think?" Was it too immoral? Too vicious? Too evil? Too American?

There was only one way to find out.

51

A SOUTHERN DOUBLE CROSS

Early the next morning, I went to Mr. Arthur's shop. As usual, he was pleased to see me. Mr. Arthur's support in any circumstance was one thing I could still count on in Cayman. Never critical, always willing to listen to anything I had to say and always supportive, Mr. Arthur had that plentiful commodity found in our childhood that becomes rarer as the years drift by—unquestioning friendship.

"Arthur," I said cautiously, "what if I found a way to double-cross Billy?"

I didn't really like to call my plan a "double-cross," but I knew that in this country where blood runs thicker than sorghum molasses it might be interpreted as something right out of a textbook written by the black-hearted Henry Morgan himself.

"I think we should sell the Caymanian to Billy," I said, paused, and waited for his reaction.

He looked at me in surprise.

"Friend Dick," he said quietly, "I never took you for a quitter. We're not whipped, lad."

He meant it as a compliment and I understood that. I could see he was disappointed, but I hoped it would only be for a moment more.

"Arthur, I can only see one way to win this fight. Let's let Billy think he's won," I said.

"But Friend Dick," he said, "If he buys *The Caymanian Weekly*, he has!"

"Arthur," I said, almost in a whisper, "We'll take his money and we'll start another print shop and publish a new newspaper."

He turned to look at me. There was no expression on his face. I didn't know whether or not he had realized what I had proposed. He didn't look up, but I could see a slight smile play across his lips. I could tell my friend Mr. Arthur was savoring the thought. After all, Billy had turned on him, too.

I shook my head and smiled. "Billy won't ask us for a covenant in the contract not to compete," I said. "He probably doesn't even know what it is. Even if he does, his offer is already on the table."

I didn't know whether or not I was on shaky legal ground but I trusted Truman and Truman had said we could sue Billy if he backed down. Either way, I didn't see any way to lose. If Billy reneged we would sue him and use the money to find another building, upgrade our equipment and keep going with our operation. My way, if the others agreed, would be sweeter—and to me, much, much sweeter.

"I'll take his money and go to Miami and outfit another print shop," I said. "After we're in operation for a while we'll start another newspaper."

He was listening.

"There are two newspapers on Cayman now and there will be two after this is over. The only difference is we'll own one and we'll be free of Dr. Roy and Billy and we won't ever have to go through this bullshit again.

"Think about it Arthur: We would be letting Billy set us up with new equipment. As it stands now we're out anyway because Dr. Roy is kicking us out on our asses. Plus, the equipment is on its last legs. It's worn out, almost worthless. Billy is going to have to replace most of it."

That was another beautiful part of my plan. The equipment that Billy bought from us would have to be replaced. That would tie him up financially even more. He would buy our company, pay for our new equipment and then be faced with the prospect of buying new equipment for our old company. It was beautiful.

I didn't have to wait long for an answer.

"Let's do it, by golly," he said firmly.

Arthur called Norberg and asked for a meeting later that morning. We found the baker busy as usual but willing to listen to our plan. He too smiled when he realized the implications of my proposal.

"I think we should ask Hunter if he's interested in investing," Norberg said, speaking of the late Clifton Hunter's son, who still held a few shares. "There's no point in creating more hostility if it's not necessary."

I agreed, and left that up to Norberg with the understanding this must all be done in strictest secrecy.

Truman was also brought into the plot. He saw no legal problems in what was being proposed. So it began.

52

END GAME

The next morning my loyal employees were in a dour mood. I learned from Sandra that Billy and the staff of the Compass had held a joyous, noisy celebration the previous evening. They had not been invited and their feelings had been deeply hurt. Their loyalty to me had cost them in terms of their personal relationships with their former friends at the Compass.

They wanted reassurance from me that everything was OK. That their lives were not going to be disrupted and that they had not made a bad choice by sticking with me. I could only offer silence. Nothing traveled faster in Cayman than a secret.

No way could I explain that a big part of what I was doing was for them. And it was. I had worried after the initial confrontation with Billy about the employees who had chosen to remain with me. I knew that Billy would never hire them after he had taken over. They had made their choice. Billy's victory would not only be over me, but over everyone who had worked for me, who had stood up for me in the bleak early days—anyone who had ever been my friend.

Everyone in the islands was aware a fight was looming. Few were privy to the actual details but enough information had leaked so that sides had formed in the community in anticipation of a nasty fight. Word quickly spread that Billy had offered to buy the Caymanian and that I was on the way out.

It took Billy three days to make his decision. He called Truman and accepted our terms.

I anticipated exhilaration, perhaps even stronger than the day I fired George, but it didn't happen. Cayman was a bright, colorful, charming island in the warm sunshine—everything that I had ever wanted or hoped to find in my life.

But today there was no joy. I had come here to run a newspaper.

267

I wanted to build it into the finest publication in the Caribbean. I enjoyed my work, suffered the guilt of my professional indiscretions, and cherished my thin victories.

I had not enjoyed the constant pressure and the apprehension that came from not being trusted by the bureaucrats. First, there had been the problem with my employees. I had won that round. There had been the trouble with the work ethic of the islanders. I had that under control. There had been the politicians and the parliament. I had dealt with it and could still hold my head high. There had been the government's attitude. Now, there was the flicker of grudging respect from that quarter.

Finally, there was Dr. Roy. Had it been an isolated incident, I would have coped. As it was, coming with a string of obstacles for month after desperate month, it had been shattering—more so because the entire episode and all of its aftermath was based on one huge lie from a guy I had once trusted as a friend. I had given him everything he had wanted, and then came that knife in my back.

I was preparing a rejoinder to batter both Billy and Dr. Roy. They had purchased an empty shell. The name was valuable but the equipment was junk. They would have the building, as long as Billy managed to tread on Dr. Roy's good side anyway.

Billy thought he was buying me off. That was what he was paying for, why he had mortgaged everything he owned. I would be out and he would be top-dog of the island's press again. What he hadn't accomplished with work and competition, he would accomplish with his checkbook and kinship.

It was ironic, too, that I had done to Billy what he had done to me in the beginning. I had a complete copy of the mailing list along with all of the financial information. I was walking away with every piece of documentation that I could carry that might help me with the new company.

When we established our publication, I would send every former subscriber a free subscription, just as Billy had done with the Compass. "We're back!" I would shout.

Billy had been so incredibly naive that it was almost larceny. And that was when I finally realized what was causing me so much misery in the face of such achievement. Sure, Billy and Dr. Roy had stabbed me in the back at every turn in recent months. But both had made certain I knew exactly where they stood.

As for me, I was for once acting like a shrewd businessman. I had never told Billy that I was going to leave Cayman. He simply inferred that I would. He had been too naive to put it in writing. Legally, he would have nothing to complain about when we opened our printing

268

company and hit the street with our new publication.

So why was I depressed? Was it that this was simply not the Caymanian way? In Cayman, a handshake is a contract. Well, it wouldn't be any longer after the ramifications of this were publicized.

It gave me some comfort to remember that Billy had skimmed thousands of dollars from the newspaper's advertising revenues with the Carib Advertising Agency, but even that had been up front. Billy had explained it to the directors and they foolishly approved it. Understood it, no, but never-the-less gave their blessing.

My plan was devious from the beginning. It was good business but it was intended to be a personal blow to Billy's pride as well as his wallet. Within a week, he had raised enough cash to consummate the sale. Mr. Arthur got $25,000 and Norberg $15,000. My 5 percent ownership gave me $5,000.

There was no ceremony as I turned over control. I wasn't even there. I walked out of the office in the early afternoon and strolled to the quiet, familiar harbor to watch the ships.

53

A NEW DAY BEGINS

A new company was immediately incorporated. It was called Cayman National Publishing Co., Ltd. and the new directors were Mr. Arthur, Truman, Norberg and Dick Gentry.

We opened an account at Barclay's Bank and arranged for our $25,000 overdraft. I put myself on salary along with several key employees, including Nolan. We leased office space in a new building under construction on the main square. We could be seen from our old location. It would be several months before completion. In the meantime, I flew to Miami to look for printing equipment. I decided on two new Japanese-made presses, a smaller one for the commercial printing work and a larger one for a tabloid-sized newspaper.

I spent $15,000 for the equipment and arranged for it to be shipped to Cayman. I negotiated with our long-time supplier, Southern Paper Company, to send us a full supply of paper products.

Everything was on schedule.

More than that, my life entered another phase. It was no secret that the newspaper battle had ended in Cayman. For all the public and the government knew, Billy had won. He had driven the American interloper out and into the dust. I was the loser in an international brawl played out before an audience of disassociated players. We had provided a few weeks of amusement, but no one thought their lives would be affected one way or the other.

In general, it was believed that I would pull up stakes and sneak back to America, my interlude in the tropical sunshine over.

One thing I had learned about the British colonial service during my years in Cayman was they were a randy bunch of characters. There were so many assignations—some even ending as public disputes in divorce court—that hardly a week went by without a new and glorious tale of who had been caught in whose bed by whose angry wife or husband.

Still, a modicum of decorum was demanded for the highest rungs of the British civil service. It would not have been appropriate for His Excellency, for example, to be found under the bed. The same applied to the high court officials and members of the government with departmental portfolios.

Although several British policemen at times flaunted their appetite for sexual adventure—one even set tongues wagging by openly bringing an associate's wife to a civic theatre opening—such indiscretion by the top officers, such as the commissioner or other department head, couldn't be tolerated.

When my old nemesis Police Commissioner Doty announced his resignation, rumors were immediately ignited that the pompous martinet had been caught in some indelicate situation. It could have happened. Myself, I suspected it was all about money. It is hard to live as a civil servant in paradise and not grab at the brass ring if it ever presents itself.

Fortunately for Doty, he had maintained a friendship with Interbank's Jean Doucet, and there was an immediate job available as security chief for the bank, which Doty quickly grabbed.

Still, Doty had been an excellent police administrator and was held in some esteem by both his officers and many local Caymanians and British expatriates. Following his unexpected resignation, his officers decided the appropriate gratitude for his efforts should be the obligatory cocktail party.

I was surprised when an invitation arrived. Doty and I had been at odds almost since my arrival. We had never found a neutral path and neither of us had hidden our distaste and distrust of the other. I had no strong feelings one way or the other about his resignation. For all I knew, he had most likely done what many Caymanians and expatriates had done before him: taken the golden bait offered by the celebrated, flamboyant Jean Doucet.

The French Canadian banker was held as a brilliant, almost mystical figure, a man who was shaping his own destiny for greatness. There were many who wanted to be linked with him. To be honest, I had thought about it myself. But I was still potential poison to some in the government and would have been a liability for him. Few were aware that Interbank was a house of cards.

Doucet's end actually came soon after mine. He had begun to sell gold certificates to clients. When a purchaser bought gold, he received a certificate, not the heavy metal that Doucet held for safekeeping in the bank. A rumor circulated that the bank didn't have enough gold on hand to pay all its depositors on demand. Few banks do, but there

271

was no coalition or Federal Reserve to rescue him. A bank run began. Interbank quickly collapsed.

Doucet collected his 60 or 70 employees in the lobby and gave them each $100 and his best wishes for the future. While the stunned employees gaped, he rushed to a private jet and vanished. He was found in Europe and returned for trial. Since there was no deposit insurance of any kind in Cayman depositors lost their money. Nolan and Risë were among those who lost everything.

The courts determined Doucet had defrauded his customers and he ended up bankrupt—that is as far as anyone knew; there's always Switzerland—and he was sentenced to serve nine months in the Cayman jail. But at the time of the party for the departing police chief, Doucet and Interbank were at their shining, glorious zenith with no hint of the scandal ahead.

The commissioner's party, rowdier than the norm for its kind, was almost over when Doty got around to acknowledging my presence. Neither of us had failed to appreciate the generosity afforded by the open bar.

"What will you do?" he asked.

"Go back to Texas, maybe," I answered, still not trusting anyone with my true plans.

He looked around the group, then turned to me and quipped quietly and discreetly with a rueful smile: "What are they going to do around here without us stirring the pot?"

I smiled, taken aback by this surprising intimacy, and held my drink up to toast the comment and our silent, secret reconciliation.

So, in the manner of things like that between men, it was over. The antagonism, the animosity, the rivalry, the resentment, the mistrust— gone. We were simply two people who, for whatever reasons, had been kicked about a bit on the ironshore and now both of us, at least in that blink of time, were in perfect harmony with one other, if not with the rest of the universe.

"Good luck," he said, and walked away to rejoin the revelry.

"And to you," I replied, holding up my glass.

Another invitation was for dinner at Ron Soley's house. This too, was surprising. I had said no more than a dozen words to the Royal Bank of Canada's manager since the infamous banking series, which had electrified the local government officials and united them against me. He, of course, had been the banker who had vocalized the immortal word, "crap."

It was near the end of the evening when I decided to mention it. Ron rolled out the after-dinner cart and its assortment of liqueurs, which traditionally signaled the official end of the assemblage.

"Well Ron," I said, sipping my Tia Maria, "Are you about ready for another banking interview?"

He laughed far too heartily, but he did laugh.

"Oh, no!" he said, "Let's don't go through that again!"

There was no acrimony and I could feel the sense of relief that surged through our small gathering. The evening turned mellow and we stayed for a few extra drinks.

There was no more mention of the article but I could feel—just like the incident with the former police commissioner—that the unpleasantness had crawled to its hole of conclusion. It was over. For whatever sins I had committed, I had completed penance. I was forgiven.

Olive Miller, the government's information officer, stopped me on the street and asked me what I planned to do now that I was leaving the islands.

"It's a pity you can't find something here," she said. "You and your wife really like it here, don't you?" She appeared genuinely concerned but who knows how she would have reacted had she, or anyone else, known my true plan.

It was no surprise that I got a letter from Dr. Roy's attorneys—Maples and Calder, which would eventually morph into Ugland House—asking me to vacate his house, or whoever's house it was. Dr. Roy had inherited it from his sister, or so he claimed. Other relatives said a signature on a document giving it to him was questionable and a lawsuit entangled the heirs. In many ways, Cayman is like every other country. I never learned how it was settled.

I was as anxious to leave the house by the ironshore as he was to get me out. I had no desire to remain among the ghosts. The reason I had not moved was the same old problem: There were simply no suitable accommodations available without buying a house and I was wary of making such a commitment yet.

We moved in temporarily with Nolan and Risë at their home in Bodden Town and started looking purposefully for suitable quarters.

Nothing was available. Nothing.

I told Mr. Arthur and Norberg about my housing problem. They had no answers except to assure me, "Something will turn up."

The days passed but nothing turned up. Our level of anxiety grew and I began to question whether or not this was worth it.

Finally, we heard about a possibility on South Sound. It turned out to be a very private and secluded house on a beautiful little inlet—exactly what I was looking for.

It was one of those charming Caymanian houses open to the elements with large, screened-in porches all around, yet plenty of privacy because it was far from the road. There was plenty of lawn and

273

so much undergrowth you couldn't see the house from the road.

If you followed a walkway for 100 feet you had your own small private beach. There was a rowboat that went with the house. Martha and I were delighted. Once again I was optimistic about building another business in Cayman.

Jay Hargest was making steady progress with Cayman Office Supply and although we were nowhere near declaring dividends, I felt strongly that this business could grow into one of the largest retail establishments in the islands.

There was little doubt that our printing company would be successful. We had brand new presses and people who were willing to work hard for success. I fully intended to share my good fortune with the employees through bonuses, and even equity.

Then it happened. Billy found out.

54

ENOUGH IS ENOUGH ALREADY

A chill descended again over all of our lives.

I was expecting him to be gunning for me. In my mind I went over what I would do when he confronted me. My physical health had never fully recovered from the bout of ulcerative colitis and I still tired easily, but I was certain I could handle myself in any situation.

I wasn't looking forward to a confrontation with Billy since I wasn't especially proud of my tactics, but I found myself wanting to get on with it. I made myself available in every way short of marching down to the office to call him out. I knew he was looking for me. I spent several nights at the Galleon Beach bar, his favorite haunt, but he never came, and there was no final showdown between us.

Billy had no intention of coming after me. Instead, he was devastated that Caymanians had been involved in the ploy. He told Mr. Arthur and Norberg that he could have expected something like this from a foreigner, but not from fellow sons of the soil.

It didn't take long for the information to sweep the island. Most Caymanians saw it as a double cross by my hand. I hoped that thought would not have traction.

That night, Elsworth Terry, Nolan and Risë's landlord, showed up at the apartment. He was furious. "I didn't rent this to two families," he said. "I want both of you out of here!"

He was vehement and refused to listen to reason. He wanted both of our families to vacate the property immediately. I told him we were on our way out but he wasn't placated. I could tell there was more behind his fury and it didn't take much genius to figure it out.

Nolan and Risë were philosophical about the turn of events but it created a terrible problem for them, too. We assured them they could stay with us in our new house until they could find a new apartment.

The next day, our prospective landlady for the beautiful little home

275

with its own boat by the sea called to tell us the family members had met to discuss leasing the house. I could tell from her tone that something unpleasant was afoot.

"They decided it might not be a good idea to rent the house at this time," she said. "We're not certain what we want to do with it."

She refused my pleas to reconsider or to let me talk to the family.

This was the first time I began to feel a little desperation. Not only did we have to find an apartment, Nolan and Risë did too. We were in the winter tourism season and there was simply nothing to rent.

Housing had once been only a distraction for us. Now it was the central issue of our concerns. I had hoped for more help from my Caymanian friends and business associates. Not getting that help puzzled and depressed me.

Then, I got a disturbing telephone call.

"You had better leave," the caller warned me. "There's talk about putting some ganja in your car. You get caught with it and it's an automatic five years in Jamaica. You're a white man. You won't come back." I recognized the voice. It sounded like a policeman I had known.

Maybe there was a real threat; maybe not. What it was to me at that time was sinister. On top of everything, I began to imagine my "enemies" trying to have me jailed by placing marijuana in my car.

The government had shown some sympathy for me in recent weeks, but they thought I was leaving. Now, they all knew what I had done and the frost had started to coat my life again. I knew I could not count on any official assistance.

No matter that in all probability I could have made my case with the court that I had been framed. It wouldn't have taken much to convince anyone in authority that I was an unpopular target in the islands and I had never seen any indication that the courts were corrupt. But that didn't matter any more. I was growing extremely weary of being a foreigner in a foreign land. The police hierarchy now distrusted me, the government had never fully approved of me, the parliament suspected me, and it was beginning to look as if most Caymanians were again shunning me.

Risë brought home another story that added to our apprehension. Her upstairs neighbor, Hamish Drummond, was an American insurance agent married to a Caymanian. Hamish bore a slight resemblance to me, which had caused him some dismay that afternoon.

"Hamish just told me a couple of Caymanians threatened to whip his ass at the grocery store," Risë told Martha.

"Hamish said they accosted him, believing he was Dick Gentry!" she said.

Hamish had no idea why they were after me and had skedaddled as quickly as possible after convincing them he was not the infamous, backstabbing, newspaper mogul, Dick Gentry.

That evening, Martha and I walked over to Pedro's Castle and sat on the rocky bluffs to watch the sunset. It was a sight we had seen countless times during the last three years and we never tired of it. It was our little twilight ritual and a perfect way to end a hectic day. There was always the promise of a new start that might turn out perfect. This night there was something powerfully sorrowful about the day's end. I think the true nature of our situation was taking solid shape in our minds.

We had free reign of the beach around Pedro's Castle. It was one of the oldest structures on the island, the subject of legends.

The massive stone walls of the home rose behind us. More than one entrepreneur had attempted to turn it into a commercial business. Most believed William Eden had built the place in the late eighteenth century. Dr. Roy, a descendant of Eden's, believed this account.

The latest owner, the legendary diver Tom Hubble, told me Pedro Gomez, a pirate, had built the house in 1631. Hubble said Henry Morgan himself once had a bedroom on the top floor. Tom said coins dated from 1500 had been found on the property and a young girl killed there by lightning in 1877 still haunted the place.

Tom was turning the old building into a restaurant.

Tom was a mysterious character if ever there was one. I had heard of him months before I met him. The talk was that he could free dive as much as 100 feet and often did to catch fish for his supper. Another story said that he had discovered a treasure ship somewhere off Grand Cayman and made secretive, periodic trips to plunder its gold whenever he needed cash. The story was that people tried to follow him but he always lost them. He made regular trips to Switzerland to stash his gold, I was told.

He had very little to do with anyone in Cayman. Before his arrival in George Town, he had worked in Jamaica as dive manager of the resort Playboy Club in Montego Bay.

James Jones, renowned for his books "From Here to Eternity" and "The Thin Red Line," used Hubble as a character in his book, "Go to the Widowmaker." At least that was the story that went with the local legend about Tom. I never asked him about it but then you didn't get into the hairy details with him.

Years later, I looked for Tom in the book. After many pages I was ready to give up when I came to this passage:

"...Once they were up and cruising, the co-pilot had come back to sit with them. He was a stocky, small, sandy-haired American with pale eyes and blond lashes…(he) was about as famous in The Trade as Villalonga, della Valle or the Pindar brothers…he specialized in free-diving and hardly ever used the lung anymore…and could do a hundred to a hundred and ten or twenty feet free diving…He had a strange smile with his pale eyes and blond lashes, a totally self-centered, non-caring, self-absorbed one, but with a strange secretiveness tucked away in it somewhere…"

I first met Tom when he came into the office asking if I could print copies of some of his drawings. I looked them over. They were quite good pencil drawings of Pedro's Castle and he wanted to sell reproductions. I thought they would make excellent artwork for a short piece on the building and asked if I could use one for *The Caymanian Weekly*.

He was delighted and I struck up a friendship with the mysterious diver that lasted until I left the island. I was welcome on his private property at any time to fish or just sit and watch the ocean, and I spent many a lazy afternoon there fishing for grouper off of the high bluffs near the castle. I vividly remember the final visit.

To the east, a three-quarter moon began rising over the sea beyond the castle. "Isn't it beautiful," Martha said. "I've been so happy here."

I did not say anything.

"I knew the minute the plane touched down that I was going to be happier here than anywhere else I've ever been," she said. "I thought we were going to fit in here. And we did. Cayman is really for people like us. We're different. We always have been. And for a while there we had it all."

She turned toward me, and I could see her tears.

I hadn't said anything about leaving. But her words were like the first stone of an avalanche. Everything is stable. Then the first rock tumbles. After that the whole side of the mountain falls on you.

Sitting there quietly on that rocky precipice it tumbled down on us with finality.

It had reached the end.

55

AMEN

I decided not to tell many people about our latest decision. Only my closest friends and associates involved in the company were told. My shop foreman Bob was the first. He was sorry to hear my decision but he knew what I had gone through and assured me he would have the new plant up and operating as soon as possible. I'm sure he saw an opportunity for himself in my absence and I was all for him.

I couldn't tell Truman, Mr. Arthur, or Norberg. I had made my decision and couldn't face the righteous arguments I knew they would mount. I was uncomfortable for weeks knowing my salary was a financial drain. The equipment was purchased and the employees were in place. There was no way they would understand how I felt. I just didn't have enough juice left to try to make anything work any more.

The choice was clear. It had once been the time to come and now it was the time to go. The office supply store I had founded was up and running. Jay was proving a capable manager. It was prospering. But, I would walk away from it all.

I wanted to go home.

Martha and I left Stephen and Alison with Risë and Nolan and flew to Miami. As we took off for the last time from Cayman International Airport, I was overcome with a sense of relief. We had made our decision and now we had to build another life.

We rented a car in Miami and drove north. In Ocala I called the publisher of the Ocala Star-Banner and asked him if he remembered offering me a job a long time ago when I called from New Mexico. He remembered and within two days I was working as a reporter.

Within a week, I had written Mr. Arthur, Truman and Norberg long letters explaining my position and why I was not coming back. A true friend to the end, Mr. Arthur wrote back, forgiving me completely for my actions and expressing his thanks for what I had done for the

279

company. "I will always be your friend," he wrote.

In two weeks Risë packed Stephen and Alison aboard a *Cayman Airways* jet. When I saw a stewardess leading them toward the international reception area in Miami, all of my anxieties over The Cayman Islands melted away and the door to that part of my life began to close.

Nolan and Risë stayed on in Cayman. Desmond Seales offered Nolan a job selling advertising for his Nor'wester. Eventually the job took them to Miami and they bought a home in Coral Gables. After several years their marriage fell apart and they divorced

She's happily remarried, recovering, and lives in Florida. Nolan returned to Mississippi and also remarried.

Desmond eventually got himself arrested. He and his wife at the time, Carol Fox Seales, were charged with theft in the early 1990s when the couple owned a real estate and property management firm. They allegedly used some of the firm's money suspiciously to support Desmond's venture into television. He started a local station, CITV, which required more cash than Desmond had. The judge gave Desmond's wife 18 months and Desmond three years in the slammer. He also smudged his M.B.E. medal that was awarded him by Her Majesty for his publishing service to Cayman.

The judge recognized Desmond prior to sentencing as a "pillar of society, a leading publisher, a business entrepreneur and a Member of the Order of the British Empire."

Before too long, Desmond was back in business. I have always suspected that if a young Desmond had moved from Trinidad to New York City instead of The Cayman Islands, he would today be a competitor of Donald Trump's.

Martha and I continued our search.

We moved to Idaho, Washington State, Texas, North Carolina, California and Georgia, where each of my four grandchildren were born. She became a registered nurse and alcohol and chemical abuse counselor, and was drawn into nursing management, eventually becoming nurse executive of a huge, state psychiatric hospital.

We returned to Hawaii once a few years ago and I was editor of a business magazine but we didn't stay long. It's never better the second time around in spite of all of the memories. My enjoyment and use of alcohol faded as the years passed. I live in the past a lot these days but some people do that.

More and more people have discovered The Cayman Islands. Some 4,500 satellite dishes keep the islands tuned in to the rest of the screwed-up world these days. The *Caymanian Compass* still publishes. Ursula Gill, the writer I hired as a reporter so many years ago, became the Compass's editor. At my Caymanian Weekly, Ursula had been given leave to have a baby, and was replaced by the poor, alcoholic Grant who had staggered down the ramp to "a new life."

Mark Rice married a daughter of Mary Lawrence and has four grown sons. He owned one of Cayman's successful advertising agencies. He told me that his mother-in-law has run for just about every legislative election since I left.

"She's never won," he added.

Two of the companies I started are still in business although they have changed hands.

Susan Roy, the darling little Scot who tried to call Howard Hughes for me that day at the Lobster Pot, went to work with David Parchment, in the local print shop that I helped create. Yes, the same David who abandoned me for Billy and who might have changed my life if he had fulfilled his promise to "meet me later and talk" on that very first day I set foot in The Cayman Islands.

Bob Hodges struggled with the printing company for a couple of years after I left, then left the islands himself, divorced again and drinking heavily, I heard.

The islands hold a pirate festival every year to celebrate their real and imagined history. A booze festival would be more realistic. Alcohol clobbered more people than the pirates ever did.

The Honorable Truman Bodden, O.B.E, became Cayman Islands Minister of Education and Planning, and later the Leader of Government Business. The executive council is more fragmented today than it was in the 1970s, I am told, but is still the political seat of power.

In 2002, I heard that a young legislator named McKeeva Bush, who was threatening to take the reins of government, was forming a new political party. I asked Mark Rice who was this whirlwind wunderkind? "Dick," he emailed back, "you hired McKeeva right out of school and trained him as a pressman. I had to let him go because all he wanted to do was sing religious songs."

The islands suffered along with the U.S. as the stock market tumbled in the new millennium. Tourism and land sales both fell off. A buyers' market was created, with sales generally falling about 20 percent in the first two years of the new century. There were setbacks, depending on your point of view. The government changed the height limit for condos and hotels in their perspective zones from three to seven stories, although there were some limits placed on existing structures to protect some properties. The legislature also passed a law limiting planning and zoning challenges to surrounding property owners only, ending the practice of allowing anyone to protest. I heard they had a bad hurricane.

Recent visitors have also found an increase in traffic, especially around George Town, where as many as five cruise ships at a time release hordes of tourists to jam the fragile infrastructure. Time moves on.

Many have died. Dr. Roy, my friend Mr. Arthur, George.

Eric Bergstrom was awarded the M.B.E. for his tourism work. He and Suzie divorced. She married the island's premiere dive master, Bob Soto. I heard Eric inherited his share of the family fortune and moved with a new wife to a big ranch in Arizona.

Benson O. Ebanks, the member of ExCo who spoke for the government, was defeated for election to the legislative assembly in 1988 and retired from politics to manage his little grocery store and gas station in West Bay, where he can still be found today.

Tom Hubble died in Grand Cayman at the controls of a small airplane. It tricked him one day coming in for a landing. It was that same little Cessna 150 two-seater that a friend and I bounced around in when we flew around the island one day shooting pictures of the wrecks at East End. Tom's Pedro's Castle is still a local attraction.

Three years after I left, Billy Bodden stuck a pistol to his temple and blew his brains out. I was told he couldn't overcome demon rum and other sorrows. I often think about what Dorabella meant that day long ago when she said, "Poor Mr. Billy."

"I tried to use Billy as a salesman for a while," Mark Rice told me. "It didn't work out..."

I heard it took Billy two separate attempts to kill himself.

Funny thing. Some days I'm overcome with a deep sadness about the deaths of my island friends. Even Billy and George. I suppose it's because of the great influence they all had on my life and because there was no closure—only imaginary confrontations late, late at night.

Jim Bodden mellowed in the years after his election, dropping any talk of full, internal, self-government. Long after I left The Cayman Islands, he was elected by his fellow members to the executive council and eventually named Minister of Tourism, Aviation and Trade. He held his seat in Bodden Town until his death in 1988 at the young age of 53.

Bodden and I had one last personal conversation before I left the islands for good. I received a telephone call from him asking if I could come by his office.

"I understand you're leaving," he said.

"Yea, time to go," I answered.

"You know," he said, "I've always wanted to start a newspaper here. I thought you might be interested in the editor's job."

Surprised, I told him I would have to give it a lot of thought.

We never spoke again and he never started another newspaper, but I still think about the offer and what it meant, sometimes.

In 1994, Jim Bodden's statue was placed in Heroes' Circle opposite the Government Assembly Building in George Town. The islands are a sensitive, forgiving land. And they love pirates. Dr. Roy should be up there too, not as a pirate, but as the elder statesman of the country.

To this day, I never knew why Billy, who pioneered journalism in The Cayman Islands, walked away from *The Caymanian Weekly* and opened the door for me. Perhaps there was justification. If someday they put him up there beside Jim Bodden that will be okay with me.

It's been decades since Martha and I saw North Sound disappear behind the wings of the Cayman Airways BAC1-11.

But I think about my great adventure and what it all meant.

The Cayman Islands introduced me to a world that I would never have believed if I hadn't seen it. Men shook hands to forge a contract. Unbelievably, they told the truth when the truth could be offensive and harsh. How many politicians in America walk up to the editor and say, "I'm disappointed, so-and-so died and I had hoped it was you." But you came to expect the truth, and even learned to speak it yourself.

Perhaps my journey could have been historical for the Caymans. In the end, I changed nothing significant about the islands, but they changed me.

Dr. Roy thought God sent me but I think it was all illogical timing. It would never have happened without that singular convergence: Billy walked out on the board in George Town just as this restless reporter chased a story to break the boredom one lazy afternoon in Beaumont, Texas.

And what brought the collapse of my great adventure. Misunderstanding? A joke gone off track? Fate? George? Circumstances? God? The awful truth—it was I.

Did I lay down my burden on the beach at Little Cayman joyfully looking up at ole Crux that magical night? No, you can't dump anything completely. You re-adjust the straps and make it ride more comfortably for a while. Maybe, if you're very lucky, a few trifles roll out and drift away with the tide. Then you pick yourself up. And there you are.

But what Martha said as we sat by the sea at Pedro's Castle watching the sunset is true. Nothing has ever been so magical.

And so we moved on, two Knights of the Southern Cross...

Afterword

RETURN TO THE RUINS

Many years later, when I read over the previous pages of this manuscript and wanted to type 'THE END,' I could not do it. Like Yogi Berra said, it ain't over 'till it's over. But I was afraid if I returned it would awaken the demons I have hidden from myself for more than three decades. I might be arrested, threatened, beaten or drowned. Or worse, forgotten. "Who the hell is Dick Gentry?"

I felt comfortable contacting three of my former employees, Susan Roy, the little Scot who had helped me try to track down Howard Hughes; Ursula Gill, who had worked for me as a reporter and Mark Rice, my faithful art director at *The Caymanian Weekly*. Mark and I had exchanged a few emails. He had given me the little bit of news I acquired over the years.

I planned to go late in the off-season in order to be able to afford the trip. Without dwelling on my sudden decision, I arranged a room at the Spanish Bay Reef Resort at the north end of Grand Cayman. I thought an old friend, Nancy Sefton, an American artist who contributed to the newspaper occasionally, owned it. But Nancy was long gone from the islands. Still it was a great choice. It is an all-inclusive resort, which means food and bar tabs are included. It sits right next to the still-empty lot where the woman complained to me decades ago in a letter about sand thieves.

My delight at the reception my trip evoked from Ursula and Mark was immediately tempered when they told me Susan Roy had died six months earlier in an auto crash. She was the first of many of my old friends and foes who had not waited around for my return.

The sky was clear and blue on my flight down. Martha was still in shock. I had told her to "take off next week; we're flying back to Cayman."

I had a great look at the eastern end of Cuba as we raced above. It's

284

very rural with few paved roads. All green and brown and rumpled before it pours suddenly into the sapphire sea. There are miles and miles of beach unimpeded by the wounds of civilization. Someday, promoters will go nuts fighting over that property.

As we rushed in from the sea and screamed over George Town, I tried to get my bearings. It didn't look that much different, but it was hard to tell. Then we were down. I felt queasy. The old terminal was history and a new modern complex greeted us. It only took moments to clear customs and obtain the required 30-day visitor's visa. Not even a wee flash of recognition from the young customs agent.

We rented a small car and set out for our hotel. The road snaked through downtown on Shedden Road and then turned north on West Bay Road along Seven-Mile Beach, a distance of about nine miles. I was immediately lost. Everything was different. This was old territory for me, but now new and confusing. Offices and shops had sprouted everywhere. Traffic was scary. It took a few hours to get used to driving on the left side. That's a mistake that kills tourists in Cayman and may have killed Susan.

Driving along the famous Seven-Mile Beach, hub of the tourism industry, most of the older hotels I had known were gone. Huge resorts under construction appeared to have been stopped in mid-step. I had yet to hear about a visit from vicious Hurricane Ivan, which had challenged even the strongest Caymanians.

We survived the drive and checked in for a late lunch. Storms were blowing across the Caymans, and this day was no exception. We unpacked, ran to a beach hut to unwind and watched the strong breeze bulldoze the waves. Morning would come soon enough to begin our look back.

Ursula Gill had offered to pick us up at the airport, but I told her I wanted a car. She would give us a tour tomorrow. Ursula had worked for me until Billy Bodden took the reins of *The Caymanian Weekly*. He folded my old company into his new Compass.

Ursula divorced herself from her husband Casey Gill long after I left. They have some great, very successful kids. Ursula owns her own large home conveniently located not far from downtown and we stopped to see it and have a quiet talk.

Originally from Germany, Ursula told me she may eventually leave the islands and return to London, her home before Cayman.

There are several newspapers operating in Grand Cayman at last count, but the largest by far and the most influential and financially successful is Billy's old *Caymanian Compass*, now a daily newspaper in a huge new, bright yellow building. I drove by it several times during my short stay, but never had time to drop by and see the publisher—an old

285

friend - Brian Uzzell.

Brian and his late partner at the time walked into my office almost four decades ago and announced they were going to operate an advertising agency. They rented an office from Dr. Roy on the second floor of his building. Naturally, I had yet to trust a single soul in Cayman and suspected they all had to be up to no good, and this pair was literally right over my head. They had to be hucksters, I thought. Everyone was.

As it happened, Brian turned out to be one of the many decent British expatriates I met. We enjoyed a few drinks and solved the world's problems a time or two. I had wondered about him over the years. When I learned that he had battled his way to ownership of the largest newspaper on the island after I left, I could only think, "Brian accomplished what I had wanted but botched. You go Brian!"

Another of my old employees worked for Brian. Walwyn Clark—remember, he was one of those Jamaicans I fired and rehired within hours—called me during my stay, but I ran out of time before I could see him again.

Ursula drove us almost completely around the island, and passed the apartment in Bodden Town we had shared for several weeks with Risë and Nolan before the landlord kicked us all out. It's still there, although like many houses on the south side of Grand Cayman it was shattered by Hurricane Ivan and is now just a roofless relic.

We stopped at Pedro's Castle, now a national park. The government took ownership of it and recently completed a $9 million renovation. The grounds look like a palatial estate.

Martha and I walked to the rocky bluff at the edge of the sea at Pedro's. The hurricane had shredded the vegetation to the coral base and we could see the rugged coastline for miles. In the distance was the bluff where the "end of the world" came crashing down long ago when Martha said, "It's over."

Farther west, we could make out the ruined cabins where Mark Rice and his first wife had lived. Next to it was where George and Erleen had once settled. Below the bluff was the little cove where I walked down that morning to find George and coax him back to work. That would have been the predecessor of the coming storm had I recognized it.

As I was walking around the park grounds, I saw an older man on a ladder changing a bulb. I introduced myself and learned he was William Eden, the same name as the founder of Pedro's hundreds of years ago.

"Do you remember Tom Hubble?" I asked. "He used to own this place for a while, and was a diving legend in the Caribbean."

"Of course I do," he said. "He was killed in an airplane crash."

"I knew him," I said, "Do you know what happened?"

Of course he did. Tom began giving flying lessons a few years after I left and he was approaching the airport for a landing with a student. They crashed into the ground. No rhyme or reason was ever found as far as Mr. Eden knew.

So many of my friends and foes are under ground. The latest was my dear little Scot, Susan Roy. Susan's life had turned bitter in recent years. Her husband Hugh was diagnosed with cancer and he had slit his wrists one morning in the bathtub. He was dead when she found him.

Susan would have been able to answer all of my in-depth questions about the two companies I had started before I left—the printing company and the office supply firm. She could have told me about Brian Uzell's march to conquer the Compass. She had worked for "my" printing company until her recent death.

As for the office supply store, Jay Hargest, the American I had hired to manage the shop, had divorced and returned to America. I never quite understood what happened to the store. Not really hard to understand if you are familiar with island life, but I did locate the printing company, still in business and full of surprises.

I wanted to pay my final respects to Mr. Arthur and Dr. Roy. I easily located Mr. Arthur's grave, but Dr. Roy's eluded me after an afternoon-long search. Both had died within a few years of my departure.

Bud Gordon, the writer I found at *The Caymanian Weekly* the first day I arrived, was also dead. He never found what he was looking for in Grand Cayman. Bud and his wife divorced. She moved away and Bud tried to open and operate a private care facility.

My friend Ed Oliver, probably the premiere artist on the island, and the man who invited Martha and me into his home for our first Christmas supper and our first taste of island fellowship, had also died from cancer. His wife returned to the U.S.

Ursula stopped for lunch at a small restaurant near East End overlooking the ocean. We sat and watched waves roll over the reef a few hundred yards out. The untrained eye wouldn't have seen the few rusty rails breaking into occasional view above the waves. They were the remnants of two large cargo ships which took a wrong turn many years ago. We had a marvelous picnic out there once. I wondered if that old cannon we discovered was still hiding out there on the sandy bottom.

Ursula drove us through the national Truman Bodden Recreation Center, a sprawling complex of public playing fields and courts. Truman had become a very important person in The Cayman Islands in recent years. He had risen to become the chief minister. A sea change in politics swept him out of office in the early 1990s, and he was relegated back to the private sector again, where he slowly built one of the largest law firms ever owned by a native son.

Truman and Hilda, his significant other during my early years in Cayman, had married but were soon divorced. He remarried, had two children, and divorced again. Truman and Hilda had been the closest friends to Casey and Ursula before Truman and Casey dissolved their partnership. I didn't know if I would be able to see Truman this trip.

The next morning Martha and I decided to drive to George Town and walk down to the old office, visit the harbor, and see if we could make it to the house where we had lived, just south of the harbor. Dr. Roy had owned it.

It rained, man it rained.

We were soaked when we went to one spot we knew would never change. It was the little grocery shop just north of the harbor on Church Street that had been owned and operated by Mr. Arthur and his family almost forever. Right across the street from the store was his Cayman-style home with his tiny print shop in the front yard, now preserved by the family as a historical property. It was in that little shop where I first told Mr. Arthur that George and Erleen had betrayed me.

It's a short walk across the road from the little store to the little house. The walk can be deadly. A truck killed Mr. Arthur's grandson, a tragedy he never got over. It was this same spot where he crossed one day not too many years ago. He was lost in thought, not paying attention. Another truck; another tragedy.

Inside, I asked if anyone was kin to the late Mr. Arthur.

His daughter, Arthurlynn, responded warmly. As we talked, many memories of the old times resurfaced. Behind and above the small checkout counter hung a portrait of Mr. Arthur, dressed in his standard white shirt and pants. I asked if she remembered the printing shop that Truman and I, Norberg and Mr. Arthur had started when *The Caymanian Weekly* folded.

She told me it was still operating just a block away. I left, promising to send her a photograph I had taken on my first day in Cayman. It was of Mr. Arthur and David Parchment, the shop foreman who had mysteriously warned me of "something I needed to know" and then failed to show up to tell me what it was. I found out what it was the hard way. I sent the photo, and it arrived six months later.

"Well," Arthurlynn told me, "David is the manager of the shop!"

This was going to be a short but interesting walk in the rain.

The print shop we had started was not where I left it. It had been moved from the downtown area proper and established in a neat, white, out-of-the-way building.

Martha and I walked in and found no one in the front office. I could hear a small press running, and the smells were familiar. We were at the right place.

In a few minutes we were discovered, semi-recognized, and enjoyed a terrific, short reunion with people I couldn't remember but who welcomed me as a friend and brother. Unfortunately, David was in Tampa visiting his cardiologist and would not be back in time to see me. Disappointed, I left my wishes for his good health.

Employees in the shop told me that David felt responsible for Susan's recent traffic death. She was feeling ill and David insisted she quit early and go home.

We tramped on through the warm rain to the harbor area. We paused for a few photos at the remnants of old Fort George. There was a historical marker explaining what this hallowed ground represented. "It was saved from destruction," the marker read in bronze letters, but my question was, "By whom?"

"That's the spot where they tried to run over Desmond," I told Martha, "and over there is where Bodden drove up and stopped the bulldozer from shoving the rest of the fort into the sea."

The area around the harbor has changed. There are fancy shops and fancy bars everywhere. The spot where Dr. Roy's house stood is now a multi-storied shopping center. It was also the exact spot where another nail was added to my coffin when the old man first spotted my mother-in-law, Agnes.

The government named a nearby street for him and there's a monument across from his former home, which says, "Dr. Roy's Ironshore." There's little doubt that he was a great man in his time. I just wish he had kept his sense of humour as he got older. I could have owned my own piece of the ironshore. Oh, well.

That's where the lobster boat *Gulf Star* capsized, I pointed out to Martha, "and right in front of us here is where the graceful *Sharon Michelle* was beaten to death by the waves, right here by Dr. Roy's Ironshore."

We continued our walk down South Church Street to locate our old house across from the Ironshore. The huge trees that had surrounded it were still there, but apartments had replaced the little house.

I had to see what happened to my old office at the newspaper. There are some specialty shops there now. I found what I thought to be the area where my old desk would have been. As employees watched me nervously, I poked around and gawked at the sparkling diamonds around me. I was in the middle of an expensive jewelry shop.

As one of the young clerks approached me, I told her, "I used to sit right there!" I think she was happy when I walked out into the rain again.

We were awaiting the arrival of Mark Rice for lunch. I was to meet him in the parking lot of Kirk Supermarket. Before he arrived, I marveled at how much better the selection had gotten since the time the market had been on the corner next to my old office.

I would have recognized Mark anywhere. Time had not taken too much of a toll on him. He was heavier, and a little grayer, but he still had his long, thick hair and his speckled gray beard. He was still married to Mary Lawrence's daughter.

We went to one of his regular retreats and enjoyed a quiet lunch as we tried to eliminate the years and get to know one another again. His original family home is in Oregon, but he has made his life here. "I couldn't be anywhere else," he told me.

After I gave up on Cayman, Mark continued with his marketing and artistic talent. He started his own agency and at the height of his business, he had revenues of more than $1 million a year and employed almost a dozen. That was before the hurricane and prior to the popularity of desktop publishing.

"Everyone began thinking they could save money, design their own ads and didn't need me any more," he said. And then along came Ivan.

Mark showed me a book of devastating photos entitled "Spirit of Cayman—The Aftermath of Ivan." The authors were Sheree Ebanks and Karie Bergstrom, two sisters.

"They've got to be Suzie's kids," I said.

Mark said the September 2004 monster hurricane had changed the course of history in the country. Because it had not claimed lives, the media around the world generally ignored it.

The reality is that it had destroyed or heavily damaged most structures on the south side of the island and many inland. Most of the homes and shops were uninsured and the scars remain. Mark said he was without power for six months. The sand covered up some of the homes of his neighbors. It will still be years before the country will be fully restored.

Mark said the government was so worried about tourism that it tried to prevent news reports on the devastation reaching the U.S., Great Britain and the rest of the world. The message still got out, and tourism, the largest source of income for The Cayman Islands, suffered. Fortunately it is recovering today. As Mr. Arthur would have said, "Praise be to God!"

Mark insisted we meet him again at his favorite haunt, Durty Reid's, owned by none other than Reid Dennis, a partner of Billy's at the old *Caymanian Compass*. Reid was the photographer who let me use his dramatic photos when the northwester sank the *Gulf Star* and *Sharon Michelle* in Hog Sty Bay 315 on Dr. Roy's Ironshore. He was also my "friend" who helped me celebrate both the Marine Corps birthday and my firing of the traitor George Heon at a memorable night at the Galleon Beach Club. He still laughs about my getting so drunk that I fell backwards off the bar stool.

I managed a short visit with him at his bar near Bodden Town. Reid lost his leg in Vietnam and was facing an operation at the Tampa VA Hospital, which he hoped would allow him to get out of his wheel chair and walk again.

As hard as I tried, I could find no information during the brief time I was in Cayman about Police Chief Doty, Governor Crook, and Interbank's Jean Doucet. They were gone, but not forgotten. Ms. Sybil McLaughlin, the clerk of the legislature who used to castigate me for my spelling, rose to become Speaker of the General Assembly. I managed to avoid running into Sybil during my return trip. She is considered a national treasure in Cayman.

I began to sense closure about my life here in this paradise. The edginess I felt had stopped stalking me and apprehension was replaced with growing confidence. It's incredible when you finally get the courage to grapple with old ghosts. Obviously, I wanted to track down more people, but I was running out of time.

Although there was some trepidation, I hoped to see Truman, but I was going to let it be his decision. Truman never understood why I had abandoned the islands. Perhaps he thought I ran out on my friends and partners. In a way, I did.

But I set out intentionally by myself to see Desmond Seales, and the man who had been a strong leader of the government during my day, Benson O. Ebanks.

I found Benson one afternoon sitting under a roof on the porch of one of his buildings. He owns a building supply store and enjoys a brisk business. He sits behind a large desk where he can observe the activity around him. He said he was "thrown out of office in the early 1990s," probably about the same time as Truman.

He has a cash box on his desk and obviously knows the price of every nut and bolt in the place, because customers come to the porch, show Benson the part they need, and he gives them a price. Of course there is no sales tax, so it always rounds off easily. At the same time, Benson's in touch with the rest of the world. During our conversation, interrupted occasionally by customers, he called the U.S. several times ordering supplies on his credit card.

Obviously, Benson is wealthy enough to avoid sitting under the porch all day parceling out pipes, bolts, and nails, lumber and plumbing supplies.

"The main reason I do this is for the people up here," he said, sweeping his hand around. "They need this business in West Bay."

West Bay, at the northern tip of Grand Cayman, is close to George Town, but still remote. A few tourists come to the turtle farm, but it is generally free of tourists. Real estate is less expensive, and there are still undeveloped plots of land.

I might have recognized Benson on the street, although we have both changed a lot. He's much heavier and grayer than I remembered, but then so am I. We both admit to a few medical concerns.

Mainly, I just wanted to see him again. We weren't friends, but we were not enemies either. He had some great ideas in the old days that challenged my thinking, and perhaps pointed me toward my sluggish cooperation with the government.

I asked him about the offshore banking community. I had heard the secrecy laws had been weakened.

"Beginning in 1985, the U.S. Attorney General was allowed to speak to The Cayman Islands Attorney General," he said, "It worked well."

My conversation turned to the smaller two islands. I wouldn't be able to visit the Brac and Little Cayman this trip.

"Those people on Little Cayman are trying to build a hotel," he said. "They need a hotel like they need another hole in the head."

We parted in more agreement than ever.

I was determined to see Desmond Seales.

Desmond is a survivor. I knew that he was publishing the Cayman Net News, a daily competitor to the Compass. It is printed by web press in Florida, and flown back daily to Grand Cayman for distribution. Usually, it is a dozen pages or so, filled with local and international news. Desmond has always believed in a confederation of Caribbean nations. It has never happened before, and I personally doubt it ever will.

Desmond is always able to work out some trade program with the airlines to transport his products, free or in exchange for advertising. On the flag of his front page, there's an overline that says, "36 years of publishing for Cayman." He's including his old Nor'wester Magazine in the mix. Good.

I located his office, and walked inside to a very efficient looking arrangement, from the office design to the crop of bustling employees at their desks. In the far corner of the huge front room, I saw a glass-enclosed office with a dark man reading behind a large desk.

"Can I help you sir?" an attractive young woman asked as I looked around.

"No thanks, I'm here to see that guy," I said, pointing to the man in the glass office.

I gently eased her aside and walked directly in and stood before the man at the desk.

He was startled, and sat up behind his desk to look at me.

"Hi Desmond," I said.

He looked back, smiled, but said nothing. He was probably thinking about how he would escape if I proved dangerous.

"You know me?" I asked. "You once did."

He looked closely, but could not identify me and shook his head.

"Well, it has been at least 33 years, I'm Dick Gentry."

He paused just for a second as that sank in, then leapt to his feet and shouted: "Dick!" extending his hand.

We tiptoed through the past years for a few minutes, talking about old, unimportant things. I would have recognized him anywhere, even after all these years. Nothing about him was different. His mannerisms, his enthusiasm, and his pride in himself and what he had accomplished. No matter how I tried to slice it, here was another man who had made it work and was hanging on to his dream.

We talked about Fort George and the day when bulldozers attacked. He's resentful that his name is nowhere to be found of the monument, and I don't blame him.

I touched briefly on his trip to the slammer, and found him in total disagreement with the verdict. He thinks he was persecuted. Desmond believes himself to be Cayman's "Nelson Mandela" and he may be to some extent. Unlike the vast majority of blacks in the Caribbean, who have no chance of breaking the invisible chains that have stymied them for the past 400 years, Desmond has all the necessary skills to succeed. He wants desperately to spread some of the wealth not only to himself, but also to other blacks.

When our visit ended, Desmond gave me a brotherly hug, copies of his newspaper and a video about his company, starring himself. I told him I wanted one more thing.

He looked at me skeptically.

"I want one of your front pages autographed to me by 'Desmond Seales MBE!'"

It's framed today on my wall, "To Dearest Dick Gentry from Your Best Introduction to Cayman, Desmond Seales MBE."

I can't say more because even I cannot afford to run afoul of the "PC Police" but let me just add this: The more things change, the more things stay the same. You'll understand when I talk about: "THE ROLLOVER."

*   *   *

293

I went by to pay my respects to Jim Bodden, the first official hero of The Cayman Islands. His life-sized statue is in the newly designated Hero's Park across from the Legislative Assembly Building. In the old days, before all of the confounded banks arrived, you would have been able to see him from my desk. But that was before he was a hero.

It was pure bad luck that his genes assigned him a short life span, dead of a heart attack in his mid-50s. I'm not sure if there's anyone around today with enough gumption to stir things up as he did in his short legislative career. I still wonder if I missed the boat when I didn't pursue his offer to manage his proposed newspaper, which he never got around to publishing.

Looking at Jim's metal face above me—which looks as much like me as it does Jim—I couldn't help but think of his nemesis, Mark's mother-in-law and my former "political editor," Mary Lawrence. Mark had given me her telephone number.

She wasn't even surprised when I called her.

The veneer of "we picked up where we left off" is used superficially to address social reunions. Not here.

She was still angry with me and we argued for the first five minutes about why I wanted her out of my office. My argument was, and still is, that you can't have a political writer running for the office they are covering. Martha was listening to my conversation and when I was finished, she told me I had defended myself "pretty good." Mary had a different opinion.

She told me that she and her late husband Jim had started their own newspaper, on their kitchen table, and it had published for three years in the 1980s.

"Our purpose was to tell all the people the truth!" she said. It began as a weekly and turned into a daily. "Jim and I worked on it while raising our six kids."

Mary has had a very interesting life, and her fascination with politics continues.

"We're having a political meeting tonight at the community hall in Bodden Town, and you need to be there," she said, "if you are really interested in knowing how this country works."

I told her I doubted I would be able to attend, even though I wanted to.

She then launched into a tirade about how much better an editor I would have been if I had gotten out of my office more and not behaved like a mole, hedgehog, turtle or something. I cannot remember, but it was not a compliment.

She also had a bone to pick with me about my interview with Teamster would-be President Jimmy Hoffa.

294

"You know I was there with you," she said, "and you certainly didn't treat me very well after the interview."

She told me exactly what we were all wearing, including Mrs. Hoffa, and said she could still remember every word said.

She also lit into me with a withering attack for "tearing up my story about Richard Nixon and flushing it down the toilet!"

Obviously, she had been there, and had written a disparaging story about Nixon, who had pardoned Hoffa.

`I doubt that I flushed it down the toilet, but I did begin to recall the article she was talking about. She had lambasted Nixon and I thought it was inappropriate. This was before Watergate. And I was the boss.

God bless you, Mary.

Our time was trickling down to another exodus. We both dreaded it.

"It's beginning to feel like we picked up right where we left off," Martha said. "I love it here."

Later, lunch was special. I had managed to track down Sandra Parchment, my most faithful employee at the newspaper. She was now the office manager of the classy Lacovia Condos on Seven-Mile Beach. She said she would come for lunch, along with Mark and Ursula.

When she walked in, I was flabbergasted. She had not changed at all. She looked like she was coming to lunch from her old job at *The Caymanian Weekly*. Sandra was the one employee who never faltered during all of our tribulations. She had done well for herself and we spent an afternoon laughing about the events of our lives thirty years ago. When they left, I hoped that I would see all of them again. I walked each one to the parking lot.

As I walked back by the front desk, an impressed clerk told me I had received a telephone call from, "Mr. Truman Bodden. He asks that you call him."

I would have recognized Truman anywhere because he looks so much like his father, Mr. Arthur. Put Truman in a starched white shirt, white pants and cap, and he would be his dad all over. But he was dressed in casual slacks and shirt and he wanted to take us to one of his favorite restaurants in the community of Batabano overlooking the North Sound.

It was a Saturday, and tomorrow we would leave for home.

Truman has at least eight attorneys working for him now and perhaps 20 assistants. I suspect he's the go-to law firm in Cayman when you need legal help.

We spoke in general terms about the changes in Cayman. The tax-haven industry is no longer as secret as it once was. You can't hide illegal profits any more.

295

"The U.S. puts up strong (meaning irresistible) arguments when it wants something," he said.

It was reminiscent of what Hoffa had told me 35 years ago: The U.S. government can squeeze anybody!

Anyone can establish an offshore account, but you can't hide illegal profits any more. The computer has also done to banks what it had done to my friend Mark Rice's advertising agency; cut them down a notch or two. Since banking is now mainly on the Internet, it has trimmed the number of employees and locations to store records. Our reunion with Truman was friendly and informal. He has done well.

Theoretically, someone with a license, bank account and computer could start a bank in Cayman from his or her condo on the beach. But that brings about the major changes I found upon my return. And they are huge. Actually, since he orchestrated the government for many years, many of the changes may be the result of Truman's influence.

And if I were a native Caymanian, I wouldn't blame him. But for expatriates, it could be the end of the world that we once knew there.

Year by year, step by step, the Caymanians made it more difficult for some expatriates to live and work in Cayman. They are terrified about the potential cultural and political changes ahead which could theoretically show them the path taken by the Arawaks and Caribs.

Since my visit only lasted a week, I'm not going to pronounce myself an expert on "the Rollover." But since my return was more than 30 years since my last exit, I am able to walk through the imaginary doorway from the past and identify what I think has changed, and what has not.

According to Desmond's newspaper, Chairman of the Cayman Protection Board David Ritch—occupying the post today that was held for the actual first time ever in the 1970s by my late friend and Caymanian Weekly board member Norberg Thompson—the number of work permits issued has increased from only 300 in 1973 to around 24,000 in 2006. And out of a total population today of almost 52,000, a little less than 32,000 are Caymanians. So a lot of expatriates are on the payrolls. My permit in the 1970s was $75 a year. The manager of the hotel where I was staying in 2006 pays about $7,500 annually.

Great Britain has signed on to European Union law that now says if a person resides in a country legally for at least eight years, they are entitled to permanent residency and eventually the right to vote. My sources in Grand Cayman tell me that of 24,000 work permits, non-Jamaicans hold only about 4,000. But read on...

So, ostensibly to protect the native Caymanians from work permit/population overflows and allow the sons and daughters of the soil to break the ceiling protecting the executive jobs now held by expatriates, the Rollover requires any expatriate worker with more than seven years of residency to leave the country for at least two years before trying to come back and work. Good luck rolling back.

I asked every Jamaican who would talk to me about their feelings on the Rollover. To a person, they were sad but philosophical about it. Several of them had to leave within months. They had no voice, although Desmond was trying to give them one. I saw several letters in the competing Compass accusing him of continuing to stir the pot.

It's a fierce debate, and the outcome may determine the course of The Cayman Islands. There are a multitude of arguments pro and con. Many fear overpopulation and eventual political control by poorer Jamaicans, and they also get nervous when Brits, Canadians and Americans begin to pile up on the beach. Others believe it is grossly unfair to make all expatriates pick up and leave the property they have accumulated just because of the fear they will become a permanent part of the community.

There is a cautionary tale here, and the statistics don't always jibe. Chairman Ritch notes that of the 36,000 in the entire labor force, Caymanians compose 18,300. Of the total force, the largest percentage of workers is in construction, more than 18 percent. Less than 10 percent compose the elite financial community. Although the overall population is now declining slightly, construction continues to boom. There are massive building projects, from roads to entire all-inclusive, community complexes. Frankly, between traffic and new construction, the island is a sprawling mess. Repair from the hurricane is nowhere near completion. Who's doing the actual labor? Not Europeans and Americans. Jamaicans are.

One recent news article I read said a new constitution was being proposed, "which does not appear to have the support of a majority segment of the population." A new constitution is being proposed for 2009, after being delayed from 2008. There are several slippery slopes being negotiated.

Should His Excellency the Governor have less powers of discretion? Can The Cayman Islands define what a Caymanian IS? Moreover, will Great Britain approve or not approve? The Caymans cannot approve a new constitution unilaterally, unless they want full independence. That is still a very bad word.

Anyway, you can argue this Rollover conundrum any way you want. There's no solution in today's economy to please everyone. Nothing much has changed very much in 400 years. The black man was literally and figuratively imported in chains with nowhere to return when his labor was done.

Of course the cultural conundrum is as simple as black and white. Always has been.

My own advice for Cayman is what His Excellency the Governor told me the Caymanians must do:

"I have an impression that incoming tourists see signs of untidiness in Cayman," His Excellency said. "My impression is that the Caymans have not yet finally made up their minds what kind of tourist resort they intend to be.

"It is far from clear whether Cayman has enough natural attractions to bring tourists here en mass. On the other hand, if you want a 'get away from it all place,' then you have to accept artificial restraints on development. I have a feeling that the latter is nearer to being right in Cayman. But restraint is never a popular word."

He got that right. By the way, that was a quote from my 1973 *Caymanian Weekly* by Governor Crook.

The Cayman Islands today make no bones about wanting wealthy expatriates to come and retire. The requirements are simple: You can apply for a 25-year permit if you have an income of $180,000 annually without the need to be engaged in employment. It's cheaper in the lesser islands; only $90,000 annually. Oh, you must also invest almost $1 million in the country, or $300,000 for the lesser islands. And there is a one-time fee of about $18,000. Entrepreneurs can apply for a 25-year certificate to start a business. The applicant must be worth at least $1 million with even a higher permanent source of annual income. They must employ at least 10 Caymanians.

Now, with all of this being said, my friend and former reporter Ursula, read these comments and told me what I have always tried to tell reporters: "Whenever you can, get the facts from the source." She sent me a copy of the official government report.

The year I returned to the islands to complete my epilogue, 2006, the government reported there were 24,865 work permits in force. Far less than 50 percent—10,828—were Jamaican. There were 1,487 American permits; 1,822 UK; 1,949 Canadian; 3,414 Asian and about 7,000 from the rest of the world, including 180 from Cuba.

Also, since 2003 there are two new departments under the Chief Immigration Officer: The Work Permit Board and the Business Staffing Plan Board. If a business has at least 15 expatriate workers, it must provide the staffing board with each job detail for review and approval. The Work Permit Board deals with businesses with less than 15 employees and individuals.

The term limit on how long an employee can remain continuously in the Caymans on a work permit is what is called the "so-called rollover policy," the immigration regulators say.

"Seven years is the maximum length of time a work permit holder can work continuously in The Cayman Islands. After this period the board cannot normally grant the person any further work permits until he or she has left the island for a period of at least two years."

There is an exception for certain expatriates who were legally working an aggregate of five years on Jan. 1, 2004, the year the new law was passed. At the board's discretion, the employee might be granted a permit for a period not exceeding three years to allow fulfillment of the eight-year provision so as to apply for permanent residence. (One exception would be expatriate civil servants).

Those who have been aboard between eight and 15 years were given three years to apply for permanent residence.

As far as becoming a Caymanian, for an expatriate who has no close Caymanian family member, the law requires 15 years of residency before applying for Cayman Status. It is not easy to interpret the laws, and those laws are always under review, so if you want to conduct business or live there make sure you have lots of money and then talk to a Caymanian attorney.

The growing worldwide problem of crime is understated in Grand Cayman, but my friends tell me it is embedded there and not necessarily under control. I'm sure the Governor would summon me again for a scolding if I wrote a story about the increase of vandalism, theft and gangs, but I would have to do it anyway if I were there. The islands still want to show a scrubbed-clean face to visitors.

All in all, The Cayman Islands are in better shape than the vast majority of Caribbean nations.

*   *   *

Sunday morning was a sad, beautiful day. The storms passed and for the first time, the waves were smoother and the sea cleared to blue-green, spectacular transparency. We took bikes from the resort in the morning and rode into the vast Cayman Islands National Park nearby.

It had been a lifetime since I struggled with bicycle pedals, but the farther we rode, the healthier I felt. Long ago, I remembered this series of mangroves and canals was part of the great scheme of a developer, to create a massive housing development. Today, it is home to birds, bugs, colorful iguanas and passing memories. The paths up and down the carved-out water canals—waiting for homes-that-will-never-come—are wonderful trails. The canals drain into the still pristine North Sound. A town called Stingray City is out there. We peddled leisurely back to our hotel in the morning sunshine and I realized at long last why I was feeling much lighter.

That afternoon we packed our bags, had a last meal and left for the airport. There was a quick glimpse of the remote North Sound before we disappeared into the clouds. Soon, we were approaching Atlanta. We didn't say much.

That's it.

THE END

BIBLIOGRAPHY

Craton, Michael. Founded upon the Seas. Kingston, Miami: Ian Randle Publishers, 2003.

Cooke, Jean, and Ann Kramer and Theodore Rowland-Entwistle. History's Timeline. New York: Crescent Books, 1981.

Parry, J.H., and Philip Sherlock. A Short History of the West Indies. London, Basingstoke, New York, Toronto, Dublin,

Melbourne, Johannesburg, Madras: MacMillan St. Martin's Press,1971.

Household, Geoffrey. Prisoner of the Indies. Boston, Toronto: Little, Brown and Company, 1967.

Marx, Robert F. Port Royal Rediscovered. Garden City, New York: Doubleday and Company, Inc., 1973.

Meredith, James. Three Years in Mississippi. Bloomington, London: Indiana University Press, 1966.

Diaz del Castillo, Bernal. The Discovery and Conquest of Mexico. Kingsport, Tennessee: Kingsport Press, Inc., 1956.

Griffiths, John. The Caribbean in the Twentieth Century. London: Batsford Academic and Educational, 1984.

Hirst, George S.S., ed. Handbook of The Cayman Islands, 1908. Kingston: Times Printery, 1907.

5758547R0

Made in the USA
Lexington, KY
11 June 2010